AF081781

75 AMAZING INDIANS
WHO MADE A DIFFERENCE

75 AMAZING INDIANS
WHO MADE A DIFFERENCE

VISHAL K GUPTA
VISHAL GUPTA

Vitasta

ADVANCE PRAISE

In a brilliant and subtle manner, the authors made the contemporary high achievers from broad cross-sections to communicate their life-changing experiences with the readers through this book. The book kindles the aspiring Indians to have heroes in their lives.

–**Putta Vimaladitya IPS**
Dy Inspector General of Police, Kerala

Just after India has celebrated 75 years of independence, here is a book celebrating 75 famous and not-so-famous contributors to national growth. All these Padma awardees represent the indomitable and resilient spirit of India and will motivate countless from the future to emulate them. Easy to read and packed with information and inspiration, this volume needs to be in the hands of every one who loves India.

–**Swami Narasimhananda**
Ramakrishna Mission

The book drives through intimate glimpses into each lives motivation, challenges, and personal journeys of each individual. The inspirational nature of the narrative not just informs but strives to readers for their own potential and contribution to society. As we celebrate their achievements, let their stories inspire us to weave our own threads into the rich tapestry of our nation, etching our own paths towards a more luminous future like it inspired me.
I loved reading about Ratan Tata, Mary Kom, A R Rahman, Illayaraja and many others.

–**Sanjeev Kumar, IAS**
Principal Secretary, Government of Gujarat

The power of purpose! It showcases the best of India - where people of diverse backgrounds make an impact regardless of where and how they started. Each narrative brims with optimism for what lies ahead. Inspiring!

–Gerry George
Managing Director, IMU Health (Malaysia)
and Tamsen and Michael Brown Family Professor of Entrepreneurship at Georgetown University (USA)

Amazing and inspiring! Finally, a book about great Indian role models to learn from! Once
again proving "greatness is made" and not born as anyone with the right learning mindset,
hard work and self-belief can succeed in their pursuits!

–Sharavan Goli
Chief Operating Officer, Coursera
(One of World's Largest Online Learning Platform)

"This is a fabulous book that takes you on an inspiring journey through the minds of 75 amazing Indians, who contributed to Nation Building in their own unique ways. The book also highlights the common traits of grit, humility, self-belief, and compassion, which shone bright in the lives of these people. A must read for people who aspire to realise their true potential and build a life of their dreams ."

–Dr Himanshu Rai
Director, IIM Indore

DEDICATION

To all dreamers, thinkers, and doers, in India
and everywhere else.
–Vishal K Gupta

To all young Indians who dream big and aspire
to make a difference.
–Vishal Gupta

Published by
Renu Kaul Verma
Vitasta Publishing Pvt Ltd
4348/4C, Ansari Road, Daryaganj
New Delhi – 110 002
info@vitastapublishing.com

ISBN 978-81-19670-99-4
© Vishal K Gupta & Vishal Gupta
First Edition 2024
MRP ₹ 495

All Rights Reserved.
No part of this publication may be reproduced, stored in a retrieval system, or transmitted in any form, or by any means—electronic, mechanical, photocopying, recording or otherwise—without the prior permission of the publisher. Opinions expressed in it are the author's own. The publisher is in no way responsible for these.

Edited by Soumitro Das
Cover and layout by Rohit Gautam
Printed by Vikas Computer and Printers

Contents

Introduction   *xiii*

Science And Engineering   xxiv-31
   Kiran Mazumdar Shaw   1
   Brahma Singh   5
   Thirumalachari Ramasami   9
   Koppillil Radhakrishnan   13
   Padmanabhan Balaram   17
   Nambi Narayanan   20
   Madabusi Santanam Raghunathan   24
   Vijay P Bhatkar   28

Civil Services   32-49
   Parveen Talha   34
   Vinod Rai   38
   Venkataraman Krishnamurthy   42
   Moosa Raza   46

Trade and Industry   **50-91**

    Shiv Nadar   52
    Azim Hashim Premji   56
    Venu Srinivasan   60
    Anand Gopal Mahindra   64
    G V Krishna Reddy   68
    Adi Burjorji Godrej   71
    Nagavara Ramarao Narayan Murthy   75
    Rajendra Singh Pawar   79
    Anil Manibhai Naik   83
    Ratan Tata   87

Sports   **92-155**

    Mithali Raj   96
    Mahendra Singh Dhoni   100
    Rahul Sharad Dravid   104
    Pankaj Advani   108
    Mary Kom   112
    Pullela Gopichand   116
    Pusarla Venkata Sindhu   120
    Bachendri Pal   124
    Viswanathan Anand   128
    Abhinav Bindra   132
    Harry Boniface Prabhu   136
    Love Raj Singh Dharmshaktu   140
    Arunima Sinha   144
    Deepika Kumari   148
    Devendra Jhajharia   152

Social Work — 156-185

- Saalumarada Thimmakka — 158
- Anil Prakash Joshi — 161
- Hari Pal Singh Ahluwalia — 165
- Arunachalam Muruganantham — 169
- Tulsi Gowda — 173
- Bindeshwar Pathak — 177
- Baburao Hazare — 181

Literature & Education — 186-201

- Sitakant Mahapatra — 188
- Ruskin Bond — 191
- MT Vasudevan Nair — 194
- Shekhar Gupta — 198

Medicine — 202-219

- Neelam Kler — 204
- Devi Prasad Shetty — 208
- Tsering Landol — 212
- Suresh Hariram Advani — 216

Arts — 220-287

- Saroja Vaidyanathan — 224
- Ilaiyaraaja — 228
- Channulal Mishra — 232
- Ajoy Chakrabarty — 236
- Hari Prasad Chaurasia — 240
- Zakir Hussain — 244
- A R Rahman — 248

Sudarsan Pattnaik	252
Naresh Chander Lal	256
Ram Narayan	260
Naseeruddin Shah	264
Shiv Kumar Sharma	268
Amitabh Bachchan	272
Kattassery Joseph Yesudas	276
Teejan Bai	280
Manoj Bajpayee	284

Public Affairs   **288-297**

Ujjwal Nikam	290
Ravindra Chandra Bhargava	294

Others   **298-317**

Chandi Prasad Bhatt	300
Balkrishna Vithaldas Doshi	304
Chewang Norphel	307
Jadav Payeng	311
Simon Oraon	314

Conclusion	*319*
End Notes	*329*

Introduction

When the Roman Senate ordered Julius Caesar, conqueror of Gaul, to disperse his troops, he instead led the 13th legion under his command across the river Rubicon on the northern border of Italy, in clear violation of Roman law. At the time, Roman generals were forbidden by law from entering Rome with a standing army. To do so was treason. As Caesar made the momentous decision to cross the river at the head of his soldiers, he is said to have declared *Alea iacta est*, a dramatic Latin proclamation that later became famous in English as *the die is cast*. Crossing the river with the army to enter Italy put Caesar in an irreconcilable opposition to the Senate, turning him into a traitor and making the expression *Crossing the Rubicon* forever synonymous with passing a point of no return.

Caesar's historic decision on that fateful day was memorialised in *Parallel Lives*, a series of profiles of notable personalities from ancient Greece and Rome, written by the philosopher Plutarch. Over the next two millennia, Plutarch's biographical account became the source of information on ancient heroes. To this day, *Parallel Lives* remains one of the most read biographical books of all times. The libraries of the Florence Court, French philosophers Montaigne and Montesquieu, Genevan philosopher and composer Jean-

Jacques Rousseau, and American philosopher Ralph Waldo Emerson, all had copies of the book. The French emperor Napoleon Bonaparte considered the book a guide for ruling well. The first American president George Washington, who had *Parallel Lives* in his personal library, tried to model himself on the heroes described in the book. His contemporaries Thomas Jefferson and Alexander Hamilton read Plutarch's book, as did most American leaders that came after them, including Abraham Lincoln, widely considered among the greatest presidents of the United States. The 26th American President, Theodore Roosevelt, kept a copy of the book in his breast pocket, noting that, 'I've read this little volume close to a thousand times, but it is ever new.' Indeed, well through the early twentieth century, *Parallel Lives* was considered essential reading in much of the western world, especially in the United States.

In 2013, the American author and journalist David Brooks gave a talk at Yale University titled 'Who Would Plutarch Write About Today'? Brooks's reference to the ancient philosopher's work may seem pretentious to a modern audience, yet his inquiry into who Plutarch would choose today is fascinating and compelling. Unfortunately, Brooks himself never answered his question, leaving others to delve into it, and discuss and debate their selections.

We reformulate Brooks question, asking instead: Who would Plutarch write about in India today? This reformulation of the original question is not as strange as it may seem at first glance. Plutarch was certainly aware of India, and the ancient country finds mention in his writings. He also recognised the valour and courage of the Indians, recounting the brave fight put up by King Porus against Alexander's marauding hordes. Of course, Plutarch wrote about the great battle on the shores of the river Hyphasis (modern Beas) from his vantage point as the chronicler of Alexander. It was only much later, when Indian historians began to turn a critical eye towards their country's history, that our understanding of the battle became more balanced and nuanced.

Plutarch profiled forty-eight Greek and Roman men, who he believed had achieved great success and made a mark in history. His main interest was in understanding 'what sort of a man was he?' (all were indeed men), exploring matters of personal character.

Our approach starts with Plutarch, yet departs from him in critical ways by broadening the scope of the inquiry to answer 'what sort of a person is s/he?' as well as diving into 'what did s/he do?' We take a gender-neutral approach as men and women now have equal rights and responsibilities to engage in the public sphere in most countries, including India. Women have long played an influential role through the ages in India, from Meerabai to Razia Sultan to Rani Laxmibai. The great patriot Subhash Chandra Bose fielded a women's regiment as part of the Indian National Army during the Second World War, decades before women in the armed forces became acceptable in many parts of the world. Since Independence, many women have played a remarkable role in shaping the trajectory of India. Thus, the decision to include men and women in our selection of Indian heroes is in keeping with the zeitgeist of our times.

Plutarch's reasons for selecting the personalities he discussed are not well understood, and the Greek philosopher never explained it in his own writings. Indeed, most books that focus on prominent individuals of a country tend to cherry-pick the people they discuss. We wanted to be transparent about our intent and method of choosing the Indians we cover. In this spirit, we describe our logic in detail.

Unlike Plutarch, we wanted to be objective about our selection of personalities worth discussing. We were interested in subjects who would be interesting to read about, and from whose stories one could learn about achievements and success. Selecting a pre-defined number of people from a population that was about 130 crores (1.3 billion) when this book started was challenging, to say the least. Trying to make sense of their lives, their journeys and their dreams, the challenges they faced and the setbacks they had, from dispersed and scattered archives and documents, then cohering the narratives into a book that one could take on a plane or keep on the bedside table to read, compounded the challenge. Our solution to this problem was to identify the heroes from the list of Padma awardees in India, a list which recognised outstanding achievements across a wide range of activities or disciplines.

Considered the highest civilian honours of India, Padma awards were instituted in 1954, and then reorganised in 1955 into three tiers: Padma Shri (distinguished service), Padma Bhushan (distinguished service of high order), and Padma Vibhushan (exceptional and distinguished service). Since then, awards across the three categories have been announced annually on the Indian Republic Day, except for brief interruptions during the years 1978-79 and 1993-97 when no awards were given. The awards are presented by the President of India in a formal ceremony at the imposing *Rashtrapati Bhawan* (Presidential Palace) during the month of March/April where the awardees are presented a *sanad* (certificate) and a medallion. Awardees also receive a small replica of the medallion, which they can wear during formal state events, if they want. Padma awards are a rigorous, independent measure of achievement, allowing us to focus our efforts on men and women with impeccable credentials in different fields.

In Plutarch's time, achievement was based usually on leading troops and winning military battles. In the present times, achievement can be in various spheres. Accordingly, the Padma awards are given across various walks of life, which gives us a broad cross-section of achievers from which to select eminent personalities. The awardees we discuss include artists, social workers, lawyers, scientists and engineers, business tycoons and entrepreneurs, doctors, teachers and writers, civil servants, and sportspersons, among others. Despite their diverse backgrounds, they share one common feature: all are high achievers who have made a mark in their field. One group of prominent people you will not find discussed in this book: politicians. One could endlessly debate the pros and cons of excluding politicians from our list of Indian heroes, but let's just say we wanted to keep politics out of this book.

We started with the list of Padma awardees after the turn of the century. We deleted from our list all non-Indians (e.g., Lia Diskin of Brazil and Barry Gardiner of United Kingdom) and people already deceased at the time work on this book started (e.g., Abdul Jabba of Madhya Pradesh and Manmohan Mahapatra of Orissa). As we mentioned earlier, politicians were eliminated as well. From this much shorter list, we identified the 75 Indians discussed in this book. Shortlisting just 75 high-achieving Indians from the hundreds of Padma awardees was not an easy task. We tried to be representative across several dimensions in our selection: field of distinction, home-state, gender, religion, and so on. Women and minorities were well-represented among the recipients of India's highest achievement awards. The 75 people we discuss here come from different states of India, from Mary Kom in the East to Ram Narayan in the West, and Hari Pal Singh Ahluwalia in the North to Kattassery Joseph Yesudas in the South. They span across the socio-economic spectrum from the richest Indians (e.g., Narayan Murthy and Ratan Tata) to those who live off the land (e.g., Tulsi Gowda and Saalumarada Thimmakka). Regardless of their geographical affiliation or socio-economic status, all Indians discussed here distinguished themselves through their extraordinary achievements.

Our list includes Indians of different religions, including Muslims (Zakir Hussain), Christians (Simon Oreon), and Parsis (Adi Godrej). Religious diversity has been, and remains, a uniquely Indian phenomenon. No other country in the world, in the present times or ever in history, is as religiously diverse as India. Indians of different religious stripes have co-existed for millennia and they will continue to live together for as long as one can see in the future. This book reflects – and celebrates – the religious diversity of India, by showcasing Indians across the religious spectrum.

At this stage, some might wonder why we decided to focus on 75 Indians in this book. India won its independence in 1947, after a long and brutal fight for freedom. At the time of Indian independence, many world leaders and public commentators thought there was little chance this young nation would survive, let alone thrive. Yet, India not only survived, but also expanded and grew, so much so that it is now one of the largest economies in the world, among the countries with a highly educated populace (even though it often does not feel or act accordingly). When work on this book started, India was getting ready to celebrate seven-and-a-half decades of independence. The popular press was buzzing with discussions of India@75, which helped us make the decision to focus on 75 Indians.

The format of this book is biographical, in that we present short narratives about Indian heroes, one chapter per person. The 75 chapters are organized into ten fields: science and engineering, civil service, trade and industry, sports, social work, literature and education, medicine, arts, public affairs, and others. Each chapter is written with the goal of summarising the trajectory of the hero's life, highlight the work they have done, and recognise some of the challenges and setbacks they faced on the way.

There are few major countries with a history as rich as India that have been as biographically neglectful of their prominent men and women. Biography has been surprisingly absent as a legitimate form of knowledge in India. The Harvard-educated historian Dinyar Patel attributes the lack of biographical tradition in the Indian canon to 'Marxist and post-colonial traditions' that equate achievements with elites, and thus unworthy of serious inquiry.[1] The Stanford scholar Abbas Milani considers the absence of biographies to be an intellectual failing of Islam, which for several centuries was the de-facto state religion of much, though not all, of the Indian subcontinent.[2] The Indian historian Vikram Sampath believes that Indians are 'plagued with a constant sense of apologia' about their achievements, resulting in derision of their heroes.[3] Whatever be the cause, the end-result is that biographical accounts of prominent men and women have been almost ignored, or even shunned, in India (although well-educated Indians are quick to embrace biographies of western heroes).

Plutarch hoped that the ancient personalities in *Parallel Lives* would be examples to emulate for generations to come. We share the same dream. We agree with Plutarch that there is much to learn from people who have made their mark. We hope that readers find the mini-biographies in this book inspiring and the high-achieving people discussed here, role-models.

Every society needs positive role models, successful people who we can look up to and be inspired by. Good role models motivate us to strive to realise our true potential and overcome our weaknesses. Having role models inspires us to do better in life. Argentinian football (soccer) player Lionel Messi had French legend Zinedine Zidane as his role model when he was growing up, labelling him his 'hero'. The entrepreneur Valentina Lopez, founder of travel site 'Happiness Without', considers Anita Roddick of The Body Shop as her role model, inspiring her to 'be ethical and see the business world in a humanitarian sense'. A whole generation of singers in India grew up considering the melody-queen Lata Mangeshkar as their role model. Tens of thousands of Indian cricketers, wannabe or actual, consider Sachin Tendulkar their role model.

A common lament in India is that there is a dearth of positive role models in society. Whether in business or sports or scientific research, most Indians have no good role models that inspire them to aspire and achieve. While systematic research on role models is missing in India, a small study done on post-graduate students (Masters level and beyond) at a regional Indian university provides some guidance: Only about 11 percent of surveyed students reported having role models outside their immediate family and their educational institution. The Annual Survey of Education Report, which focused on Indian youngsters in the 14-18 age group, revealed that 40% of the youth in the country do not have any role models for the profession they are considering.[4] Narayan Murthy, a co-founder of Indian software giant Infosys (and a Padma awardee discussed in the book), observed that 'the number of role-models that our youngsters can look up to is decreasing. How many people in our public life can you be proud of for honesty, courage, commitment, and hard work? And that number is dwindling'.[5] For a country of more than 130 crore (1.3 billion) people, considered the world's most populous country, it is unfortunate that most Indians, adult or youth, struggle to name even one or two role models that inspire them.

We (the two authors of this book) found it difficult to accept that the world's most populous country lacks role models. Instead, we felt that the problem was that there was little to no awareness about Indians who had been successful in their chosen field. In other words, role models exist, but people do not know about them. Consider the Indian javelin thrower Neeraj Chopra, who gained tremendous fame after winning India's first ever individual track-and-field Olympic gold. Before Chopra clinched the gold, most Indians did not even know his name and were unaware that India had medal prospects in javelin at the Olympics. Indeed, his success took most Indians by surprise. Yet, as is well-known, what seems to be overnight success often takes years of hard-work. Chopra was not a rookie when he competed for India in the 2020 Tokyo Olympics, as he had already won several medals (including gold) at international sporting events. The lay Indian, however, knew little to nothing about him before the Olympic gold and remains largely unaware of his journey and years of toil and perseverance that came before his stellar performance at the Olympics.

Why do Indians know so little about successful Indians worth emulating? For us, the answer to this question was straightforward: Dearth of biographical efforts in India, coupled with no consistent archival or scholarly data available about the lives of Indians who matter. As a result, a biographer interested in notable Indians, living or dead, is forced to reconstruct lives from 'fair or faux' artifacts, which are few to begin with, and often difficult to access, if not completely inaccessible. Dismal archives, shoddy record keeping, and stunning neglect of biographical accounts in India make writing an authoritative account of prominent Indians particularly challenging.[6]

Trimming any life to a handful of pages and to corral into a readable, reliable, and cogent narrative that captures the complex interplay of dreams and defeats, forces of history, desires and frustrations, and individual talent and perseverance is a herculean task under the best of circumstances. Our work in the present book was made more challenging by the few pages afforded to each person discussed here. Yet, this difficult task was rendered acceptable and rewarding by the deplorable alternative of allowing these lives to drift into oblivion. In our writing, we worked hard to ensure that the weight of 'received opinion', or of myths and rumors about a notable personality (such as Ratan Tata and Amitabh Bachchan), does not influence our mandate of biographical impartiality. At other times, usable artifacts were largely absent, leaving us with no option other than to seek interviews with the personalities themselves (e.g., Brahma Singh).

We understand that enthusiastic readers who might have hoped to see one or the other of their favorite Indian heroes (Sachin Tendulkar, Ameera Shah, Lata Mangeshkar, or Arnab Goswami, perhaps) in this book would be somewhat disappointed with our selection. To questions about 'why not X?' or 'why not Y?', our response is simply that this book is not the final work on the subject. We recognise, indeed welcome, similar books that identify eminent Indians using other criteria. Our hope is that this book will spur further interest in the life and work of notable Indians. If, after you finish reading this book, you find yourself picking up another biographical book about amazing, incredible, high-achieving Indians, or searching for information about other Padma awardees, we will consider our present work to have been successful.

75
AMAZING
INDIANS WHO MADE A DIFFERENCE

Science And Engineering

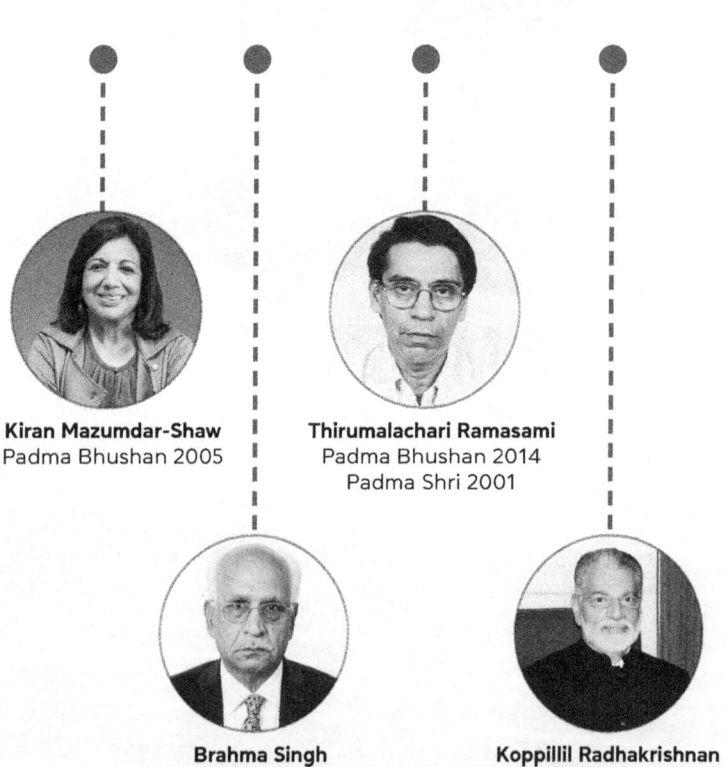

Padmanabhan Balaram
Padma Bhushan 2014

Madabusi Santanam Raghunathan
Padma Bhushan 2012
Padma Shri 2001

Sankaralingam Nambi Narayanan
Padma Bhushan 2019

Vijay Bhatkar
Padma Bhushan 2015
Padma Shri 2000

AWARDS

Kiran Mazumdar Shaw
The Self-made Female Billionaire

She wanted to follow in her father's footsteps. He was a brew master. She too trained to become one. The breweries of the 1970s, however, were no place for a woman, or so she was told.[1] A chance meeting with a visiting Scottish entrepreneur led her to start her own business. Within a short time, the company was making good money. *Financial Times* put her on the '50 Women in Business' list. Forbes counted her among the most powerful women in the world. Kiran Mazumdar-Shaw, India's first self-made female billionaire, received the Padma Shri (Trade and Industry) from the Government of India in 1989 and the Padma Bhushan (Science and Engineering) in 2005.

Kiran was born on 23 March 1953 to progressive middle-class parents. Her father was the head brew master at United Breweries, which at the time was owned by Vittal Mallya, father of the tycoon-turned-fugitive Vijay Mallya.[2] Like many middle-class girls of her time, Kiran wanted to be a doctor. When she did not make the merit list for medical college, she was disappointed.[3] Her father told her: 'If you can't get into medical school through meritocracy, then you don't deserve to go to medical school. If you really want to go to medical school, then work hard. You'll get into medical school through merit. If not, do something else.'

Kiran decided to pursue an undergraduate degree in zoology from Bangalore University. When she finished college, she decided to make her career in the same field as her father, which took her to Australia for a graduate degree in brewing.[4] Upon her return to India, she found it difficult to find a job as a brew-master in the country. Her father had already retired from United Breweries to start his own business, a malting company in the town of Baroda. The new venture did not work out the way he expected, and the family lost a good deal of money ('I want to forget it like a bad dream', said Kiran's mother, decades later).

Frustrated with her inability to find a job with an Indian brewery despite her education and family connections, Kiran applied and landed a job in Scotland. The plan was for her to intern for a few weeks with a small malting company in the sleepy village of Gurgaon near Delhi, and then fly to Scotland to begin her career with a brewery.

The morning of her departure for Gurgaon, Kiran received a telephone call that was to change the course of her life. 'This is Les Auchincloss from Biocon Biochemicals in Ireland. Can we meet today?' Kiran met Auchincloss at The Express Hotel in Baroda, where he laid out his proposal. His company had been sourcing some raw materials from India, but now wanted to set up a local branch. He had come to Baroda in search of a partner who would start and run Biocon India. A few minutes into the meeting, he asked Kiran to be his partner.

Kiran declined his proposal. Having just helped her father wind up his business, she had no appetite for another entrepreneurial venture. Give up her overseas job in Scotland to struggle with a new business in India? No way, Kiran told Auchincloss. When he asked to meet her again in Delhi, she introduced him to the founder of Barmalt, which was considered among the top companies in India's nascent malting industry. After the meeting, Auchincloss told Kiran, 'Thanks for the introduction, but I do not want a business partnership with Barmalt. I want an entrepreneur and I want you to be that entrepreneur.' He would mentor her, he promised. She would not need much money to start, he assured her, nor would she need any business expertise. It was clear he really wanted her as a business partner.

As the evening dragged on, Auchincloss made another attempt to convince Kiran. 'If you do not enjoy the work after a year, I will make sure you get the same job, or some other, in the brewing industry there', he told her. Kiran accepted the offer. Auchincloss had some enzymes and $3,000 cash with him which he gave to Kiran to start Biocon India. The next morning, Kiran left with Auchincloss to visit a Horlicks plant in Nabha district of the state of Punjab. The plant was owned by a Scottish businessman, who was willing to let Kiran do trials with Biocon enzymes in his facility.

Kiran and Auchincloss agreed to locate Biocon in Bangalore (now Bengaluru), a city where Kiran had grown up, gone to school (Bishop Cotton Girls' School), and done her undergraduate degree (Central College). Her father had a strong network in the brewing industry in the city, which would make it easier to gain access to customers. After a few weeks of training in Ireland, Kiran returned to India, and launched Biocon. The initial days were anything but easy. 'I had a lot of foolish courage because when I started the company, I found I had huge credibility challenges to overcome', says Kiran about her startup days. 'I was a 25-year-old woman with no business experience; I was trying to pioneer a sector called biotechnology which nobody had heard of. I had huge challenges from getting financial backing to even getting people to work in the organisation.'

Kiran initially focused on two enzymes, *isinglass* (obtained from dried swim bladders of tropical catfish for clarifying beer) and *papain* (derived from the papaya fruit for cooking meat).[5] Within a short time, Kiran was exporting enzymes to markets in North America and Western Europe, becoming the first successful home-grown Indian biotechnology company. It was not long before Kiran was able to move out from the rented premises where she had started the company to a large spacious facility. Since then, the company has grown tremendously, launching an initial public offering in 2004, which was oversubscribed.[6] Kiran had not only become a successful entrepreneur in her own right, she also practically launched the biotechnology sector in India.

Kiran is one of the few self-made female billionaires in the world. Her advice for aspiring entrepreneurs: 'There are no shortcuts to success. Don't be in a hurry to succeed. It is okay to make mistakes. But we should learn from our failures.'

Brahma Singh
The Horticultural Scientist

Early in his career at Defence Research and Development Organisation (DRDO), Brahma Singh wanted to work in Leh in the Indian region of Ladakh. His bosses, however, did not agree to send him there.[1] Several years later, when DRDO told him to join the Field Research Laboratory (FRL) in Leh, Singh did not want to go there. Leh is located at nearly 11,000 feet above sea level. For those not used to living at such heights, the low oxygen levels can cause dizziness, headaches or even acute mountain sickness. Acclimatising to high altitude air is even harder for older people as it becomes difficult to breathe and puts additional strain on the heart to pump more blood.

When Singh left his family in Delhi to work at Leh, there was no way he could have foreseen the changes that were going to happen in his life. What initially seemed like a 'punishment posting'—shunted to an undesirable location—turned out to be the start of the best phase of his professional career. The work Singh did in Leh opened many new doors for him, paving the way to receive the Padma Shri in 2014 for his contributions to science and technology.

Singh was born in 1941 to a farming family in Palari village of district Muzaffarnagar in Uttar Pradesh, the fifth of eight children of parents who could neither read nor write. The family was well-respected in the community, and the land provided a comfortable living. His parents had few expectations from their children. The thinking was that the kids can study if they want, and when done with school, they can come work on the farm. Singh had little interest in farming, so he decided to continue with school.

Singh started his professional career with a faculty position at Haryana Agriculture University, after a PhD from Indian Agriculture Research Institute (IARI) in Delhi. However, he soon got tired of the repetitive work of a professor, 'teaching the same thing to students year after year', as he describes it. By this time, he was already married and had three small children. Most people in his position would have stayed in a job that gave Singh status and a middle-class lifestyle without much work. Singh, however, decided to take a different path. He applied for a job with the DRDO, which had a strong interest in vegetable cultivation because it wanted to ensure good supply of fresh vegetables and fruits to armed forces in difficult remote areas.

Singh started at the DRDO as Senior Scientific Officer. It was at this time that Singh made his first trip to Leh for work. He fell in love with the place and requested to be sent there on a more long-term basis. His request was denied. Over the next few years, as Singh moved up the organisational hierarchy, he worked in different parts of the country: Mysore (Karnataka) in the South and Tezpur (Assam) in the East. In Tezpur, his team identified the hottest chilly in the world, *bhut jolokia* or ghost pepper, measuring more than one million Scoville Heat Units (SHU).[2]

In 1991, he was asked to join the laboratory at Leh as Director. The laboratory had been mismanaged and the DRDO had been told to either shut it down or fix it. Singh was seen as someone who could run things well. By now, Singh was past 50, his children had grown up, and there were no family accommodations for officers in Leh. Singh did not want to go.

Leh was unlike any other place that Singh had worked in before. 'Whatever I had studied, nothing was applicable there. Winter, summer crops grow in the same season', he observed. Instead of lamenting the unexpected turn in his career, Singh decided to learn about Leh and its issues by talking to anyone who would chat with him. He introduced small-scale interventions, such as experimenting with an underground polyhouse to harness solar and soil heat for cultivation. He led the development of new technologies for 'protected cultivation' to grow different kinds of vegetables in Leh. Soon, he earned the reputation as an officer who listens to people and does not pretend to know everything.

When some farmers came to ask for help to get rid of a weed that was growing everywhere, Singh volunteered to look it up in the IARI library on his next trip to Delhi. Singh's search in the library yielded results no one expected: What Leh farmers thought was weed was sea buckthorn, a multipurpose plant with tremendous potential for the region. Singh convinced the farmers to protect the natural growth and cultivate the plant, developing and sharing the technology for growing it.

After five years in Leh, when Singh was transferred back to the DRDO headquarters in Delhi, he continued to support sea buckthorn cultivation. At a seminar he organised to promote sea buckthorn an entrepreneur offered to set up a factory to make a beverage that could be bottled and sold widely. When the DRDO asked the entrepreneur for an exorbitant sum of money to license the technology for making the beverage, Singh intervened to make the technology readily available for commercialisation. India is now known for seabuckthorn-based nutraceutical, pharmaceutical and cosmeceutical products.

For many, retirement is a time to hang up their boots and

look back on their life with satisfaction. Singh saw retirement as a time to do more, embark on new initiatives. The DRDO had made him an Emeritus Scientist, only the second person to receive this honor in the organisation's history. Around 2004, then President APJ Abdul Kalam, who had been his boss at DRDO, invited him to work at the sprawling *Rashtrapati Bhawan* (President House) estate in Delhi. For the next three years, Singh worked on several novel projects there: herbal garden with medicinal plants, musical fountain garden, and a spiritual garden with plants important to different religions.

Singh's passion for his work is reflected in the various activities he has undertaken during his retirement. He runs the Professor Brahma Singh Horticulture Foundation (BSHF) to disseminate knowledge about the latest horticulture cultivation practices. In 2022, he was elected President of the Indian Society of Vegetable Science. 'Nothing is impossible', Singh notes, 'as long as you work hard with sincerity and honesty.'

☙❦❧

Thirumalachari Ramasami
Pioneering Advances in Leather Science

Born on 15 April 1948, Thirumalachari Ramasami is a technologist-turned-scientist and a scientist-turned-civil servant.[1] He is a distinguished researcher and leather scientist and served as Director of the CSIR-Central Leather Research Institute at Chennai from 1996-2006. In 2006, he assumed the role of Secretary, Science and Technology, Government of India and continued in the position till 2014. He is now affiliated with the Anna University, Tamil Nadu where he teaches both graduate and post-graduate students of the Department of Leather Technology the fundamentals of leather science.[2]

Ramasami completed his secondary schooling in 1963, from the G S Hindu School in Srivilliputtur, Tamil Nadu; senior secondary from St. Joseph's College, Tiruchirapalli, Tamil Nadu; in 1964; he went on to obtain a bachelor's as well as a master's degree in leather technology from the University of Madras in 1969 and 1972, respectively. He did his PhD in Chemistry from the University of Leeds, UK in 1976. He was a post-doctoral candidate, first at the Ames Laboratory at the Iowa State University from 1978-80, and then at the Wayne State University, US from 1981-83.[3] He worked as a visiting fellow at the University of Newcastle upon Tyne during 1983-84.[4] He returned to India in 1984 and joined CLRI in the capacity of Assistant Director.

Ramasami assumed the Directorship of CLRI in 1996. CLRI (Central Leather Research Institute) is a central government research and development laboratory set up to transform the leather industry into an industry that is innovation-driven. The organisation aims to conduct high-quality research and provide inputs to the leather industry in the form for knowhow about testing and technological certification for leather manufacturers. This is a leadership role. The laboratory is working towards promoting the national agenda for becoming a world leader in leather, leather products, leather chemicals and allied areas.[5]

Under Ramasami's leadership, CLRI acquired a truly global status for high-quality research, with about thirty percent of papers published worldwide for leather and allied areas, and registering more than seven per cent of patents worldwide. It also has a prominent position in fashion forecasting and has launched a large number of public-private partnerships to drive progress in leather in the country.[6]

Under his leadership, CLRI became a hub for academic research and industry partnerships in leather technology. Close to 900 tanneries in Tamil Nadu implemented sustainable initiatives and went green in just about eighteen months. His initiatives to improve the functioning and efficiency of the leather industry and tanneries helped save 250,000 jobs, resulting in INR 3500 crores of annual export and INR 6000 crores as annual turnover.[7] Under his leadership, the CLRI won two landmark awards – the CSIR Special Technology Award in 1998 and the Third World Network of Scientific Organisation's Technology Award for outstanding Science and Technology (S&T) innovations for the Micro Enterprise Sector in leather, in 1998.[8]

Ramasami has a large number of publications and patents

to his credit, establishing his stature as a renowned researcher and scientist. He has 230 research articles, 41 patents and 12 process know-hows relating to various aspects of leather production and leather research to his credit.[9] Many of his patents have been commercialised and deployed by industry. His research cuts across multiple domains: applied and basic research, inorganic chemistry, leather and chemical technologies, leather and environment related technologies, and the chemistry and applications of Chromium,[10] a silvery metallic chemical used in the tanning of leather.

Post his retirement from CLRI, Ramasami assumed the role of Secretary, Science and Technology (S&T) at the Government of India in May 2006 where he earned the unique distinction of being one of the longest serving secretaries in the government. As the Secretary, S&T, Ramasami undertook major initiatives to overhaul the research ecosystem in the country, especially in the centrally-funded R&D organisations. Schemes were introduced to attract talent to R&D and science, to rejuvenate R&D in Indian universities, stepping up international S&T collaborations, initiating public-private partnerships and de-bureaucratising research and making public-funded R&D organisations accountable.[11] He was a key contributor in drafting the 2013 Science, Technology and Innovation policy of the government of India.[12]

Recognising his research and contributions to the sciences, the Government of India conferred on him the Padma Shri in 2001 and the Padma Bhushan in 2014. He was also given the Shanti Swarup Bhatnagar award, the highest award in science in India given by the CSIR (Council for Scientific and Industrial Research) for notable and outstanding research, in the chemical sciences in 1993. He was also given the 'Vasvik Prize for Environmental Technologies' in 2004 for his work on the development of a pollution control system in leather industry and the 'Vasvik Prize for Chemical Sciences' in 1997 for his research on the development of chromium-based tanning agent, Alcrotan. He has also served as the Indian co-chair for the Indo-US Science and Technology Forum, as well as the US-India Science and Technology Commission.[13]

Talking about his philosophy of science and technology, especially for developing countries Ramasami mentions, 'I think we have to look at a science policy for people. It should enable faster and sustainable inclusive growth of the nation, and open our space for strategic partnerships for sustainable global growth by also serving the needs of the unserved, underserved markets of the world. People say, the world is flat. Could science policy serve to make it even? It is one thing to be flat, it's another thing to be even. And on this, I'd like to finish... Every lecture of mine I finish with Mahatma Gandhi. He says, "Economics that hurt the moral being of an individual of a nation are immoral and sinful." Therefore, I would like to talk about technologies for the pro-poor world.'

○○○

Koppillil Radhakrishnan
Leading India's Space Odyssey

The Mangalyan was India's first and cheapest interplanetary mission. It made India the first nation in Asia to reach the Martian orbit as well as the world's first nation for doing so in its maiden attempt. The man behind Mangalyan was Dr Koppillil Radhakrishnan. He was the Chairman of the Indian Space Research Organisation (ISRO) as well as the secretary of the Department of Space from November 2009 to December 2014, the period during which Mangalyan was conceptualised, designed, launched and set into the Martian orbit.

Radhakrishnan was born on 29 August 1949 at Irinjalakuda, in the Thrissur district of Kerala. Completing his schooling from Irinjalakuda, he pursued Electrical Engineering from the Government Engineering College, Thrissur. He did post-graduation in management from the Indian Institute of Management, Bangalore and obtained his doctorate degree from the Indian Institute of Technology, Kharagpur.

Radhakrishnan joined ISRO in 1971 where he worked on different projects such as the SLV-3 which was India's first satellite launch vehicle, the ASLV and the PSLV.[1] As a young engineer in the early 80s, Radhakrishnan was given the responsibility to lead ISRO's budgetary planning by the Chairman (Prof) Satish Dhawan and was asked to prepare a 10-year plan for the programme. It was a great opportunity for Radhakrishnan to learn and prepare to become a future leader even as he closely watched and imbibed many qualities from Prof Dhawan. Over time, he developed the ability to prepare reliable reports, an ability which is often lacking in many other scientists.[2]

As the Chairman of ISRO, Radhakrishnan elaborated and led a more diverse portfolio which included projects such as the MARS mission, the Lunar Mission, the GSLV, the Tsunami warning center, and a 24x7 disaster management center. Since June 2013, many successful missions such as PSLVs, the MARS orbiter mission and the GSLV-D5 were launched with the use of indigenous cryogenic technology.[3]

Launching the GSLV-D5 had been a great challenge for ISRO as there had been many unsuccessful attempts since 2001. This was only possible after a lot of ground tests especially for the indigenous cryogenic technology to ensure that it worked properly.[4] Later, five foreign satellites were launched which were an endorsement of the country's space capability.[5]

Mission Mangalyan was India's first mission to the planet Mars which had to overcome many challenges. The first was to launch a spacecraft with indigenous payloads, in a short span of about fifteen months. Many technological obstacles had to be surmounted; this included providing an enlarged shielding to the spacecraft so as to protect it from harsh operating conditions, thermal and radiation hazards and creating an onboard self-governance mechanism for the Orbiter to handle long communication delays and other contingency situations. Radhakrishnan, along with his team members, was able to deal with such challenges by proactively factoring in various design considerations. Not only did the team overcome the challenges, it also completed the project at a very low cost. The Mars mission was built using a modular approach that involved the use of technology developed earlier, with suitable modifications, saving both time and money.[6]

With Mangalyan, India became the only nation at the time to reach Mars on its first attempt. It also spent the least amount of money to do so. India's Mars mission had the price tag of about $74 million, about a tenth of the $671 million that the Mars program of the National Aeronautics and Space Administration (NASA) of the US cost.[7]

After the successful mission of Mangalyan, Radhakrishnan and his team started working on developing technology for a manned space mission.[8] As always, they were aware about the challenges such as providing a life support system to the crew, lessening the failure rate and an escape system in an emergency. The country's space agency has recently tested the atmospheric re-entry module.

Success has brought Radhakrishnan many awards. In 2014, he was awarded the Padma Bhushan for contribution to science and engineering, especially in the field of space science and technology. In the same year he was named as one of ten 'people who mattered' in the reputed science journal *Nature*.[9] Some of his other other awards include ISRO's Lifetime Achievement Award, the Allan D. Emil Award of the International Astronautical Federation, Ernst & Young Lifetime Achievement Award, Technovation-Sarabhai Award of the Indian Electronics & Semiconductor Association.

Radhakrishnan wants young students to work on key technological, social and environmental issues our world is facing today. He motivates young students by saying that 'exactly what you want to do and where you want to see yourself is really up to you and your passion in life, but we all need to be looking for better ways and means for realising an improved living environment for humankind while we walk on our way to personal growth. Particularly, we make a living by what we earn; we make a life by what we contribute.'[10]

Surprisingly, Radhakrishnan has not only been ahead in science and technology, he has also been an enthusiastic and active performer in the field of arts such as Carnatic music and Kathakali. He was attracted to the world of performing arts from his childhood and had even taken formal training in both.[11] While serving as Chairman of ISRO, he performed in the Good Knight Soorya Festival, an annual celebration of India's cultural diversity.

Padmanabhan Balaram
Mastermind of Molecular Symphony

An acclaimed biochemist, Padmanabhan Balaram is known for his work on natural peptides, which are short chains of amino acids. Balaram has also been the Director of Indian Institute of Science (IISc), Bangalore and is recognised for making valuable contributions to the design and synthesis of model peptides, particularly disulfides, an important component of the structure of proteins.

Born on 19 February 1949, Balaram completed his Bachelors' degree from Pune University in 1967, graduating in chemistry. 'I would have sat for the civil services examination since I had no intention of doing research until I attended IIT Kanpur. It was there that I first experienced the thrill of working in a lab', remarks Balaram.[1] He obtained his Master's degree in Chemistry from IIT Kanpur before moving to the United States for a PhD. After returning to India in 1973, he joined the IISc Bangalore as a Lecturer.

Coming from a chemistry background, Balaram's work has predominantly been in biology. Remembering his initial working days, he points out that his work in peptides was actually influenced by the department he was appointed to at IISc. He started work as a Lecturer in the department of molecular biophysics headed by G N Ramachandran, who had discovered the triple helical structure of collagen. 'I was little less than 25 years old when I came to the department. Ramachandran was an established and senior figure. I quickly realised that one had to do something in which he was interested; otherwise, you wouldn't have a good time in the department. After listening and attending seminars, I began to work in the field of polypeptide conformations, stereochemistry which I thought was a fertile field for a chemist', remembers Balaram.[2]

Being the only person in the department who had training in organic chemistry, Balaram was expected to perform chemical as well as biological work. Balaram started by making small peptides (fragments of proteins) through chemical synthesis. While working, he came across an unusual amino acid that was not available in his catalog. He decided to manufacture the amino acid that nobody had done at the beginning of their careers. Working on amino acids, Balaram realised that he could mimic the structure of proteins, through conformationally or stereochemically constrained amino acids.

The research and study of the crystallisation of amino acids made Balaram curious about proteins and peptides. He then started working on protein biochemistry and enzymes. His primary work has been in the area of polypeptide chemistry and protein biochemistry. Using a variety of techniques for his research, Balaram was often viewed as a generalist rather than a specialist by his peers. 'I have never been particularly specialised, be it nuclear magnetic resonance or crystallography or computational methods or infrared spectroscopy. At some point I have used all of them', said Balaram in one of his interviews.[3]

On working with Isabella Karle, who was the world's leading expert in the field of crystallography, Balaram recalls that she had agreed to work with him and had asked him to send her some crystals. 'You could say that the postman played a major role in my career', said Prof Balaram. Karle and Balaram had a fruitful collaboration. They published their first paper in 1985 and their last paper was published in 2014. Karle was in her mid-60s when she collaborated with Balaram. He believes that age should not be a factor in determining whether a person should work or not.

In his career spanning decades, Balaram has seen tremendous changes around him. He has seen how students, student-teacher relationships and technology have evolved with time. How with time the teaching standards have come down and education is nothing more than a war for percentages. He is of the opinion that there is a need for good teachers who are able to develop deep interest in different subjects in students.

Balaram, a genius in the domain of biochemistry, has not only contributed excellent work but has also collaborated with a number of foreign and Indian authors to spread knowledge like a beam of light. Balaram has been a mentor and guide to numerous students and an inspiration to many during and after his professional career.

Balaram has been conferred with many national and international awards for his contributions in the field of peptides and biochemistry that has furnished a platform for further research. In 2014, he was conferred the Padma Bhushan for his contributions towards science.

Nambi Narayanan
Integral to India's Satellite Launch Vehicle Development

Espionage scientist and a traitor... The year was 1994, when Sankaralingam Nambi Narayanan made it to the headlines. The head of the Indian Space Research Organisation's promising cryogenics division, Narayanan was allegedly accused of espionage and trading India's space secrets in exchange for money and other perquisites to foreign agents.

Narayanan was born in a middle-class family on 12 December 1941 in Nagercoil village in Kanyakumari district, Tamil Nadu. Young Narayanan was fascinated by aeroplanes and graduated in Mechanical Engineering from Madras University. 'I always had a fascination for aircraft and flying objects', remembers Narayanan.[1] He was a bright student and rose through the ranks that won him a scholarship to Princeton University to study rocket propulsion systems.

On returning to India, Narayanan joined ISRO and worked with the stalwarts of India's space programme. 'When I began working with ISRO, the space organisation was in its infancy. We never really had a plan of developing any rocket systems. We were planning to use rockets from the US and France to fly our payloads', observes Narayanan. Recognising his potential, Narayanan[2] was given the responsibility of developing homegrown Indian rockets.

The ambitious project of homegrown rockets was soon put on hold in November 1994 due to a scandal—one that turned the life of a zealous scientist upside down. On the morning of 30 November 1994, Narayanan was pulled out from his house by police officers and taken to a nearby police station only to be asked to wait for the boss. The boss did not show up until next morning when suddenly Narayanan was put under arrest. Journalists gathered in front of the station and within hours Narayanan was declared a traitor. The newspapers started calling Narayanan 'the man who sold rocket technology to Pakistan, after falling into a honey trap set by two women from the Maldives'.[3] Narayanan's life was never the same again.

Narayanan was produced before the court. 'The judge asked me whether I confess to the crime. I asked, "What crime?" They said, "The fact that you have transferred the technology." I couldn't understand anything,' he remembers.[4] The media reported that apparently a tall athletic woman from Maldives named Mariam Rasheeda had enticed ISRO's top scientist into selling her the secrets of rocket technology. She was allegedly working for Inter-Services Intelligence (the spy agency of Pakistan) and weeks later the police caught Fauziyya Hassan, a Maldivian friend of Rasheeda. Following their arrests Narayanan was not only arrested but also subjected to torture when he refused to 'make a confession' or make false accusations against top ISRO officials.[5]

Narayanan was blamed for corruption and violating laws of secrecy, among other charges. He tried to convince the officers that he was being framed since rocket secrets could not be transferred via papers. Now, nearing eighty years, he says that the Kerala police had 'fabricated' the case and that the technology they talked about did not even exist in 1994 in India. 'How can I sell a technology (cryogenic) that was not existent in India in 1994? Why on earth would any entity want to cultivate me as a spy to sell them a technology (Vikas/Viking Engine) which was available in the open market and as common as brinjal', mentioned Narayanan in one of his interviews.[6]

Narayanan reminisces that his interrogators used to beat him up and make him answer questions for thirty hours without letting him sit. He was kept in a high security prison along with a 'serial killer' who had beaten his victims to death. Despite his constant pleas, Narayanan had to spend 50 days in captivity which included nearly a month in prison. A month after this, the Central Bureau of Investigation (CBI) took over the case from Kerala Investigation Bureau and after two years, in 1996, the case was closed due to lack of evidence. Narayanan along with five others, including the then ISRO Deputy Director D Sasikumaran who were charged with espionage, were released.

Later the federal detectives said that no evidence points towards the exchange of confidential documents from the space agency to Pakistan. No money was found in return for drawings of engines. ISRO held an internal investigation that proved that no drawings or important information relating to cryogenic engines were missing.

Finally, Narayanan rejoined ISRO, but this time only as an administrative worker. However, his ordeal had not ended. The government in Bangalore tried to reopen the case and take it to the Supreme Court. The case was finally dismissed in 1998. In 2001, Narayanan finally retired. The struggle for redemption cost his family and him not only financially but physically and mentally as well.

In 2018, the Supreme Court of India directed a high-level panel to compensate Narayanan with a sum of INR 50 lakhs. The court also stated that the police action against Narayanan was wrongful and that his basic human rights were jeopardised and he was compelled to face 'cynical abhorrence'.⁷ The court also prescribed measures to be taken against the officials who had caused 'tremendous harassment' and 'immeasurable anguish' to Narayanan. Moreover, the state government later decided to payout INR 1.3 crores as compensation. The case had a political fallout, with a section in the Congress targeting the then Chief Minister of Kerala, late K Karunakaran over the issue, that eventually led to his resignation.⁸

Narayanan had to fight for his dignity for more than 20 years. On 16 March 2019, Narayanan was awarded the Padma Bhushan. Narayanan played a prominent role in developing the Vikas Engine which was used for the first Polar Satellite Launch Vehicle (PSLV) launched by India. The engine has been used in most of the historic missions of ISRO, such as the Chandrayaan (India's moon mission) and Mangalyaan (India's Mars mission).⁹

Narayanan finally got his name cleared from the supposed 'scandal' that almost destroyed his life.

❊❊❊

Madabusi Santanam Raghunathan
Maths Genius

Madabusi Santanam Raghunathan is an Indian mathematician born on 11 August 1941 at Anantpur, in present-day Andhra Pradesh. His father had a timber business and mother belonged to a family of academicians. Raghunathan's maternal grandfather was a renowned Professor of English who had written for the prestigious *Cornhill* Magazine, a popular Victorian magazine published monthly from London. Though Raghunathan's father was into business, there were talks about science at home and his father used to encourage children to learn science.

Growing up in such a family, Raghunathan was an unusually bright student and completed his schooling from the Madras Christian College High School in the year 1955, at the young age of fourteen. At school, an interesting incident happened with Raghunathan when he absent-mindedly left the examination hall along with the Sanskrit answer booklet in which he had to answer the questions. When the examiner found one answer script missing, they identified that it was Raghunathan. He could only manage this situation when the headmaster stood up for him and vouched for his integrity and ethical conduct.[1]

The University of Madras had a norm in those days of not

admitting a student if he/she was less than 14 years and six months old. Raghunathan therefore had to move to Bangalore and study Intermediate at St. Joseph's College from 1955-57. He then enrolled for a B.A. course in Mathematics at the Vivekanand College in Chennai. Subsequently, he enrolled for a PhD at the University of Mumbai and successfully defended his dissertation in 1966. He was immediately appointed as an Associate Professor at the Tata Institute of Fundamental Research (TIFR) at the young age of 25 years.[2] He continued to work at TIFR till his retirement. He also served as the Professor of Eminence as the DAE (Department of Atomic Energy)-Homi Bhabha Chair Professor at TIFR. Presently, he is the Head of the National Centre of Mathematics at IIT (Indian Institute of Technology), Bombay.

Raghunathan also held visiting faculty positions at institutions around the world. He holds the distinction of being invited to speak at the 1970 International Congress of Mathematics (ICM) at Nice, France at the age of 29 years. The ICMs are held every four years and mathematicians from around the world look forward to being invited to speak at the event. So far, a very few Indian mathematicians have been invited and Raghunathan was one of the first to represent India at this prestigious scientific event.[3]

Raghunathan's work mostly lies in exploring 'discrete subgroups of Lie groups', defined by the mathematician Sophus Lie. It was found that the examination of the discrete subgroups of the Lie groups have tremendous bearing on geometry and the number theory. This is the area that attracted Raghunathan's attention and he addressed this topic through his research, thereby emerging as one of the undisputed leaders in this field.[4] One of his conjectures, known as the 'Raghunathan conjecture' has been extremely influential in understanding the dynamics of flows and their application in real life.[5]

In a book titled *A Panorama of Pure Mathematics* published in 1977 by a French mathematician, Jean Dieudonne, established Raghunathan as an individual who contributed to the field of mathematics. Raghunathan was only in his mid-thirties at the time.[6] Raghunathan published *Discrete Subgroups of Lie Groups* in 1972, which has now become a classic.[7]

Describing Raghunathan's work and his contributions to the field, S G Dani, Professor of Mathematics at TIFR observes, 'Raghunathan's work is characterised by uncommon ingenuity on the one hand and dexterous use of techniques from a variety of areas in mathematics, on the other hand. He embodies the rare combination of a modern mathematical genius with an urge to do pioneering work and a scholar in the classical mould interested in imbibing and propagating ideas. He is an enthusiastic teacher, ever eager to explain intricacies of various topics to students, both inside and outside the classroom'.[8]

Raghunathan has played an active role in promoting the study of mathematics in India by serving on the board of various scientific bodies. He was a member of the executive committee of the International Mathematical Union and also the Chairman of the governing council of the Mehta Research Institute at Allahabad. He served as a member of the National Board of Higher Mathematics since its formation in 1983 and went on to become its Chairman in 1987. The board promotes the study of mathematics by providing scholarships to talented students at the masters and PhD levels, conducting competitions such as mathematics Olympiads, mathematics training and talent search competitions, and also organising conferences. The board was instrumental in organising the prestigious ICM, held at Hyderabad in 2010. This was the first time that ICM had been held in India.[9]

On the current and future state of mathematics in India,

Raghunathan states that 'while we have indeed come a long way in the post-independence era, the future poses some serious questions. There is increasing paucity of talented young people taking to mathematics, and our means to meet the problems seem to be quite meagre in comparison to the socio-economic factors responsible for it'.[10] Raghunathan is however optimistic about the future. He observes that 'while the numbers in India are small and on the average Indian mathematicians may not have a good standing, the peaks are world class'.[11]

Raghunathan has been honoured by international agencies for his contributions. On 14 July 2000, he was inducted as a Fellow of the Royal Society of London. He received the Srinivasa Ramanujan Medal of the Indian Academy of Sciences in 1991, the Shanti Swarup Bhatnagar Award in 1977 and The World Academy of Sciences (TWAS) Award in 1991.

The Government of India recognised his contributions to science and conferred on him the Padma Shri in 2001 and the Padma Bhushan in 2012.

888

Vijay P Bhatkar
Architect of India's Param Supercomputers

Vijay Pandurang Bhatkar, a pioneering Computer Scientist best credited for developing India's first supercomputer, *Param*,[1] was born on 11 October 1946 in Akola district of Maharashtra. Bhatkar completed his bachelor's degree in Electrical Engineering from Nagpur University in Maharashtra, a master's degree in engineering from MS University in Baroda, Gujarat and a PhD from IIT Delhi.[2] Bhatkar was a top student throughout his education, finishing his engineering degree when he was only eighteen years old.

In 1971, after Bhatkar had completed his PhD, he was chosen to be a part of Indira Gandhi's (then Prime Minister of India) Electronics Commission (EC). Around that time, Intel had developed the microprocessor and Bhatkar proposed an education program on microprocessors that was introduced in engineering colleges. Bhatkar also went on to start the Electronic Research & Development Centre (ER&DC), India's largest electronics R&D lab at Kerala when he was just 31 years old. The lab became a harbinger of India's electronics revolution and was instrumental in designing devices such as colour TV, colour TV telecast equipment, low power transmission, and a microprocessor-based traffic system.[3]

The most important phase in Bhatkar's career came in the

late 1980s. Rajiv Gandhi, the then Prime Minister of India met the then US President Ronald Reagan in 1987 and requested him to sell the Cray supercomputer to India. The request was denied and the Cray was only allowed to sell the previous generation supercomputer to India and that too for weather forecasting purpose only. A US official had remarked that if it was used for any other application, 'then forget about the chip, even a pin will not be allowed to come to India'.[4]

Rajiv Gandhi met Bhatkar and asked him if India could develop a supercomputer. Gandhi had asked him 'Can we do it?', to which Bhatkar answered, 'I have not seen a supercomputer as we have no access to supercomputers, I have only seen a picture of the Cray! But, yes, we can.' The next question was, 'How long will it take?' Bhatkar answered immediately, 'Less than it will take us in trying to import Cray from US'. Finally, the Prime Minister asked, 'How much money it would take?' Bhatkar responded, 'The whole effort, including building an institution, developing the technology, commissioning and installing India's first supercomputer will cost less than the cost of Cray'.[5]

In order to develop indigenous technology, the Government of India set up the Centre for Development of Advanced Computing (C-DAC) in 1988 that was charged with the goal of developing a supercomputer for India. The centre was built as a society comprising of scientists under the Ministry of Communications and Information Technology and the then Department of Electronics.[6]

The rest is history. Within three years, the team of scientists at C-DAC rolled out India's first supercomputer Param 8000 in the year 1991. In order to prove to the world that India has developed its own supercomputer, Bhatkar took it to a conference and put it as an exhibit. A US newspaper published a news report on this event with a title, 'Denied supercomputer, Angry India does it!'[7] The speed of Param 8000 was 5 Gflops (1 Gflop equals '1 billion floating point operations per second'), making it the world's second fastest supercomputer at that time. Reflecting on this event, Bhatkar responds, 'Great nations are not built on borrowed technology.'[8]

The Param 8000 laid the platform for the development of Param series of supercomputers. In 2002, Param 20000 achieved a top speed of 1 Tflop (1 Tflop equals '1 trillion floating point operations per second').[9] Based on his experiences with the Param supercomputers, Bhatkar went on to develop the National Param Supercomputing Facility (NPSF) through which a nationwide access to high performance computing could be provided.

Bhatkar is also credited with establishing many of India's top computing facilities such as the Electronics Research and Development Centre (ER&DC) in Thiruvananthapuram, Kerala, the ETH Research Laboratory and the International Institute of Information Technology (IIIT), the India International Multiversity, all in Pune, the Indian Institute of Information Technology and Management, Kerala (IIITM-K), and the Maharashtra Knowledge Corporation (MKCL).[10]

Bhatkar has also served on prestigious government bodies such as the Scientific Advisory Committee to the cabinet of the Government of India, governing council member of the CSIR, India, a member of India's IT task force, and as the Chairman of the eGovernance committees of the governments of Maharashtra and Goa.[11] In 2017, he was appointed as the third Chancellor of the Nalanda University, a centrally-funded institute of national importance in Rajgir (Bihar).[12] He also served as the Chairman of the Board of Directors of IIT Delhi from 2012 to 2017.

Bhatkar is an ardent promoter of the synthesis of science and spirituality. Multiversity, an educational initiative he started in Pune, aims to impart 'Integrative Education' to students and which seeks to dissolve boundaries between different disciplines and promote holistic learning by integrating science, culture and spirituality.[13] He believes that, 'Liberation is truly achieved when one dedicates themselves to understanding the synthesis of science and spirituality'.[14]

In recognition of his contribution to science and technology in the country, the Government of India conferred on him the Padma Shri in 2000 and the Padma Bhushan in 2015.

☙☙☙

Civil
Services

Parveen Talha
Padma Shri 2014

Vinod Rai
Padma Bhushan 2016

V Krishnamurthy
Padma Vibhushan 2007
Padma Bhushan 1986
Padma Shri 1973

Moosa Raza
Padma Bhushan 2010

Parveen Talha
Trailblazer in Narcotics Control and
UPSC Leadership

If you want to serve the country, she says, you have to be on the decision-making side of the table. Her own career exemplified her philosophy. Over the course of a long career as a civil servant, Parveen Talha racked up many firsts: first Muslim woman in the Indian Civil Services, and first officer from the Indian Revenue Services to become a member of the Union Public Service Commission, among her many achievements. In 2014, she was honoured by the Government of India[1] with the Padma Shri in recognition of her contribution to the civil services.

Parveen was born to an upper middle-class Muslim family in Lucknow, the capital city of the state of Uttar Pradesh. Her lawyer father was active in the Indian freedom struggle. Her mother was a graduate in arts, which was uncommon among women of her time. Like many Muslim families at the time, Parveen's family found itself at a crossroads when India got independence. Some of her uncles decided to relocate to the new country set up for Muslims, but her parents made the decision to remain in India. They did not know it at the time, but their decision was to have a major impact on Parveen's life.

The secular zeitgeist of independent India allowed Parveen's parents to raise their two children—a son and a daughter—similarly. 'Neither my parents nor my relatives treated my brother and me differently', Parveen says. She was sent to one of the best schools in the city, Loreto Convent, which had a storied history dating back to the 1800s. Her parents firmly believed in the value of education, and the family climate stressed academic excellence. While Muslims are a numerical minority in India, Parveen's parents never considered religion or community to be an impediment to what their children could achieve in independent India. 'I do not even consider Muslims to be a minority in India. I think we are the second-largest majority in the country', Parveen declares.

Parveen finished her schooling with a first division in the Senior Cambridge Exam, which was in prevalence in India during her teenage years. Her good performance in the school exams led her father to encourage her towards trying for the Indian Civil Services, entry to which required passing a national-level exam. He motivated her with examples of woman who had been successful in making it to the civil services, including Anna Rajam George from Kerela, the first woman to join the Indian Administrative Services after independence. At the same time, her father also told her that if she did not make it through the examination for the civil services, she could try to be a teacher. During college, Parveen started studying for the civil services as well as worked hard to excel in her education in case she needed to pursue a teaching career. After finishing her Masters of Arts degree from Lucknow University, she joined Loreto College as a teacher in 1965.

Parveen fulfilled her parents' dreams and aspirations when she passed the civil service exam to join the Indian Revenue Service in 1968. She was an idealist, driven by the passion to make her family proud and serve her country. 'We were fortunate to follow the generation that had led India to freedom in 1947. They had passed before the country could realise its full potential. I saw our generation to be responsible for the next phase of India's story', Parveen says.

At the time, there were few women in the civil services. She was the seventh female officer in the custom department. Almost all senior officers were men, who did not really understand how to do deal with women subordinates in a professional manner. 'To be honest, they did not know what women could and could not do', Parveen states.[2]

As Assistant Collector of Foreign Travel Tax, she was one of the highest-ranking women in the civil services, but it was not a valued position in the hierarchy.

When she reached out to her superiors about her role, she was told that she could not be given a better position as she was a woman. For the first time in her life, Parveen felt that her gender was limiting her. It was not clear to her what she could do to deal with the gender bias she faced, so she simply focused on working hard in her job. She also shared her predicament with senior officers. As time passed, Parveen realised that her lack of experience in roles that allowed her independent charge was becoming an impediment to future growth. Frustrated with the situation, she reached out to higher officers. Fortunately, a senior officer sympathetic to her plight recommended her for a position with independent responsibility.

As the country's first female Deputy Narcotics Commissioner, Parveen was sent to Uttar Pradesh, where opium production and smuggling was a big issue. Unlike many of her peers who preferred to remain in the safe confines of their office, Parveen chose to be in the field, travelling widely in the areas in her jurisdiction to control drug farming and trading.[3] Her work ethic earned her the reputation of an upright and honest officer who could not be corrupted or tempted.

Parveen also served as Director General of Training at the National Academy of Custom Excise and Narcotics (NACEN), which is now the National Academy of Customs, Indirect Taxes and Narcotics. The institution is an apex training institute for the Indian government for capacity building of civil servants. Parveen helped NACEN get international acclaim, when she led the institution to become the World Custom Organisation (WCO) Training Institute for the Asia-Pacific Region. Under her leadership, the custom department played a major role in controlling the smuggling of Ozone Depleting Substances by introducing new focused training programs for custom officers.

In 2000, Parveen received the President's medal for exemplary service. Shortly after her retirement in 2004, she became a member of the Union Public Service Commission. No other Muslim woman had ever reached the heights that Parveen achieved. 'A big problem in the Muslim community in India is that people who have been successful have not extended a helping hand to their less successful brethren. There are few positive role models for young Muslims who want to succeed.' While Parveen does not define herself in terms of her religion, there is no doubt that her success is an inspiration for young Muslim men and women who want to be successful.

888

Vinod Rai
A Stalwart in Public Financial Accountability

Vinod Rai served as the Comptroller and Auditor General (CAG) of India from 2008 to 2013. He was the man behind unearthing many of the scams that the nation read about during the years 2010 to 2013. Scams such as the 2G scam, coal block allocations called Coalgate, the Commonwealth Games scam not only shook the people of India but also led to political upheavals in the country that eventually led to the end of Congress rule at the centre and the election of the BJP government led by Narendra Modi.

Rai was born on 23 May 1948 in Ghazipur in western Uttar Pradesh. He completed his schooling from the Birla Public School in Pilani, Rajasthan. Thereafter, he obtained a bachelor's and a master's degree in economics from the Delhi School of Economics, where he was taught by Manmohan Singh, who was later to become the country's prime minister. Rai also obtained a Master's degree in Public Administration in 1988 from Harvard University, USA.

Rai was a 1972 batch Indian Administrative Service (IAS) officer who started his career in Nagaland, where he showed signs of unusual independence, courage and grit. Once, while still a young trainee officer, he came to know about the death of a district collector who had been killed by militants.

The body of the collector had been abandoned as no one was willing to retrieve the body for fear of militants. Rai called his driver and asked him to drive without telling him where they were headed. Only midway did he tell his driver where they were going.[1]

Rai later moved to Kerala and started his administrative career there as the sub-collector of Thrissur District. He went on to become the collector of the city and spent eight years there. He was given the title of second *Sakthan Thampuran* (translated as 'powerful ruler') for the work he did for the development of the Thrissur City. Later, he was appointed as the Principal Secretary (Finance) in the State Government of Kerala. He also served in senior positions in the Ministries of Commerce and Defence for the Government of India in Delhi. Prior to his appointment as CAG, he served as Secretary, Financial Services and Additional Secretary in the Banking Division which had jurisdiction over banks and insurance companies under the Ministry of Finance.

Rai was the kind of civil servant who knew how to get work done in the government. He has been instrumental in many reforms in India, including the overhaul of the administrative structure of Indian railways, which entailed introducing accrual accounting. He served as the chairman of the Banks Board Bureau, a body set up by the Indian government to reform public banking in India. He has also served as a director on the boards of a range of financial institutions, including ICICI Bank, the State Bank of India and the Life Insurance Corporation of India, and is a distinguished visiting research fellow at the Institute of South Asian Studies, National University of Singapore.[2] However, he will always be remembered for his tenure as the CAG of India.

Rai was appointed as CAG of India with the backing of the then finance minister P Chidambaram. But he served up uncomfortable audit reports that pinned many government departments beyond the baseline. Rai observed, 'Accountability becomes more important when public funds are involved. This is because public funds come from taxes, which we have to pay. Because there is compulsion to pay, we need to know how the money is spent. This is why governments have higher accountability to its citizens'.[3]

As the CAG, Rai reported startling revelations and grave shortcomings on the government's functioning. In November 2010, CAG released the first of a series of audit reports that would make headlines: the allocation of 2G telecom spectrum. CAG estimated the presumptive revenue loss to the government incurred by the telecom ministry at INR 1.76 lakh crore (1.76 trillion), a sum that became the subject of controversy.[4] He further produced a string of audit reports disclosing corruption within various levels of government in fields as varied as the 2010 Commonwealth Games, the allocation of coal blocks, wasteful expenditure on the fertilizer subsidy, lapses in Air India Limited's acquisition of aircraft, holes in defence spending, the sale of sugar mills in Uttar Pradesh, and anomalies in the award of contracts to exploit natural gas reserves.[5] The findings of the three reports—a collective loss of about INR 2.2 lakh crore (2.2 trillion) to the exchequer.[6]

Rai came under intense and vituperative attack from ruling party politicians. There were charges that the CAG was wrongly adjudicating on policy instead of merely auditing a government department for the possibility of financial irregularities.[7] But to most ordinary Indians, Rai had become the new national hero—someone who had used his official post to do the job that the Constitution of India envisaged for him and in the process demonstrated how politicians were ganging up to strip the national exchequer.[8]

Ordinary people who had no clue as to what the CAG does, suddenly became, thanks to Rai, aware about the powers of this office. Rai is the first of 30 Indian CAGs, who will be remembered for showing us that the government and politicians can be made accountable, if statutory bodies simply do their job. Rai managed to face relentless political pressure with unflappable élan. 'I am convinced that it is his personality that has allowed him to unleash the power of the office of the CAG', said a senior IAS officer who had worked with him in Kerala. 'He takes leadership. He works like a general commanding his forces.'[9]

Recognising his contribution to the country, Rai was conferred the Padma Bhushan for civil services in 2016.

Venkataraman Krishnamurthy
Father of Public Sector Undertakings in India

Venkatarman Krishnamurthy started his career as a technician of electrical installations at two airfields during the Second World War.[1] By the time of his retirement, he had been at the helm of four large public sector undertakings in the country: Bharat Heavy Electricals Limited (BHEL), Maruti Udyog Ltd., Steel Authority of India Ltd. (SAIL), and Gas Authority of India Ltd. (GAIL). He had also been the Chairman of Indian Institute of Management at Ahmedabad (1985-1990), Indian Institute of Management at Bangalore (1982-1984), and Indian Institute of Technology at Delhi (1990-1993), among others. The Indian government recognised his contribution to the civil services with the Padma Shri in 1973, Padma Bhushan in 1986, and Padma Vibhushan in 2007.

Many admirers of Krishnamurthy consider him among the best public sector managers in India. Others compare him most favorably with the leading Indian CEOs of his generation, public or private. Krishnamurthy's management philosophy rested on five pillars: treat people with dignity, maintain constant communication with all stakeholders, create awareness of productivity and quality inside and outside the organisation, develop a culture oriented towards customers and the market, and constantly upgrade the technological infrastructure of the company.

Krishnamurthy was born on 14 January 1925, the youngest of three sons. At the time of his birth, the family was quite wealthy as his paternal grandfather was the largest landowner of Karuveli, a village in the Tiruvarur district of the state of Tamil Nadu. Within a few short years, Krishnamurthy's family fell on hard times. The family house had to be sold and Krishnmurthy's father moved to Madras to try something new. Soon, Krishnamurthy lost his mother. He stayed on in the village with his uncle, completed his school education there, and then moved in with his elder brother, who was already working in Madras (now called Chennai).

A relative suggested joining a three-year engineering course, which could help Krishnamurthy find a job doing war-related activities for the British government in India. When he finished his engineering education in 1943, some family friends helped him get temporary employment as an airfield technician.

When India became independent in 1947, Krishnamurthy was named Supervisor of the Madras Electricity Supply Corporation where his brief was to evaluate the assets of the organisation. At the electricity department of Madras Presidency of the newly independent country, Krishnamurthy found his first mentor, V P Appadurai, the Chief Engineer. Krishnamurthy himself describes his time there thus:

> Appadurai was always the first to enter office. Soon he found I was there before him. He also found that I had an aptitude for solving the most difficult problems with speed, and he started entrusting me with more and more responsibilities. At one point, those among the old guard at the technical directorate complained to Appadurai that he was favouring me unduly and not giving them opportunities to prove themselves. Appadurai, on his part, ignored such protests and said that he would encourage anyone coming up to the same standards. It did not bother me either, because at a very young age I got important responsibilities like working on

the designs of the Periyar and Kundah hydroelectrical projects and making a presentation to then Prime Minister Jawaharlal Nehru on the achievements of the erstwhile Madras Electricity Department. My stint there gave me the opportunity to be associated with the beginning of the development activity of independent India.

In the early 1950s, the Planning Commission—set up by the Government of India for economic planning to develop the new country—invited applications for its natural resources division for the Second Five-Year Plan. At the end of his one-year deputation in the Commission, Krishnamurthy decided to take the Central Engineering Services (CES) exam, which helped him get promoted to Senior Research Officer with the Commission to work specifically on power development.

Krishnamurthy believes that joining the Planning Commission was the turning point in his career as his five-year stint there gave him a ringside view of policy making and taught him to look at problems in a holistic manner. 'I doubt if I would have been able to achieve the successes I did later in my professional life if it had not been for my years there', he shared.

In 1960, Krishnamurthy left his secure CES job to join Heavy Electricals (India) Ltd as an Officer on Special Duty for K B Mathur, who had been tasked with setting up new power equipment manufacturing plants after his retirement from Railway Board. In Mathur, Krishnamurthy found another mentor. As he wrote years later:

> Mathur was a wonderful boss, and it was he who helped hone my managerial capabilities. He delegated responsibilities and made people working under him feel empowered, a lesson which I put to practical use when I reached positions of authority later. Between four and six every evening, over tea, he would review with me all that had happened during the day and discuss what else needed to be done over the

following week or so. The next morning, it was left to me to convey all that needed to be done to the general managers of the three plants. He never kept any files or papers on his desk, and work never got stalled.

In the 1960s, when the prevailing sentiment was that Indian executives can manage only small organisations as they had limited managerial experience and talent, Krishnamurthy went on to head BHEL. He showed, 'for the first time in India, the ability of a CEO to lead a large multi-unit, high-technology, capital intensive long gestation company to high performance', an observer commented. His success at BHEL led, a few years later, to an appointment to revive the moribund Maruti Udyog Limited where he brought the 'People's Car' to life. The success of Maruti led him to, ultimately, take up the responsibility of turning around SAIL. His time there is remembered for the way he focused the steel producer on the customer and readied it for domestic and foreign markets in a competitive environment, a distant possibility before his arrival there.

Any one of his successes—building BHEL in the capital goods sector, reviving the virtual private sector joint venture Maruti, and turning around the steel giant SAIL—would have been enough to qualify him as a great CEO. Two of them put him among the best CEOs in the world. All three take him to the stratosphere, virtually beyond reach and comparison, where few business leaders, Indian or foreign, have ever reached.

❦ ❦ ❦

Moosa Raza
A Storied Journey of Diplomacy

Moosa Raza, an Indian Administrative Services officer who has held prestigious positions in the government over the years, was born on 27 February 1937 in Minambur, Tamil Nadu. Till the age of eight he studied at the local village school until he moved to Chennai to pursue further studies at Madrasa-e-Azam. He earned a first class Bachelor of Arts degree in English Literature from the Madras Presidency College. Moreover, he was awarded seven gold medals for academic distinction in the subjects of History, English, Physics, and Economics. A brilliant orator, winner of various college and inter college competitions, Raza came back to the same college to receive his post-graduate degree.

Raza went on to become an assistant professor of English at the Presidency College in 1958. In 1960, he passed the civil services exam to become an IAS officer and in 1964, he was appointed Collector and District Magistrate of Gujarat's Banaskantha district. For the next four years, he was selected to lead the Valsad district. He was involved in flood rescue efforts in 1968 as a Municipal Commissioner. In 1975, Raza became the Chief Secretary to the Government of Gujarat.

Raza was happy working in Gujarat until around 1998 when Farooq Abdullah, Chief Minister of Jammu and Kashmir (J&K)

asked for an outsider. During that time, J&K was witnessing destructive events in the valley. The activity of certain local and non-Kashmiri groups led to clashes and Jagmohan Malhotra was suddenly appointed as the new Governor.

Abdullah then reached out to the then Prime Minister, Rajiv Gandhi for help. M K Narayanan, the then Director of the Intelligence Bureau, requested Raza to go to Kashmir as the Chief Secretary. At first Raza was reluctant as he was comfortable working in Gujarat. Narayanan asked him to meet the Prime Minister himself. Finally, Raza decided to leave for Kashmir and within two years he was able to resolve all the disparities between the locals and the outsiders.

In 1988, Kashmir was witnessing an upsurge in militancy and insurgency. Raza's statistics indicated that around 3,000 Kashmiri young men were ready to cross the border to receive training in Pakistan. According to Kashmiris, the police had no Muslim representation thereby causing imbalance in the force which led to communal riots in the valley. When he learned about the problem, Raza reached out to the local CRPF chief and requested him to recruit the 3,000 youth to form three battalions.

Raza worked on a detailed scheme which was sent to the central government. Since no action followed, he had to fly down to Delhi to explain the situation to Rajiv Gandhi. 'I told him that 3,000 people were going to become militants. If you can give them jobs, take them out of Kashmir, give them national training, they will come back as responsible citizens to Kashmir. They would learn what is happening in the rest of India'.[1]

When the Kashmiri Pandits were forced to leave Kashmir, they were settled in relief camps. Their trust in the government was further eroded after the infamous Nadimarg incident, when terrorists killed twenty-four members of the Pandit community. It was important to assure them of their safety as they had been facing militancy for the past ten years. Raza, after Sushila Banerjee, was the only Chief Secretary who had tried to establish direct contact with the people by visiting villages. 'I strongly believe that you cannot allow people to be killed by militants or security forces and the only way to check these killings is to initiate measures both at the political and administrative levels. Human rights violations by security forces should not be allowed.'[2]

During Raza's tenure in Kashmir, interactions with bureaucrats, politicians and the locals helped him understand that most people in the valley are victims of misgovernance and corruption while the rest are felons. His book *Kashmir - Land of Regrets* discusses the struggles faced by ordinary Kashmiris, due to bureaucratic indifference, by linking history with current events. His book also reveals the lack of competent administration in Kashmir that had hollowed out the structures and given rise to corruption, pushing people away from the mainstream.

In 2002, Raza was sent to Uttar Pradesh as an Advisor to the Governor. While serving in Uttar Pradesh, he managed the law-and-order situation in the state. Few years down the line, he was appointed Secretary to the Government of India, under the Cabinet Secretariat in the Steel Ministry. His work helped expand and modernise the steel industry in India via policies and formulated proposals.

After 35 years of service, Raza retired from the government in 1995. Raza's work was not only limited to services, to formulating policies and to connecting with the locals; he was also a linguist, a poet, an Urdu scholar and an avid reader. He has also written several books that include *Of Nawabs and Nightingales* and *Dynamics of Islamic Law* among many others. He has also chaired the prestigious Movement for the Empowerment of Muslims in India (MOEMIN) to take up issues confronting the Muslim community, urging Muslims to follow the Quran's emphasis on peace and fraternity. His role as the chairperson was to promote education amongst Indian Muslims in order to promote the community's future in all fields.

In 2010, Raza was conferred the Padma Bhushan.

Trade and Industry

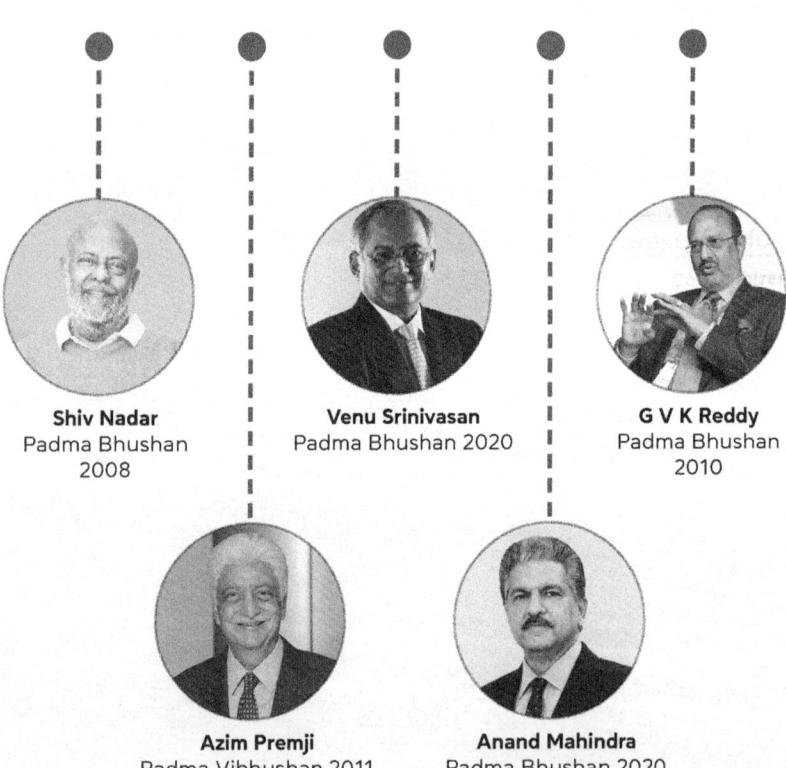

Shiv Nadar
Padma Bhushan 2008

Venu Srinivasan
Padma Bhushan 2020

G V K Reddy
Padma Bhushan 2010

Azim Premji
Padma Vibhushan 2011

Anand Mahindra
Padma Bhushan 2020

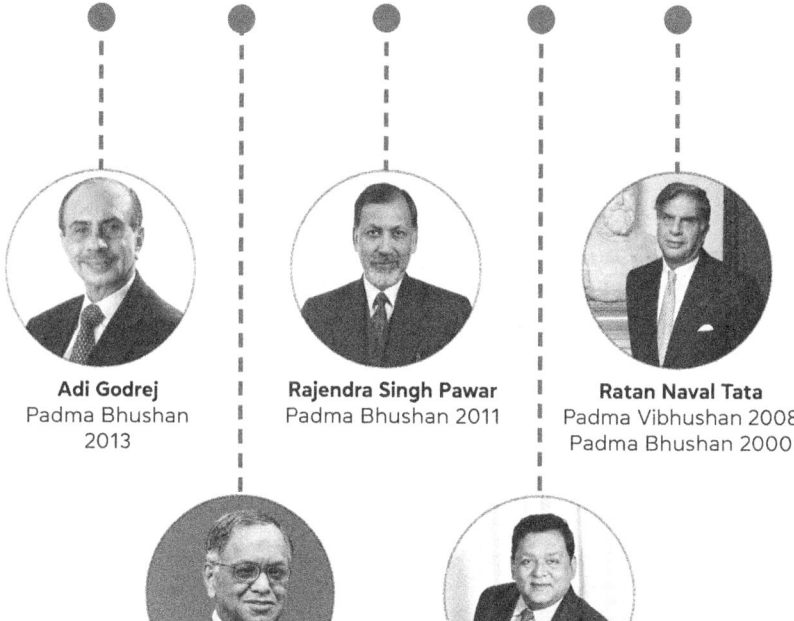

Shiv Nadar
Bringing Computers to India

There was a time when the Nadars—or 'Shanars' as they were pejoratively called—were a marginalised community of toddy tappers and coir weavers. They were not allowed to use public wells and their women were expected to leave their upper torso uncovered. The community was concentrated in present-day Kanyakumari, Tirunelveli, and Thoothukudi districts of southern Tamil Nadu. Born in this community in 1945, Shiv Nadar went on to become not only one of India's most successful entrepreneurs ranking among the richest persons in the world, but also a top philanthropist globally. Nadar was honoured in 2008 with the Padma Bhushan.

Nadar's focus on philanthropy began in 1994 with the establishment of the Shiv Nadar Foundation to invest in education. In 1996, he founded the SSN College of Engineering, named after his father, Sri Sivasubramaniya Nadar. Over the years, it has grown into a 250-acre college with units for management and computer applications, and a school of advanced software engineering in partnership with Carnegie Mellon University in the United States. Nadar and his wife also support art, focusing on contemporary and modern art from the subcontinent and offer cultural and educational programs. The Kiran Nadar Museum of Art, named after his wife, has two facilities, one in Saket (Delhi) and another on the HCL Campus in Noida.[1]

Nadar's father was a district judge, and the job involved many transfers, so Nadar studied in several schools across Tamil Nadu.[2] The Elango Corporation School, where Nadar studied from 1952 to 1954, provides free education to students from under privileged families. The facilities of the school, originally constructed in 1937, were very poor with children sitting on cracked floors and pathetic toilets with dismal water supply. Nadar visited his old school in 2011 and promised a complete makeover for the building, which now has rooftop solar plant to power all equipment, new toilets with swanky accessories, murals on the walls inside and outside the classrooms, open learning spaces, generator back-up, a public address and CCTV surveillance system, and new sleek furniture. Nadar also studied at St Joseph's College Higher Secondary School in Trichy, a Jesuit institution dating back to the mid-1800s. When Nadar visited there in 2011, he donated 350 computers to his alma mater, promising to help further as needed.

After a degree in electrical and Electrical and Electronics Engineering from the PSG College of Technology in Coimbatore in 1967, Nadar began his career at the Walchand group's College of Engineering, Pune (COEP). His education was primarily in the South Indian language of Tamil, and he did not start speaking much English until age twenty-two after completing his engineering degree. 'I came from a rural background, but I did all right', he contends.

In 1968, Nadar moved to Delhi to join DCM Ltd., a textile company, as a management trainee with the digital products division. DCM was then the fourth-largest company in India. Working a ten-twelve hours job made him realise that he wanted to do something else. In 1976, Nadar and five of his colleagues, all young engineers, decided to quit their jobs and start a venture of their own. All six young men had good jobs that paid them well, but they wanted to do more, riding on their own gumption.

The six friends set up a company to make personal computers. They had gathered enough technical expertise at DCM's calculator division, but, as with all start-ups, getting funds was the problem. To raise money for manufacturing computers, Nadar started a company to sell tele-digital calculators. This venture threw up enough cash to allow the founders to give shape to their ultimate dream of manufacturing computers in India, at a time when computers were just sophisticated cousins of the good old calculator. They also managed to rope in Uttar Pradesh Electronic Corp., a government outfit.[3] The state government held a 26% stake in the newly formed company, but within a decade, Nadar was able to buy out that stake. 'We grew up in Uttar Pradesh', says Nadar. 'I owe a huge debt of gratitude to the state.' To show his gratitude to Uttar Pradesh, Nadar set up a chain of residential schools for under privileged students and a university there.

The company founded by Nadar, his friends, and the Uttar Pradesh government, was originally named Uttar Pradesh Computers Limited (UPCL), which they renamed Hindustan Computers Limited (HCL) to ensure national resonance. This was around the time when IBM (and other foreign companies) had been told to leave India by the central government. HCL introduced the first PC in India in 1978, calling it HCL 8C. At the time, most computers used in India were the IBM 1401s that required a big data centre with air conditioning. IBM was charging around INR 500,000 annually just to lease their computer. The HCL 8C could be bought outright for INR 300,000.

When the company was barely three years old, Nadar started exploring foreign shores, deciding to set up a venture in Singapore. To meet the growing demand for computer education in India, Nadar set up the National Institute of Information Technology. 'We knew many people in the Indian Institutes of Technology and the Indian Institute of Science. We formed an advisory panel and asked them, can you help us navigate this whole thing and they were very enthusiastic about this and they were, of course, shaken up a little bit when they saw us start advertising in Bombay, selling education as a commercial project.' By 1983, HCL had introduced indigenously developed relational data-based management system, a networking operational system and client-server architecture.

In 1984, the Indian government opened up the computer market and permitted import of technology. With new guidelines and regulations in place, HCL grabbed the opportunity to launch its own personal computer. Soon, HCL became one of the largest IT companies in India.

In 1997, Nadar spun off HCL's research and development division, creating a software services firm HCL Technologies, which went public two years later. The original hardware arm, which had been listed on the stock market in 1987, became HCL Infosystems. In 2020, when Nadar stepped down as chairman of HCL Technologies, the company employed more than 200,000 people in more than fifty countries.

'Learn Hindi', he advises students. Knowledge of Hindi, he says, helped him become more competitive outside his home-state of Tamil Nadu, which has seen some of the strongest opposition to learning Hindi. 'Knowing Hindi would also be an advantage if you go to the United States as Indians are there everywhere', he says.[4]

Azim Hashim Premji
Shaping India's IT Landscape

Azim Hashim Premji was born on 24 July 1945 in Mumbai, India. His father, Muhammed Hashim Premji was a noted businessman, sometimes referred to as the 'Rice King of Burma'. Muhammed Hashim Premji had incorporated a cooking oil manufacturing business in 1945, the year Azim was born in Amalner, a small town in the Jalgaon district of Maharashtra. Hashim Premji was invited by Muhammed Ali Jinnah, the founding Prime Minister of Pakistan, at the time of India's partition to relocate to Pakistan. However, Hashim Premji turned down the request.

Azim Premji enrolled in the electrical engineering program at Stanford University, but had to quit his studies midway when his father passed away in 1966. After returning to India, the 21-year old Premji assumed control of his father's business and quickly started working on taking it to greater heights.

Hashim Premji had started a cooking oil manufacturing business under the brand name Sunflower Vanaspati. The byproduct of the oil manufacturing was sold as a soap under the brand name 787. Azim Premji realised that in order to scale this business, he would need to diversify. Working on this philosophy, he expanded the product portfolio of his father's company and forayed into bakery fats, toiletries, hair care soaps, and also products such as hydraulic cylinders and lighting products.

Yet, something bigger was in store for Premji. IBM was expelled from India on the grounds of following unfair trade practices in the country,[1] leaving a big void in the Indian computer market. The young Premji recognised the opportunity and decided to jump onto the computer and software bandwagon. He first set up a minicomputer manufacturing plant in collaboration with Sentinel Computer Corporation, an American computer company.

Azim changed the name of his father's company to Wipro (an acronym for Western India Palm Refined Oils) and refocus it from manufacturing soaps to writing software. Wipro went on to become one of India's first information technology companies to place India and its engineering talent on the world stage. The company diversified into business process services, consulting and IT enabled services. In 2004, Wipro became the second Indian IT firm (after Infosys) to earn USD 1 billion in revenues from the IT services business.[2]

While the IT industry was in infancy, Wipro under the leadership of Azim Premji set up various successful collaborations with organisations worldwide in the 1980s to assist it with building computer equipment in India. However, it was the advancements made in programming that created a strong reputation for Wipro. Premji founded a policy at Wipro for employing the best talent and then providing them with good opportunities.[3] In doing so, he leveraged India's enormous pool of programmers who were able to work for considerably lower compensation than their American counterparts. Wipro, thereby, fostered a custom software development firm for trade, essentially to the US and other countries around the world.

Azim Premji continued to hold the position of Wipro's

Chairman till 2019 and handed over the baton to his son, Rishad Premji. Under Azim Premji's leadership Wipro's stock skyrocketed and he became one of the world's richest entrepreneurs.[4] He has been recognised as one of the world's 100 most influential people by *Time* magazine twice, once in 2004 and next in 2011.[5,6] He has been regularly recognised among the most influential Muslims of the world.[7] As per Bloomberg, his net worth in 2023 stands at about USD 24 billion.[8] In 1999, Premji finished his degree from Stanford through distance learning.[9] Despite his enormous wealth, Azim Premji today is best known for philanthropy. Setting an astonishing example of giving away, Premji has donated more than 50 percent of his wealth to charity. In 2001, he set up the Azim Premji Foundation, a non-profit organisation that aims to improve the Indian public school education system. Through his foundation, he has been able to impact more than 2.5 million children in 350,000 schools across 13 states.[10,11] He believes that 'business leaders, with their ability to create businesses and ability to scale, need to play a very important role in social service'.[12] He was recognised as Asia's most generous philanthropist in 2019 when he donated USD 7.6 billion worth of Wipro stocks to charity raising his total lifetime donations to USD 21 billion.[13]

Influenced by Gandhian ideals of trusteeship that encouraged the rich to believe that they were trustees of the wealth and not the owners of it, Premji was also the first Indian to sign up for the Giving Pledge, a campaign initiated by Warren Buffett and Bill Gates to encourage the rich to donate their wealth towards philanthropic causes. He was the third non-American after Richard Branson and David Sainsbury to join this club.[14] Signing the pledge, he noted 'I was deeply influenced by Gandhi's notion of holding one's wealth in trusteeship, to be used for the betterment of society and not as if one owned it'.[15]

With a donation of INR 7,904 crores in financial year

2019-20 and INR 9,713 crores in financial year 2020-21, Azim Premji has been consistently recognised as 'India's most generous' entrepreneur.[16] Recognising him for the contributions he has made to India's growth and development, not just in the IT sector but also in education (the primary cause to which he has donated over the years), the Indian government conferred on him the Padma Bhushan in 2005 and the Padma Vibhushan in 2011. Recognising his 'conscience, integrity, and compassion that have guided his visionary giving... (with) invaluable benefit to both the nation and the world', in 2017, he was bestowed the Carnegie Medal of Philanthropy.[17]

Venu Srinivasan
Driving Innovation and Excellence in India's Industrial Sector

The TVS motor company, founded by the ambitious T V Sunderam Iyengar in 1911, is the third largest manufacturer and the second largest exporter of two wheelers and automotive parts in the world. The company reached its heights under the leadership and guidance of T V Sunderam Iyengar's grandson who is also referred to as the architect of the TVS motor company—Venu Srinivasan. Born on 11 December 1952, in Chennai, Tamil Nadu, Srinivasan is a graduate from the College of Engineering at Guindy in Chennai (India). After completing his graduation, Srinivasan pursued his MSc in Management from Purdue University in the United States.

On returning from the USA in 1979, Srinivasan started working as the CEO of Sundaram Clayton, the flagship company of TVS motors, that is involved in the manufacturing and distribution of automobile components in India. Srinivasan's zeal and dedication was seen in his work and soon after he was promoted to the position of the Chairman of TVS motor company. However, Srinivasan's life was not easy. When he was around 26 years old, his father passed away, leaving behind a relatively small family business.

Srinivasan had immense respect for his father's ability to

see far ahead of his times. He mentions that his father wanted to produce 250,000 mopeds at the TVS plant at a time when India was generating only 40,000 units. His father dreamt of the day when every Indian would own a two-wheeler. Srinivasan believes that the 'seed' his father had sown made an immense impact. He shared his feelings in an interview: 'So it is that dream . . . the seed that contained the dream is the most important inheritance that I had. And fortunately for me, with very good people and God's grace, we were able to grow it steadily from what was a small business to what is today a large Indian motorcycle business'.[1]

The company's journey began with a 50cc moped in the 1980s, a time during which Srinivasan also had to deal with labour troubles. He had to shut his factory for three months forcing the labour unions to compromise. TVS and Suzuki (the Japanese automobile giant) came into a joint venture two years after the onset of the moped business. The partnership was going well until the four-stroke revolution struck the market. The business went on fuel efficiency and at that time Suzuki was not ready with a fuel-efficient engine that worked on the four-stroke technology. 'In its own small way, we made some significant changes which saw the flow of air improving by almost thirty percent. On top of that we said we cannot, as a two-stroke, only bet on fuel efficiency because we will never be as efficient as a four-stroke', said Srinivasan.[2] Therefore, the partnership broke off.

These roadblocks never stopped Srinivasan. His knowledge, expertise and experience made him realise that the company cannot run smoothly on the model that was established seven decades ago. The company needed a policy upgrade in order to stand up to its competitors in the market. After studying about various MNCs, their technologies and performances, Srinivasan hired Professor Lord Kumar Bhattacharya from the University of Warwick to be his consultant. Under his guidance, Srinivasan started updating the plant machinery, and started exploring and investing in new technologies.[3]

Long before the call was made for indigenous manufacture, TVS rolled out the TVS Victor in 2002, making it India's first indigenously built four-stroke bike. The TVS Victor laid the foundation for producing powerful bikes such as the TVS Shogun. 'Shogun, I think, ended up defining TVS at that point and we created a new bike called Samurai. So, we went away from ruggedness and roughness which we were known for to reliability and ease of use. The Samurai was the 'No Problem' bike and on top of the moped success, Samurai and Victor were the best piece of news for TVS. The Scooty was also an important part of the revival story and today if TVS has 'enormous acceptance in the scooter market, it is because almost every scooter it has launched has been a success', added Srinivasan.[4]

From there TVS only climbed the ladder of success. Today, the TVS factories are manufacturing 300cc race motorcycles, the best-selling 125cc gearless scooters, electric scooters and even BMW bikes for the Indian as well as the European markets. However, the company struggled between 2004 and 2010, as they did not have a successful commuter four-stroke motorcycle. Then came the Apache. 'After Victor faded, we did not have great success until Apache came and today if you ask anybody they will tell you that Apache is really what TVS stands for. So, we have our scooter business on one side and Apache on the other. I think these two effectively rebuilt TVS from 2007—when we were at a low point in our motorcycle business—to 2020 where we are back', shared Srinivasan.[5]

In 2020, TVS made an entry in the electric two-wheeler space by launching the iQube scooter. Also, TVS is the first Indian company to launch a motorcycle—the Apache RTR 200 Fi—that can run fully on ethanol.[6]

Srinivasan established the Srinivasan Service Trust in 1996. The trust is the social arm of the TVS motor company and Sundaram Clayton. It works with local communities and government bodies to undertake holistic development of villages in five states of India—Himachal Pradesh, Maharashtra, Karnataka, Andhra Pradesh and Tamil Nadu. The trust works at the village level to impart skill-based training programmes, programmes directed towards women empowerment and afforestation, social and cultural development, and improving the quality of infrastructure, healthcare and education in villages.[7]

The government of India has recognised him for his exemplary contributions to the industry by conferring the Padma Shri in 2010 and Padma Bhushan in 2021. After a career spanning four decades with roller coaster rides, Venu Srinivasan stepped down as the Chairman of the company in January 2023.

Anand Gopal Mahindra
Transformative Leadership

Anand Mahindra was born on 1 May 1955 to Indira and Harish Mahindra, and is the grandson of Jagdish Chandra Mahindra, co-founder of the Mahindra and Mahindra Group. The group got its start as Mahindra & Mohammed by brothers Jagdish Chandra Mahindra and Keshub Chandra Mahindra with Ghulam Mohammed in 1945 as a steel company headquartered in Bombay. In 1947, India gained independence and Ghulam Mohammed left India to become Pakistan's first finance minister. Mahindra brothers renamed the group Mahindra and Mahindra (M&M) and started manufacturing jeeps under the brand name of Willys.[1] Today the group is involved in diverse sectors such as logistics, infrastructure, IT, financial services, automotives and farm equipment.[2]

Mahindra studied at the Lawrence School in Lovedale, a small village in the Nilgiri hills of Tamil Nadu. After his schooling, he went on to study film-making and architecture from Harvard University. After graduating from the university with distinction in 1977, he completed an MBA degree in 1981 from Harvard Business School (HBS). Recollecting his HBS days, he mentions, 'Having seen that ninety bright minds in an HBS classroom usually did better than just one, I understood that a collaborative management style in the real world would be equally effective and essential'.³

When Anand returned to India, he joined his father at the Mahindra Ugine Steel Company Limited (MUSCO)⁴ as an executive assistant to the finance director. After working for a few years at the company, Mahindra was given the task of leading diversification of the Mahindra Group into sectors such as real estate and hospitality. He was elevated to the post of President and Deputy Managing Director of MUSCO in 1989 and in 1991 the Deputy Managing Director of Mahindra & Mahindra Limited. In 1997, he became the Managing Director, in 2001, the Vice-Chairman and in 2012, the Chairman of the board and Managing Director of M&M Group.⁵

Mahindra's journey is a story of grit, determination, courage and self-belief. The group lacked technology of making a car from scratch. In order to learn, Mahindra entered into a joint venture with Ford in 1993. 'We were then making open-top Jeeps and didn't have a clue how to make a mass-market car. Thanks to a decade long alliance with Ford, we've learned how to do that', admits Mahindra.⁶

Unfortunately, the Escort car failed when it was launched in the market. However, he did not lose hope and continued working on developing a new product: a Sports Utility Vehicle (SUV), and that too without a joint venture.⁷ The effort led to the development and launch of the Scorpio in 2002. That instantly became a hit in the market. The production cost of the car was only INR 550 crores, a tenth of the cost for other car manufacturers.⁸ The car is now being exported to other countries such as Italy, South Africa and Russia.⁹ The product was so successful that it occupied 36 per cent market share at a time when the Tata Group could only capture 5 per cent.¹⁰ The group has now expanded into manufacturing other types of utility vehicles such as the XUV—a Crossover Utility Vehicle or a car-based SUV, the KUV (Kool Utility Vehicle) and many more.

Mahindra also undertook a series of acquisitions to make a mark in the farm equipment segment. In 1999, he acquired a 100% stake in Gujarat Tractors Limited, a state-owned enterprise. In 2007, he acquired Punjab Tractor Limited, and emerged as the largest tractor manufacturer in the country. In 2010, the group acquired REVA electric car company, in 2011 the SsangYong motor company and in 2015 a one-third stake in the Mitsubishi Agricultural machinery company.[11] Commenting on his strategy for acquisitions, Mahindra observes 'Going global is terribly complex and challenging. Companies from emerging markets need to be eclectic in their alliances, so that they can learn as much as possible about things like technology, procurement, and marketing'.[12]

The M&M Group today is the world's largest tractor manufacturer and India's leading seller of SUVs[13]. It combines that with a leadership position in IT, financial services and vacation ownership sectors. It is present in more than 100 countries.[14] The group operates as a 'federation of companies' grouped into sectors with each sector being led by a president. Each sector has a company that is listed on the stock exchange. Mahindra observes that 'the model resembles a private equity business. From the corporate center, we provide services—financial skills and help with branding, for instance—and monitor the financial targets very closely, but we are essentially allowing professional executives to do their job.'[15]

Mahindra is a great promoter of studies in arts, culture and humanities and believes that these disciplines can address global challenges. Donating USD 10 million to Harvard's humanities center, he observed, 'To address complex problems in an interdependent world, it is vital to encourage the cross-cultural and interdisciplinary exchange of ideas in an international setting. I am convinced of the need for incorporating social and humanistic concerns into the core values that inform the world of business and have sought to do so with tremendous support from my peers and colleagues at work and beyond.'[16]

Mahindra also runs a Project called *Nanhi Kali*, an initiative that supports education for the girl child from socially disadvantaged backgrounds. The initiative supports more than 130,000 girls today. On the initiative, he mentions that 'I am particularly passionate about the cause of girl child education through our initiative. Education is an important focus area that I believe can transform India by unleashing the tremendous potential of its people'.[17]

Mahindra has been listed among the 'World's 50 biggest leaders' by the *Forbes* Magazine[18] and one of Asia's 25 most remarkable business-people.[19] In 2020, he was conferred the Padma Bhushan by the Government of India for his contributions to trade and industry.

G V Krishna Reddy
Shaping Infrastructure Landscapes

Gunapati Venkata Krishna Reddy (GVK), Founder-Chairman and Managing Director of his eponymous GVK Group, was born on 22 March 1937 in the Kothur village of Nellore district in Andhra Pradesh. He completed his schooling in Kothur village, college from Nellore and then graduation from Hyderabad. The GVK Group's predominant focus is on infrastructure development. The group has been credited with developing state-of-the-art infrastructure in India. One of the most notable contributions of the GVK Group to the country in the recent past has been the Chhatrapati Shivaji International Airport Terminal 2 at Mumbai.[1]

The story of the GVK Group is the saga of an ambitious entrepreneur who upon his graduation not only accepted the responsibility of taking up his father's construction business but also took it to greater and unimaginable heights. Though unsure of the business, he showed exemplary resilience and willingness to learn. Reflecting on his journey over the years, he mentions, 'With very little knowledge of the trade, I was unsure of myself but gradually learned the ropes by facing the challenges, working hard, remaining self-disciplined and committed — the four virtues that remained constant in the path of my life.'[2]

GVK's first project was the development of a canal and

an under-tunnel at the right channel of the Nagarjuna Sagar Dam, at Adigoppula in Andhra Pradesh and Chamarajapuram in Karnataka. From the very outset, GVK was not afraid to take on challenges. He remembers his days of working on the Nagarjuna Sagar dam: 'When the dam was being built, the river was flowing in some portions of the dam. There was a Block 41 that had to be closed in summer before the floods came through. The government wanted a reputed contractor to take up the works. Unfortunately, everybody was scared to take up the job owing to the danger of floods.'[3]

Even though he was the youngest of all the contractors, he took on this task. He would get up in the middle of the night to plan the work at the site, and to ensure that the granite needed to create the structure at the site was transported in time. His hard work and determination led to the project being a success with an on-time completion. 'My determination and commitment aided by my hard work resulted in my company being awarded the contract. I was only 30 years old then. From the beginning, I always liked to face challenges and take risks in a calculated way. Whatever others would normally be scared to do, I would take it up and handle and execute it confidently', he adds.[4]

With his self-assured approach and consistent work, GVK Power and Infrastructure Limited has become one of the most prominent Indian organisations working in the infrastructure sector. The group has expanded to other sectors apart from infrastructure. Today, the GVK Group is helping India's development by carrying out projects in airports, power, roads, healthcare, life sciences and many others.

Hailing from a village background, GVK had witnessed the sufferings of the poor. In order to help people in the areas of health, education and basic necessities, he founded the GVK foundation. The foundation started the GVK EMRI (Emergency Management and Research Institute), a not-for-profit organisation that provides ambulance services to close to 800 million people in India today.[5] As of 2021, GVK EMRI operates ambulances in 15 states and two union territories, transporting patients from their homes to hospitals. During the peak of COVID-19, the ambulances transported about 10,000 people daily to health facilities.[6]

Remembering his earlier days, GVK mentions that once there was a flood in the Munneru[7] river and all the equipment as well as the raw material he had procured for the construction of an aqueduct on the river got washed away. Even during those difficult times, he never gave up and bought additional material from his own funds in order to complete the project on time.[8] GVK credits his wife and family for full support and encouragement. He believes that it was only due to the belief his wife, Indira Reddy, had in him that he could work doggedly in pursuit of success and excellence.

The message that he would like to give to the young readers and audiences from his life is that 'one should never be afraid of taking on challenges at any stage in life. Also, there is no substitute for hard work, self-discipline and commitment to your job and those alone will make people believe in you. Be it a big or a small assignment, focus on it and put in all your efforts and work towards making it a success'.[9]

GVK has shown that hard work, honesty and belief in oneself can propel anyone to success. Acknowledging his contributions to the development and growth of the country, the Government of India bestowed on him the Padma Bhushan in 2011.

Adi Burjorji Godrej
Architect of the Godrej Group

Adi Godrej, the patriarch of the Godrej family, is one of the richest Indians on the planet. His friends and associates, however, talk more about his humility than his wealth. 'My fondest memory of Mr Godrej and his brother Nadir is them having lunch in the same canteen as factory staff every day', shares a former Managing Director of Godrej Consumer Products, one of the companies in the Godrej Group.[1] The rich are generally associated with private jets, large yachts, and a demanding and obnoxious entourage. Adi travels in commercial airlines and does not hesitate to fly economy class. He dislikes checking-in his baggage at the airport even if he is on a long business trip across continents. He hates porters carrying his luggage and usually irons his own clothes when staying in a hotel.

Adi was born on 3 April 1942 to Burjorji Godrej and Jai Godrej. Burjorji was a son of Pirojsha Godrej, who co-founded the business with his brother Ardeshir Godrej in 1897.[2] Ardeshir started his career as a lawyer but left the legal profession after he had a crisis of conscience while arguing a case for a client. His first foray into business involved manufacturing surgical instruments. That failed to make much headway against cheaper imports. Success came with his next venture; the manufacture of locks, for which he rented a tiny shed in the Lalbaug area of Bombay. His main financier in the early days was Mehrwanji Cama, a philanthropic Parsi with substantial real-estate ownership in the city. Pirojsha joined his older brother in the business after graduating from Victoria Jubilee Technical Institute (now known as Veermata Jeejabai Technical Institute). Though the two brothers did not talk much to each other, they lived in the same house and made a good team: Ardeshir was obsessive and a visionary; Pirojsha was practical and hard-headed. Two other brothers, Hormusji and Munchersha, never joined the business, choosing to pursue other interests.

When Ardeshir died, he had no children (his wife had died young and he never remarried). Pirojsha and his sons, including Adi, inherited the family business. For the next several decades, the Godrej Group grew to dizzying heights. Yet, the house of Godrej remained united, perhaps because the flagship companies of the group—Godrej Boyce and Godrej Soaps—were privately held for most of history. For Adi and the Godrej clan, the Thursday lunch with the larger family is sacrosanct. The brothers (Adi Godrej and Nadir Godrej) and cousins Jamshyd Godrej and Smita Crishna (all directors on the Godrej board) are known to have even cancelled important business meetings for their weekly get-together.

Adi completed his schooling at St. Xavier's High School, run by Jesuit priests and considered one of the best schools in Mumbai. He started at St. Xavier's at the age of seven and finished there when he was fourteen. 'In those days, Sundays and Thursdays were off days. Saturday was a regular school day then,' he remembers.[3] Adi was a good student, finishing with the prestigious Ripon Prize in 1957 (his name is still listed among the awardees in the school hallway). During Adi's time, the school had an interesting policy for student uniforms: light beige shirt and dark-beige shorts, with students allowed to choose between a lower-priced fabric and a more expensive fabric. Adi's mother, who was herself a teacher at a Godrej school, insisted that his school uniform be made with cheaper fabric.

Adi had a very close and affectionate relationship with his mother. He credits his mother with helping him develop his confidence and life skills. 'My mother went out of her way to teach me many things that were very important at a very young age…tremendous self-confidence, way of planning, and being self-sufficient, those are some things I learned from my mother', observed Adi.

After a couple of years at St. Xavier's College, Adi went to the Massachusetts Institute of Technology (MIT) in the United States for a degree in engineering. At MIT, Adi discovered business studies, something that he did not even know existed. He studied economics there for the first time.[4] MIT was among the few places in the world offering college-level business courses. His formal education in business at MIT helped Adi when he returned to India to join Godrej. It gave him credibility with the older members of the management, who had never received formal education in business. 'Cost management, marketing, and human resource management were things I learned from MIT that were practically unknown in India at the time', he said in an interview.

As a business leader, Adi is seen as someone who understands latest trends, be it technology, manufacturing or brands. 'His command of data, his child-like curiosity, coupled with the ability to zoom in and out is extraordinary', says a former Godrej executive.' He has always believed that the Godrej Group is tied with India's destiny. He would make mass, affordable, high-quality products, and innovation would be the hallmark.' Adi believes that by 2050, India will be the largest economy in the world, surpassing both the United States and China in terms of the absolute size of the economy.

Adi's advice for large family-owned firms is 'sales is vanity, profit is sanity, and cash is reality'.[5] He advises family businesses to be careful in borrowing money, and keep their debt-to-assets ratio low.

For Adi, Godrej is responsible not only to its shareholders, but to its stakeholders too, and this includes society, employees, suppliers and customers. He supports the mandate requiring public companies like Godrej to spend at least 2 per cent of their average net profit for the past three years on corporate social responsibility. The Godrej family's most valuable asset, apart from their storied business, is 3,400 acres of land, of which 1,750 acres is covered with mangroves and rare plants. At a time when the world is talking about reducing its carbon footprint, a rich businessman owning mangroves in the heart of India's commercial capital is commendable.

'I feel strongly', says Godrej, 'that the young generation today will lead India forward very well. I find them very passionate, very international in their outlook, very dedicated. What I will add is they must be disciplined and dedicated to hard work. I think if that is added to the passion and the entrepreneurial style the young people have, the country will go places.' In 2013, Adi was recognised for his contribution to trade and industry with the Padma Bhushan.

888

Nagavara Ramarao Narayana Murthy
Founding Father of Infosys

Narayan Murthy co-founded Infosys with six colleagues, after borrowing INR 10,000 from his wife Sudha for start-up capital. The company became the first Indian firm to list on the NASDAQ and, in August 2021, the fourth to cross USD100 billion in market capitalisation. It rapidly emerged as a potent symbol of a new India, oriented towards technology and connected to the world. 'Infosys shows that it is possible for middle-class people with no family heritage of being in business to build a lot of wealth from scratch in one generation', notes Nandan Nilekani, a co-founder of the company who later became its CEO and chairman.[1]

Murthy was born on 20 August 1946 in Sidlaghatta town of the Indian state of Karnataka to a middle-class family, one of seven children. His father, a math teacher, wanted him to join the Indian Civil Service, but Murthy wanted to be an engineer. He qualified for a coveted spot at the Indian Institutes of Technology, but the scholarship he was offered was not enough to cover his expenses. Unable to afford the IIT education, his father advised him to join the National Institute of Engineering in Mysore, closer to home. He graduated in 1967 with a degree in electrical engineering, and then went to IIT Kanpur for his Masters degree on a full scholarship.

After Kanpur, Murthy had several job offers from leading Indian firms of the time, but he preferred to take up a research associate position at the Indian Institute of Management at Ahmedabad, one of only two IIMs in the country at the time. Murthy had been impressed that an IIM professor had taken the time to personally talk with him about job opportunities.[2] At Ahmedabad, he was part of the team responsible for installing a time-sharing computer system — India's first — making IIM the third business school in the world to install such a system after Harvard and Stanford. He was also involved in designing a BASIC interpreter for Electronics Corporation of India Limited (ECIL), again at the IIM. Murthy's time at IIM-Ahmedabad is said to have been very hectic, with 20-hour workdays not uncommon. Looking back at that phase of his life, Murthy believes working at IIM-Ahmedabad was the best decision he could have taken for he learned a lot more there than he could have in a corporate job.

After IIM-Ahmedabad, Murthy started Softronics, an IT services firm for the Indian market. When the firm failed to get traction in the market, Murthy closed it after about a year and a half of operations. By this time, he had already begun dating his current wife Sudha. She was also an engineer, working at the time for TELCO, a Tata subsidiary. Murthy had met her through mutual friends. Sudha's father was against their relationship and wanted Murthy to have a stable job before he would give his blessing for their wedding.

With a failed business and with little prospect of marrying his then girlfriend, Murthy started working for Patni Computer Systems in Pune. Patni was a pioneer in providing IT services and business solutions to American clients from India. Working for Patni provided Murthy a comfortable life with a confirmed monthly paycheck. A year later, in 1978, he married Sudha.

By 1981, Murthy was ready to embark on another entrepreneurial career. Six colleagues from Patni were also ready to leave their job to start a new company with him. His wife provided the seed capital for the new venture named Infosys based out of a small room in Pune. 'We were short of money, but we were very long on hope. We were very united, very enthusiastic', Murthy says of the sentiment among the partners at the startup.

It took Infosys nine months to get the first telephone line. The company quickly entered into an agreement with Databasics Corporation (DBC) —their first client, who would provide them business in the US. For first five years, DBC was their only client and Infosys became the implementer for DBC products at various client-sites in the US. At the time, there was no domestic market for software in India, so Infosys made a conscious decision to focus on the American market. 'I had learned that the absence of the market was what led to the failure of my first business. I decided to focus on the export market in my next venture', Murthy says.[3]

When Infosys was finally able to source its first computer, there was not enough space to keep it in the small office. Motor Industries Company (MICO) Ltd., a Bangalore-based manufacturer of spark plugs and other equipment, was looking for a computer but could not source one for itself. Infosys entered into an innovative time-sharing agreement with MICO, thus giving the startup company a much desired access to real estate to house the computer. In 1982, Infosys moved their base from Pune to Bangalore, in order to utilise the space provided to them by MICO.

Because Infosys had no asset base for collateral, financial institutions were not willing to support the new company. Around this time, the struggling partners heard that Karnataka State Financial Corporation (KSFC) and Karnataka State

Small Industrial Development Corporation (KSSIDC), two state-owned financial institutions, were willing to provide funds for first-generation technology entrepreneurs.[4] Instead of collateral, the criteria laid down that the entrepreneurs be professionally qualified and that the project have merit. Murthy and his team were able to secure financing of INR 24 lakh (USD 24 million) from KSFC and KSIIDC in 1983.

Infosys quickly landed a good client immediately after for the startup. The funding from the Karnataka government allowed Infosys to be independent of MICO and helped them finance their initial growth. Despite quick growth and early success at Infosys, Murthy was a frugal leader. He travelled economy class even on international flights, until the company reached a revenue of $1 billion. 'I travel by economy even today on domestic flights. We always spent less than what we earned.'[5]

Murthy was an early riser, and his hard work set an example for the partners and the employees that the growing company was quickly hiring. 'I would be in the office at 6:20 am every morning till I retired in 2011. That sent an indelible message to youngsters about reaching office on time', he noted.

In 2014, Murthy was ranked 13th among CNBC's 25 global business leaders. He had previously been listed among the '12 greatest entrepreneurs of our time', by *Fortune* magazine in 2012. He has received numerous awards, including the Padma Shri in 2000 and the Padma Vibhushan in 2008.

Rajendra Singh Pawar
Pioneering IT Education

Rajendra Singh Pawar is the man behind NIIT (National Institute of Information Technology) that has helped immensely in driving the momentum of the IT industry, as well as revolutionising the IT training industry. He has helped create skilled manpower and is now a global leader in skills and talent development. Born on 19 March 1951 in Jammu, Pawar is an alumnus of Scindia School, Gwalior. He graduated from IIT Delhi in 1972 as an electrical engineer.

After graduation, Pawar started his career with Larsen & Toubro Limited in June 1972 as a graduate engineer trainee. From October 1972 to September 1976, he worked with DCM limited in the capacity of management trainee and later as Assistant Product Manager. From September 1976 to July 1981, he worked with Hindustan Computers Limited, first as Regional Manager and later as Corporate Planning Manager.[1]

As the computer industry was on the growth trajectory in the 1980s, it faced a severe shortage of trained manpower—estimated at about 200,000 people—crucial to its growth and success. The industry seemed promising and Pawar saw an opportunity. Pawar framed the blueprint of NIIT and laid its foundation in December 1981. Fueled by innovation in the curriculum development, methodologies of learning, quality product and expansion across geographies, this was the first pioneering step that ensured Pawar's leadership in the IT training space.

Pawar ventured into the field of higher education with NIIT, setting up the NIIT University (NU) in 2009 at Neemrana, Rajasthan. Under his leadership, NIIT became the first Indian computer training and educational organisation to receive the ISO 9001 quality certification. NIIT today has metamorphosed into a global training and knowledge organisation respected by peers in the industry. Today, NIIT is one among India's top most valued organisations with a market capitalisation of more than INR 47 billion.[2] The company employs more than 3,500 people worldwide and has its operations in more than twenty-five countries including Japan, Malaysia, UK, USA, Hong Kong, India, Thailand and Singapore, among many others. In India, NIIT has been ranked as the number one company in Information Technology Services.[3]

Two key factors helped NIIT play a key role in the creation and growth of the IT industry. One was the mindset that unleashed a wave of entrepreneurship in India and the other was 'Computerdromes'. which were a huge attraction amongst students since they gave youngsters unlimited access to computers. NIIT had Automated Learning Centres for experienced professionals and managers. The centers provided their users advanced interactive video equipment, computers, disks and libraries of video content that created a wow effect and became a haven for knowledge seekers.[4]

The proliferation of computers in homes, opened a new segment for NIIT. Sharing his thoughts Pawar said, 'Taking ordinary people including housewives, children, the elderly, and yes, even India's elected leaders across the Digital Divide became another mandate for us. To mark NIIT's 20th anniversary and help build computers and technological skills among people of various ages and segments, we launched World Computer Literacy Day on December 2. For a few years, on that date, we trained thousands of people for free.'[5]

Early on at NIIT, Pawar institutionalised the Complete Quality Management System developed by the business guru Phil Crosby. His pioneering vision became an inspiration not just for NIIT but also for the entire ICT industry in India. Following NIIT's success in the IT training and capability development, the company stepped in to explore opportunities in other areas such as Banking, Financial Services and Insurance (BFSI) and also Business Process Management (BPM). Like IT, these areas required skilled manpower and NIIT's exposure in the overseas market helped them make inroads into these sectors.

NIIT established many flagship programs to cater to these markets such as the Institute of Finance Banking and Insurance (IFBI) for the finance sector, Managed Training Services (MTS), Corporate Learning Group (CLG) and also the Institute of Process Excellence Limited (NIIT Uniqua) in partnership with global BPM giant Genpact. Commenting on NIIT's evolution, Pawar mentioned, 'Today, having trained over 35 million people worldwide, and operated in 40 countries, we have evolved into a global skills and talent development organisation. This claim is supported by our push to diversify beyond IT training, where we entered into partnerships with domain experts in fast growing verticals'.[6]

Pawar has served as a member of the National Task Force on Information Technology and Software Development, has headed the Quality Committees of various industry bodies, that include the prestigious South African President's International Advisory Council on Information Society.[7] He has served as a member of the Prime Minister's National Council on Skill Development and the Prime Minister's National Task Force that was constituted in 1998 to transform India into an IT superpower. Pawar has also served on the boards of reputed educational institutions such as the Indian School of Business (ISB), IIT Delhi, IIM Udaipur and IIM Bangalore.

The year 2020 saw a paradigm shift from the offline to the online world. Educational institutions had to adapt to sustain. NIIT embraced the technological shift seamlessly. The online learning model created by NU and NIIT for the digital platform proved to be as fruitful as the offline model. Pawar saw a monumental opportunity in the COVID era that brought humans and technology together.[8] Commenting on COVID and its impact on education, Pawar observed 'The purpose of education is to help people understand the power of the human mind and recognise that technology will play an important role as a subservient tool. During COVID times we have seen the power of technology in connecting human minds across the globe. In the field of education, there are new opportunities for technology and a huge set of challenges for pedagogy. I see it as a terrific opportunity and an exciting time'.[9]

Pawar's foresightedness led to several ICT industry initiatives that played a major part in molding the IT policies of the Government of India. For this, he was bestowed the Padma Bhushan in 2011. He was awarded IIT Delhi's Distinguished Alumnus Award in 1995 and the Lifetime Achievement Award in 2022 by India's apex industry body FICCI (Federation of Indian Chambers of Commerce & Industry).

❧❧❧

Anil Manibhai Naik
Industrial Titan

In the 1950s, when many Indian families were moving from villages to cities, the Naik family was making the move in the opposite direction. Anil's father, Manibhai Naik, who was teaching at a prestigious school in Bombay, had been offered a job at a rural school in his native village of Endhal in Gujarat. Endhal was, and still is, a largely tribal village. Motivated by Mahatma Gandhi's message that 'India lives in its villages', Manibhai decided to accept the job offer. Young Anil spent the next several years studying in the village school, sitting on the classroom floor finished with a mixture of mud and cow-dung.[1] Anil's family had valued education since the days of his grandfather who was the headmaster of a gurukul, and was famous for his mathematical abilities. His father held two Master's degrees, teaching first in Bombay and then in Endhal. 'We used to be known as Master *kutumb* — teachers' family', Anil shares, 'My grandfather was the first principal in the entire geography of nearly 50 sqkm of gurukul schools. He served the poor and the villagers in Gujarat for more than sixty years. Then my father returned to rural India in 1952. He served for over forty-five years. He worked in urban areas as well. So, between my father and grandfather, they worked in South Gujarat for more than

100 years. That in essence inspired me. I asked myself, how will I do a fraction of what they have done? I am an engineer. I couldn't be a teacher like them.'[2]

Anil got a bachelor's degree in Mechanical Engineering from the Birla Vishvakarma Mahavidyalaya (BVM), affiliated with the Sardar Patel University of Gujarat. The BVM was the first engineering college in the state, getting its start when the philanthropic Birla family donated money at the behest of Sardar Vallabhbhai Patel, the first home minister of independent India. With a letter of introduction from his father in hand, Anil applied for a job with a manufacturer of overhead cranes and other steel products. His English-language skills needed improvement, he was told and was rejected for the job.[3]

After much effort, he started his career with Nestler Boilers in 1963. Two years later, Anil got a job at Larsen & Toubro (L&T), which at the time hired only alumni of the five Indian Institutes of Technology.[4] His starting salary at L&T was less than what he was making at the boiler company. 'I started at (L&T for) INR 670. On confirmation I got INR 760 and then six months later, after the annual review, I got INR 950. A month after that there was a union agreement and everyone got INR 75 more. That's how I started getting INR 1,025.'

From his early days at L&T, Anil abided by the mantra Work is Worship, as he was usually among the first to arrive to work and among the last to leave office. Working sixteen hours a day for most of his career, he says—only partly in jest—he has devoted all his energy to the company. For the first two decades of his career, he never took a day off, not even the weekly holiday. 'We had Saturdays off, and I would usually come in from a tour on a Saturday, and then go around the plant on Sunday', he says.

Anil rose rapidly from the shopfloor to the boardroom, climbing up the executive ladder at L&T, as the company is commonly known. Started by two Danes in partnership with an Indian in a small room with just a table and a chair, L&T was one of the largest Indian multinationals, with annual revenues north of INR 150,750 crores (or US$20 billion) in 2022. Within five years of joining L&T, Anil had earned two promotions and was sent to Britain for training in 1970, a significant career milestone in those days. He was just twenty-eight.

Anil's work ethic is exemplary and inspiring. 'I am the greatest disciplinarian because discipline is what demonstrates your seriousness for what you do', Anil says. 'It's not for show. Everyone should aspire to become a role model in that sense, and discipline is one of the key factors. Initially, in the 1990s, when we had to submit bids to ONGC (Oil and Natural Gas Commission), we had people who would work through the night and then straightaway in the morning go to submit the tenders. I used to sit up with them up to 2 am. I would then go home and return before they finally left the office in the morning to submit the tenders. I didn't have to do it. But my being there would give them strength. If the boss is doing so much, they would think, then so can we.'

Anil came to national prominence in the 1990s when Reliance Industries made a concentrated effort to take over L&T, acquiring a substantial stake. The corporate battle became more complicated in 2001 when Reliance sold its stake to Aditya Birla and his son Kumar Mangalam Birla. The father-son duo had unsuccessfully tried to hire Naik a few years earlier. When they bought the stake in L&T, Kumar Mangalam Birla told Anil, 'You did not come to us, so now we are coming to you.'

The battle and deal-making that followed saw the cement unit being hived off from L&T. To fortify L&T from similar takeover attempts, Anil gave stock options to employees. The company grew, and so did he and the value of the stocks. Employees became '*lakhpati* and *crorepatis*'.

Asked whether he ever thought of working somewhere other than L&T, Anil says he has applied for a job only twice, and never after joining L&T. 'Just four months after I became CEO in 1999, I got a call from a head-hunter seeking an Asia head for a multinational company', he reminisces. Anil said he was not interested, turning around to ask the head-hunter if he would help with hiring at L&T. 'That was the last call I got', he says, as people realised that Anil would never leave L&T.[5] His retirement home is across from L&T's campus in the Powai area of Mumbai. He has often said he wants to die with the factory in sight.

Anil was recognised in 2019, for his contribution to industry, with the Padma Vibhushan.

Ratan Tata
Luminary of Industrial Innovation

Ratan Tata is one of the most influential business leaders in independent India. A graduate of Cornell University's architecture program, Tata would have liked to become a successful architect himself. Life, however, took him in a different direction, one in which he excelled, but which was not his first love. He was recognised with the Padma Bhushan in 2000 and the Padma Vibhushan in 2008.

Ratan Tata was born in 1937 to Naval and Sooni Tata. While Naval was a Tata by birth, he did not enter the main Tata family until his adoption by Lady Navajbai Tata, a widowed daughter-in-law of Sir Jamshedji Tata, who had founded the Tata Group.[1] Years later, Ratan Tata praised his great-grandfather Jamshedji for having provided the Tata Group with his inspiration, his ethics, values and selflessness which have provided dignity and livelihood to thousands of citizens'.[2]

From an early age, Ratan was close to his grandmother Lady Navajbai. Ratan's parents divorced when he was 10, which made an otherwise happy childhood difficult. As his father and mother married others and started separate families, Ratan came under the care of his grandmother who taught him about keeping his 'dignity at all costs'.[3] He grew up in the astonishing luxury of a huge villa in the centre of Mumbai.

After finishing high school, he chose to study architecture at Cornell (though his father wanted him to become an engineer). At Cornell, he had to take all kinds of odd jobs, including washing dishes, to make ends meet as the Indian Reserve Bank's foreign exchange allowance was not enough to survive in America. The Tatas were not willing to buy dollars on the black market for their son to live in America.

Ratan was working as an architect in Los Angeles, when he learned about the health issues his grandmother was facing and decided to come back to India to be with her. Ratan has consistently maintained that he enjoyed working as an architect. 'But then, my grandmother, to whom I was very attached, fell very ill and I had to keep coming back to India to see her. And after a while, after I had been here so many times, one thing led to another and I just never went back.'[4]

When Ratan decided not to return to his architecture job, he also had to make a heart-wrenching personal decision. Ratan was in love with a girl in Los Angeles, but she was not willing to move with him to India. As Ratan recounted later in an interview, 'That was the year of the Indo-Chinese conflict. This conflict in the snowy, uninhabited part of the Himalayas was seen in the United States as a major war between India and China, and so she didn't come and finally got married in the US thereafter'. Ratan never married.[5]

After his grandmother passed away, Ratan moved to Jamshedpur for an internship at the Tata Group. For the next six months, he struggled, 'trying to be useful' until he landed in the furnace department at Tata Steel. In the 1970s, Ratan was promoted to management, with his first significant assignment as Chairman of National Radio and Electronics Company (NELCO).[6] Years later, Ratan admitted that, 'I don't think I would have learned as much the hard way as I did at NELCO. I am grateful to the powers that be that they gave me NELCO.' Many consider NELCO to be a key formative experience in Ratan's professional life before he succeeded the legendary JRD Tata at the helm of the Tata Group.

Most accounts of Ratan's early years overlook his work in Tata's textile business. After he successfully turned around a mill and declared a dividend, he was asked to take charge of another Tata textile unit. The board disagreed with his proposal to rejuvenate the mill and instead closed the factory. Ratan disagreed with the decision, especially because many good people lost their jobs. 'I was so disgusted by that decision that when I got my annual bonus from the Tatas, I gave it to the officers of the company. These were perfectly blameless people who now had lost their jobs through no fault of theirs because of a bad corporate decision. They had homes to run and children to educate.'

When it was announced that Ratan would be the new chairman of Tata Industries, it was seen as a signal that the succession issue had been decided. Ratan, however, knew that the top position at Tata Industries did not mean that he would be put in-charge of the Tata Group. It is the head of Tata Sons, not the head of Tata Industries, that leads the group. Ratan's ascent to the head of Tata Industries put him in competition with stalwarts like Nani Palkhivala and Rusi Mody for the leadership of the group.

Critics charge Ratan with outmaneuvering his rivals to reach the top of the Tata empire, essentially using his name to climb up the ladder. Such criticism often missed an important point. Both his rivals—Nani and Mody—saw their star fall because they spoke too much and too loosely. Nani became such a vocal critic of the government that JRD felt his political views would become a liability for the group. Mody publicly criticised the management of Tata's Tesco, which lost him precious support within the company. Ratan, however, kept his head down, worked hard, and allowed himself to develop in the job.

It is easy to forget that when Ratan was nominated to the top position at Tata, many people wrote him off, with his critics arguing that he was not up to the task. He was an essentially mediocre man who had been catapulted to the top of the Tata Group, critics charged, because of the accident of his birth and his famous last name.

'I think I would have remained an architect, regardless of my surname. I was called Tata when I decided not to go into business and become an architect instead.'

One of the world's most famous business tycoons, Ratan has lived for years in the same simple apartment in the Bakhtawar area of Colaba in Mumbai that is more suitable for a bachelor who loves reading and dogs than for someone who was at the helm of India's most respected business house.[7]

888

AWARDS

Sports

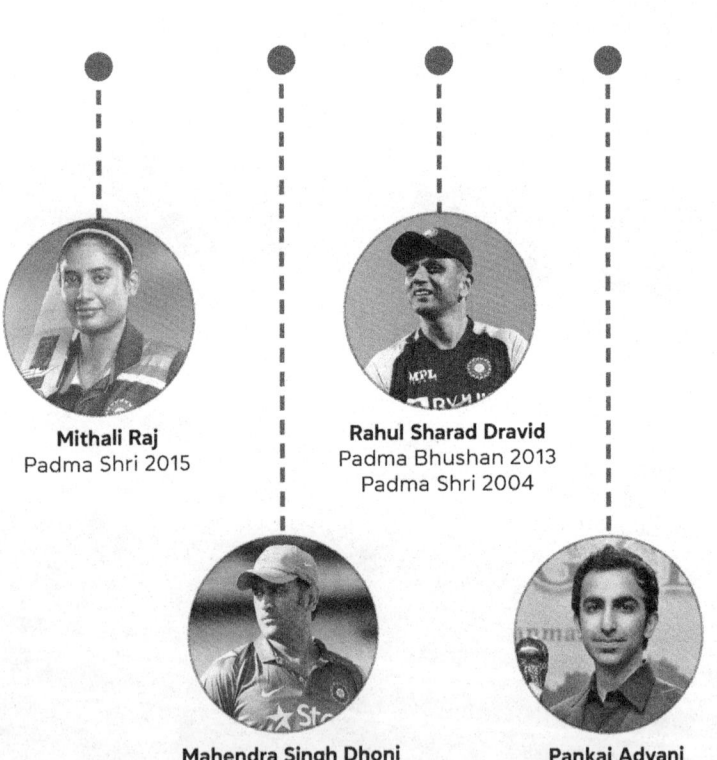

Mithali Raj
Padma Shri 2015

Rahul Sharad Dravid
Padma Bhushan 2013
Padma Shri 2004

Mahendra Singh Dhoni
Padma Bhushan 2018
Padma Shri 2009

Pankaj Advani
Padma Bhushan 2018
Padma Shri 2009

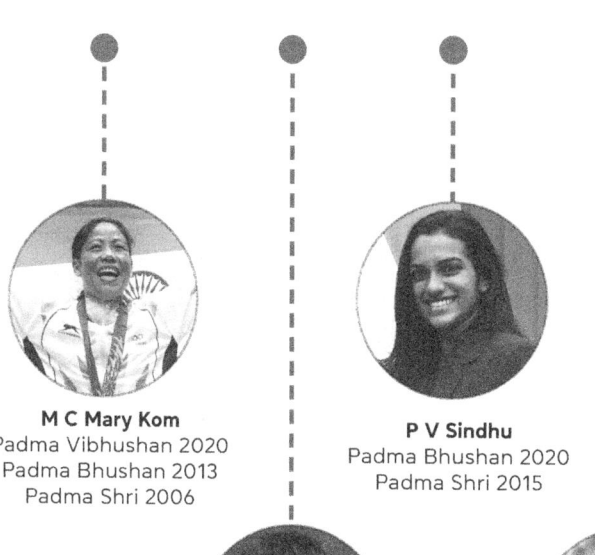

M C Mary Kom
Padma Vibhushan 2020
Padma Bhushan 2013
Padma Shri 2006

P V Sindhu
Padma Bhushan 2020
Padma Shri 2015

Puella Gopichand
Padma Bhushan 2014
Padma Shri 2005

Bachendri Pal
Padma Bhushan 2019

Sports

Viswanathan Anand
Padma Vibhushan 2008
Padma Bhushan 2001
Padma Shri 1988

H. Boniface Prabhu
Padma Shri 2014

Abhinav Bindra
Padma Bhushan 2018
Padma Shri 2009

Love Raj Singh Dharmshaktu
Padma Shri 2014

Arunima Sinha
Padma Shri 2015

Devendra Jhajharia
Padma Bhushan 2022
Padma Shri 2012

Deepika Kumari
Padma Shri 2016

Mithali Raj
Batting Through Boundaries

'Who is your favourite male cricketer?' asked a reporter to Mithali Raj, the captain of the Indian women's team, at a pre-World Cup dinner. Her response: 'Do you ask the same question to a male cricketer? Do you ask them who is their favourite female cricketer?'[1]

Mithali, who received the Padma Shri in 2015, is one of India's most successful cricketers, male or female. She is the highest run-scorer in women's international cricket, and among the all-time highest run-scorer for the country across various formats, including Tests, ODIs, and T20Is (regardless of gender). Mithali is one of the most successful captains of the Indian national cricket team, having led India's women's team from 2004 to 2022. In a career spanning twenty three years, Mithali represented India 333 times across all formats, scored a world record 10,868 runs and became the first Indian captain to lead the country in two World Cup finals. She is the only Indian captain, male or female, to have led the team in two world cup finals. Not bad for someone who was constantly discouraged by her grandparents for pursuing a 'boys' sport'.[2]

Born in 1982 in Jodhpur (Rajasthan), Mithali grew up in a traditional and loving family in Hyderabad. As a child, she learned Bharatanatyam, a major form of Indian classical dance. Her father was concerned about his daughter sleeping till late, and asked her to accompany her brother to training at a local cricket academy. While her brother played cricket with the other boys, Mithali sat by the boundary to finish her homework. Sometimes, she would also pick up a bat and try to hit a few balls.[3]

Mithali's antics caught the eye of a coach at the academy, who referred her to Sampath Kumar, the head coach of two of Hyderabad's age-group teams. Mithali did not know it then, but her meeting with Kumar was to forever change her life and alter the course of women's cricket in India. At the time, Kumar was already training some women cricketers.

Kumar was impressed by Mithali's cricketing acumen. He asked her parents to let him coach her. Young Mithali, like most Tamilian girls, was more interested in Bharatnatyam than in cricket. Yet, when Kumar convinced her parents to let her play cricket, Mithali went along with the plan and brought her dancer's dedication to cricket. 'Dance was my personal passion, but the level of cricket I had reached meant I had to understand my priorities', Mithali says. 'My parents invested a lot more time in making me a cricketer than a dancer, so I had to choose cricket'.[4]

As a school student, Mithali's cricket training was structured around her academic work. She would start training at around 4 am, go to school, and then practice some more after school. Often, she practiced as many as six hours daily. Coach Kumar was a batting purist, a stickler for technique, and a traditional disciplinarian. He asked Mithali to practice batting in narrow corridors and had her bat with a stump to ensure she was middling the ball. He 'used to hit me with a stick if the ball touched the walls', she explained in a later interview. Mithali embraced her coach's teaching style, focusing on perfecting her batting style. 'I always remember him as he taught me how to play good cricket', she shared.[5]

When Kumar had first seen Mithali play, he had told her father: 'I want the complete trust of you and your wife. I want blind support. I will make Mithali play for the country by the time she's 14.' Mithali's father thought he was saying it just to please them.

At age thirteen, Mithali was selected for the Andhra Pradesh women's team. Three years later, she made it to the national team, representing India for the first time when she was merely sixteen years old. Although her parents supported her playing cricket, they could not pull strings for her to advance through the ranks. Her father was a warrant officer in the Indian Air Force, which is a senior non-commissioned rank. Her mother was a home maker. Mithali selection to the state team and then to the national team was based purely on her merit and her coach's recommendation. Her ODI debut for India was against Ireland in England, where she scored an unbeaten 114, affirming the confidence her parents, coach, and selectors had reposed in her.

Three years later, she was made part of the Test team. Mithali was out for a duck in her first test against England in Lucknow. She scored 55 in the next test, but her true potential came through on the tour of England later in the year. She made 214, the highest individual Test score in women's cricket at the time. Her batting impressed the audience and the critics. 'That knock marked her coming of age', says former India captain Mamatha Maben, upon whose dismissal Mithali came to the crease for her historic innings.[6] 'We always knew she could bat, but that knock catapulted her to another level. We knew then that here was a role model in the making, one who would inspire future stars.'

Mithali joined the Indian women's cricket team at a time when few Indians even knew that women too played cricket. By the time Mithali retired, women's cricket had earned the kind of popularity that was hard to believe for the veterans who had been there when no one cared.[7]

'I set out as a little girl on the journey to wear the India blues as representing your country is the highest honour. It was an honour to have led the team for so many years. It definitely shaped me as a person and hopefully helped shape Indian women's cricket as well', Mithali noted upon retiring from cricket.[8]

Mahendra Singh Dhoni
Cricket Icon and Revered Captain

Born on 7 July 1981 to a middle-class family in Ranchi (capital of present-day Jharkhand), Mahendra Singh Dhoni went on to become India's most decorated cricket captain who won each one of the established ICC[1] trophies: the 2007 T20 World Cup, the 2011 ODI World Cup, the 2013 Champions Trophy, and the 2010 and 2011 Test Match Championship (awarded to the best test match team). He also led India to victory in the 2010 and 2016 Asia Cup.[2] Also, as the captain of the Chennai Super Kings (CSK) in the Indian Premier League (IPL),[3] he led his team to victory in 2010, 2011, 2018 and 2021, and to runner-up in the 2008, 2012, 2013, 2015 and 2019 seasons.[4]

Dhoni was born to Pan Singh and Devaki Devi who had migrated from their paternal village in Almora, Uttarakhand to Ranchi, Jharkhand. His father worked as a pump operator in a junior management position in MECON,[5] Ranchi. He was the youngest of the three children and had a keen interest in sports. Dhoni's first love was football and it was as a goalkeeper that he first displayed his sharp reflexes and presence of mind. His coach, Keshav Ranjan Banerjee, was so impressed by his flexibility and agility that he encouraged Dhoni to take up a sport that would provide him greater exposure. Soon, his coach recommended him to join Commando club where Dhoni stood behind the stumps as a wicketkeeper and impressed everyone.[6]

Dhoni played with the Commando club from 1995 to 1998 and sharpened his cricketing skills. Based on his performances in the club cricket, he was selected to play in the under-16 Vinoo Mankad Trophy[7] in Delhi. He performed extremely well and announced his arrival to the cricketing world. Between 2001 to 2003, Dhoni worked as an assistant to Travelling Ticket Examiners (TTE) at the Kharagpur railway station. His day job involved running from one platform to another to hand over the seating charts to the TTEs of long-distance trains that stopped at Kharagpur.[8]

On the way to getting selected to the Indian national team, Dhoni played with different teams at different times. He played with the team of the Central Coal Fields limited in 1998, with the under-19 Bihar team in the 1998-99 and the 1999-2000 seasons of the Cooch Behar trophy, and in the East Zone under-19 tournament in the 1999-2000 season. He made his Ranji trophy debut in the 1999-2000 season while he was just eighteen-years old. Dhoni was spotted by the BCCI's talent-spotting initiative when he was noticed by talent resource development officers Raju Mukherjee and Prakash Chandra in 2004.[9]

Dhoni was picked up for the India A team in the 2003-2004 season and was brought to the notice, for his good performances in the tournament, to Sourav Ganguly, captain of India's national cricket team. Dhoni made his international debut against Bangladesh in the 2004-2005 season. He also made his test debut in 2005. Though his first series did not go too well, he was picked for the upcoming Pakistan series. The Pakistan series announced Dhoni's arrival to the cricketing world and consolidated his position in the Indian team. In the second match of the series and only his fifth one-day international, Dhoni scored 148 runs off 123 deliveries, setting a world record for highest runs by a wicketkeeper.[10] The record was broken by him again when in the bilateral series against Sri Lanka in October-November 2005, he scored 183 runs off 145 balls.[11]

On the back of consistent performances both with the bat and behind the wickets, Dhoni was made the Vice-Captain of the Indian team in 2007 and also the Captain of the team for the 2007 T20 World Cup. On 24 September 2007, he led India to world cup victory by defeating arch rivals Pakistan at the Wanderers stadium in Johannesburg, South Africa. This was India's first world cup win after Kapil Dev[12] led the Indian team to victory in the 1983 ICC ODI World Cup.[13] Dhoni had made a place for himself in every Indian cricket fan's heart. He further endeared himself to them when he led the ODI team to the 2011 World Cup win, the first world cup win in the ODI format after 1983. His innings of 91 not out was crucial in clinching the title.[14]

Dhoni played 350 ODIs and scored 10,773 runs in his career. He impacted 444 dismissals in ODIs, 91 in Twenty20 internationals and 294 dismissals in Tests. On the night before his 37th birthday celebration, he became the third Indian cricketer and first wicketkeeper to show up in 500 global matches. He holds multiple records across all formats of the game: the record for most runs by a wicketkeeper (183 runs), most international matches as captain (332), most dismissals in Test matches by an Indian wicketkeeper (294), first player to score more than 10,000 runs in ODI with an average greater than 50, the most dismissals in an ODI innings (6) and in career (432) by an Indian wicketkeeper, the most dismissals in T20s by a wicketkeeper (91), among many others.[15]

Dhoni announced his retirement from international cricket on 15 August 2020, India's Independence day. From the very beginning, Dhoni struck a chord with India's booming young population, a great many of whom live outside India's metropolitan cities and who belong to the first generation to enjoy the benefits of the country's economic liberalisation. Dhoni's career, in many ways, symbolises the aspiration of this generation. He showed that people from small towns of India can also make their dreams come true.

Dhoni holds the position of Honorary Lieutenant Colonel in the Territorial Army and received a Padma Bhushan award in the army uniform from the President of India on 2 April 2011.[16] He has also been awarded the ICC Cricketer of the Year award in 2007 and the ICC ODI Player of the Year award in 2008.

Rahul Sharad Dravid
Upholding the Spirit of Cricket

Rahul Sharad Dravid is a former Indian cricketer and skipper of the Indian national team. Born on 11 January 1973 in a Marathi family, Dravid grew up in Bangalore. Dravid's father, Sharad Dravid, worked in a factory that made jams, which later led to his nickname 'Jammy'. His mother, Pushpa, was a professor of architecture at the University Visvesvaraya College of Engineering at Bangalore. Dravid completed his schooling from St. Joseph's High School and then his graduation in commerce from St. Joseph's College of Commerce.[1] Dravid grew up in a simple, serious middle class family.[2]

Dravid started playing cricket at the age of 12 and played for the Karnataka under-15, under-17 and under-19 teams. He made his Ranji trophy[3] debut in 1991 and finished his first full season scoring 380 runs at an average of 63.30. Backed by consistent performances in domestic cricket, Dravid earned his first national call in October 1994 for the last two matches of the Wills World Series[4] but could not make it to the playing eleven. He made his One-Day International (ODI) debut in 1996 against Sri Lanka. However, his international debut was not impressive as he scored only three and four runs against Sri Lanka and Pakistan, respectively.

In contrast to his ODI debut, Dravid's Test debut was

rather successful; he scored ninety-five runs coming in to bat at number seven against England. He completed his first series with an impressive average of 62.33 runs in two test matches. Remembering his Test debut, Dravid reflected, 'It meant a lot to me. I had played five years of first-class cricket to break into the Indian team. I'd scored a lot of runs in domestic cricket and got an opportunity to come on the tour of England. It was great for me, it meant so much. I never expected it to lead to anything. I remember when I was 50 not out at the end of the day and I was walking back to the hotel with (Javagal) Srinath[5] and I knew somehow that this was probably a very significant innings. I knew I had some more breathing space, I got a few more Test matches at least. It gave me a lot of confidence scoring 95 here and 80 at Trent Bridge. It gave me a lot of confidence as a player and as a person, too.'[6]

Dravid's ODI and Test careers progressed apace, just like his debut. While he had scored 15 fifties (including four scores of 90s) and one hundred by the end of 1997/98 Test seasons,[7] he was constantly in and out of the ODI team and was criticised for his slow strike rate. By the end of 1998, he had only scored 1709 runs in 65 ODI matches at an average of 31.64 and a poor strike rate of 63.48.[8] He had been labelled as a 'Test specialist' who was ill-equipped for the pace and style of ODI cricket.

Dravid's renaissance in ODI came in the season of 1998/99 where he scored 309 runs at an average of 77.25 and a strike rate of 84.65 during the 1998/99 New Zealand tour.[9] During the 1999 Cricket World Cup, Dravid emerged as the top scorer in the tournament with 461 runs from 8 games at an average of 68.85 and a strike rate of 85.52.[10] In 2000, Dravid was elevated to the position of Vice-Captain of the Indian men's cricket team. He hit his peak form between 2002-2006, when he scored 8,914 runs from 174 matches across all formats at an average 54.02, including 19 hundreds.[11]

Perhaps, Dravid will be best remembered for his innings during the second Test match at Eden Gardens, Kolkata during Australia's tour of India in February 2001. During the second match of the three-test series, India had been bowled out at 171 in the first innings. India was asked to follow on after conceding a lead of 274 runs. Dravid, playing at number six, joined VVS Laxman with the score at 232/4 in the middle of the third day with India needing 42 runs to avoid an innings defeat. Dravid and Laxman played out the remaining of third day and full fourth day building a mammoth partnership of 376 runs. India declared at 657/7 setting Australia a target of 384 runs. India went on to win the match by 171 runs. This was only the third instance of a team winning a Test match after following on and India became the second team to do so.

After a successful cricketing career spanning close to 20 years and scoring 24,177 runs in international cricket, Dravid announced his retirement on 9 March 2012. Announcing his retirement, he mentioned, 'My approach to cricket has been reasonably simple: it was about giving everything to the team, it was about playing with dignity, and it was about upholding the spirit of the game. I hope I have done some of that. I have failed at times, but I have never stopped trying. It is why I leave with sadness but also with pride'.[12]

Dravid was the gentleman of Indian cricket who was fondly referred to as 'the wall' for his performances on the field as well as his composure, both on and off the field. He made 13,288 runs in 164 test matches, and 10,899 runs in 344 ODIs.[13] His top score of 270 runs against Pakistan in 2004 were made in an innings that lasted more than 12 hours. It was the longest innings by an Indian batsman.[14]

In 2000, Dravid was named the Wisden Cricketer of the Year. In 2004, he was awarded the 'Player of the Year' award and 'Test Player of the Year' award. He was conferred the Padma Shri in 2004 and the Padma Bhushan in 2013. In 2018, Dravid became the fifth Indian cricketer to be inducted into ICC's[15] Hall of Fame.

Pankaj Advani
Cue Sports Pro

Pankaj Advani, the first Indian to win the International Billiards and Snooker Federation (IBSF) 6-Red Snooker World Cup. With a total of 24 World Champion titles, Advani was introduced to Cue sports by his elder brother. Stories of Wilson Jones, a Billiards player who lifted independent India's first world title inspired young Pankaj to pursue a career in Cue sports.

Born on 24 July 1985 in a Sindhi family, Advani studied at the Frank Anthony Public School in Bangalore, and then completed an undergraduate degree in commerce from the Sri Bhagawan Mahaveer Jain College, Bangalore. Pursuing a career in sports that is considered a recreational activity in India was not easy. However, Pankaj's family has always been supportive and understanding. 'My mother used to worry about me when I was young, but then she saw how passionate I was about the game, and she laid back. In fact, at school, I was always a bright student, but once I started playing billiards and snooker, my concentration improved by leaps and bounds. If you show your parents how passionate you are about a particular sport, they will always support and encourage you', mentions Advani.[1]

Advani started his training at the age of 10 with Arvind

Savur, a former national Snooker Champion who noticed Advani's talent in the sport. He lifted his first ever title at the age of 12 and has been setting state, national and international records ever since.

After Advani's father passed away in 1992, things went a little south. When he first represented India in the World Billiards Championship in England, he did not get funding from the Indian government. To support his love for sport, his mother had to encash an FD (fixed deposit) to fund his travel. However, everything changed when Advani lifted his first World Championship Title in 2003.

Advani won the Indian Junior Billiards Championship on three consecutive occasions—2000, 2001 and 2003. In 2003, he also became the youngest national Snooker Champion thereby setting a record. Remembering his first ever world title, Advani said, 'Representing India at the IBSF World Snooker Championships tournament has always had a special place in my heart as on this day 25 October 2021, 18 years ago in 2003 as an 18-year-old, I lifted my first ever world title in China, the coveted prize—the IBSF World Snooker Championship for India'.[2]

Moreover in 2005, Advani became the only Indian to have won the IBSF World Billiards Championship. He then went on to win the World Professional Billiards and Snooker Association (WPBSA) World Billiards Champion Pro title in 2009. In 2012, he won the World Billiards Championship, becoming the youngest individual ever to win all the world titles in English Billiards. At the age of 27, Advani also became the first player to win five Asian Billiards Championship titles. He is the only Indian to have been awarded the amateur World titles in both snooker and billiards.

Considered as one of the best billiards and snooker player to have ever emerged from India, Advani was honoured with a Padma Bhushan in 2018. When asked about this National

Award in an interview, Advani mentioned that he does not play for awards, but they do give him a sense of motivation and excitement. He believes that his National Award is not only an asset but brings glory to the entire Cue sports fraternity. 'Sport is not just about skill, technique and hard work. It is also about understanding your emotions, and how to approach the game. There is hardly anything that separates the best from the rest.'[3]

Playing for India is Advani's biggest motivation. As he mentions, 'Everybody asks me, you have won so much, what keeps you going? For me the answer is very simple. I love playing sports. I just find joy in competing, practicing and playing the game the way it should be played and continuously evolve and improve. I love my country and I love representing and winning for my country. So that itself is motivating enough, forget about other things that come along with it: name, fame, adulation, awards. Those things come automatically. I am at it because I just love doing it.'[4] He has also been awarded the Rajiv Gandhi Khel Ratna, India's highest sporting honour, in the year 2005-06.

As a Cue sports personality, Advani reckons that people underestimate their physical and mental well-being. The constant wear and tear of muscles due to bending and staying still for long durations, leads to physical ailments. Advani might win tournaments, but deep down he still feels butterflies in his stomach before any match. He believes that the true means of measuring the consistency of any sports player is by observing their yearly performances and how often the player does well. He emphasises on the mental well-being of everyone and believes that a mentally healthy nation is a physically healthy nation.

Snooker and billiards demand utmost concentration and core strength from its players. One needs to bend to a certain position and keep their feet firm on the ground. This continual exertion for the game can not only be physically but also mentally challenging. Advani seeks help from his older brother, Shree Advani, who is a sports psychologist. During championships, Advani has been suffering from upper back and muscular problems. Cue sports does not require raw physical power but demands the players to be flexible from the core.

Advani attributes his success to a deep desire to win and also to his fitness. Advani believes in working smarter than hard, considering himself an artist. He relies on his experience and decision-making capabilities when performing. The long break enforced by COVID only increased his hunger and appreciation for the game and everything that it offers.

The Golden Boy, The Poster Boy of Cue Sports or the Prince of India, Pankaj Advani dons many names. Some even call him 'Messi of Cue Sport,' but what matters to him apart from the numerous awards he has won is a small pat on the back or somebody saying something nice.

Mary Kom
The Boxing Phenomenon

Landless farmer parents. A small village without running water and electricity. One room house with a thatched roof and walls plastered with a mix of mud, cow-dung, and straw. These are just some of the reasons that Mangte Chungneijang Mary Kom, born 24 November 1982 in the village of Sagana of the state of Manipur in India, should have lived an anonymous life destined to manual labour, perhaps working in a leech-filled rice field with her parents. Yet, Mary Kom (as she came to be called), carved a different path for herself, winning the World Women's Boxing Championship multiple times (4 Golds and 1 Silver), becoming India's most-celebrated female boxer.

Mary's parents were poor, so poor that the family had to sew pieces of cloth together to make blankets to keep them warm in the cold Manipuri winters. Every morning, before going to school, Mary was expected to help out with the housework, tend to the cows, and carry water across long distances for the family. School was a one-hour trek each way, and when her shoes wore out, Mary's mother would repair them by heating iron tongs and pressing them together on the tear to join the pieces.

Mary's parents saw education as a way out of the grinding

poverty in which they lived. Unfortunately, Mary was, at best, a mediocre student. What she did like, however, was sports. At school, she participated and excelled in individual sports, which is why the principal and teachers at the St. Xavier's School suggested she pursue sports sincerely. Unable to afford the expenses of their daughter's sporting interests, Mary's father resisted until her passion for sports forced him to start looking for training options for his daughter. For Mary and her parents, sports also seemed a good way to get a government job through the sports quota. As Mary herself states, her thinking was that she 'should pursue a career in sports and get a job under the sports quota,' which would help her parents 'so they'd no longer be poor'.[1]

After much trepidation, Mary went to the Sports Authority of India (SAI) facility in Imphal. At SAI, Mary tried out a number of different sports: javelin throw, pole-vault, track-and-field, and gymnastics. She wanted, however, to do something related to martial arts as she had enjoyed watching Bruce Lee and Jackie Chan movies growing up (in Manipur at the time, Hindi movies were banned by militants, so Manipuris had no access to them). Around that time, SAI was introducing women's boxing at its facilities. A Manipuri, Dingko Singh, had won the gold in the 1998 Bangkok Asian Games, which generated buzz around boxing in the state. A chance meeting with a Manipuri boxer, Debika Chiru, a boxer training at the SAI helped Mary decide to pursue boxing.

Training was difficult and challenging. Mary's hard-work began to pay off when she won her first State Women's Boxing Championship. A local newspaper published the winner's photograph, which is how her father found out that she was training to be a boxer. He admonished his daughter for her interest in boxing, which he considered a violent sport, not appropriate for women. Mary persisted, and when she did not relent, her father agreed to continue to support her financially. Gradually, she started winning at the nationals, and after an initial defeat in her first international tournament in Bangkok, Mary started winning internationally too. A silver at the 1st World Women's Boxing Championship in Pennsylvania (USA) started her international medal haul. Subsequently, she won four World Championship golds.

Mary's story would remain incomplete without talking about her married life. Mary met a fellow Manipuri, Onler Kom, during a training session in Delhi. After some resistance from her father, Mary married Onler, who promised to support her career. After her marriage Mary took a four-month break from boxing. Many in her family and among her friends imagined she would no longer be able to box. Mary proved them wrong! Not only did she compete, she managed to retain the title in the Third World Women's Boxing Championship at Podolsk in Russia, and then also won the gold at the Fourth World Women's Boxing Championship at New Delhi.

When Mary had twins, she took a two-year break from competing. Six months after her delivery, Mary had started to exercise and build up her stamina again. At the time, even Mary's father advised her to quit boxing. 'Now that you're a mother, its enough', he said. 'You will be tired. Stop boxing. You have won so much, earned enough, and you have a job. You have achieved enough.'

The twins were barely a little over a year old when Mary left for the training camp for the selections for the Fourth Asian Women's Championships. She was sick and in pain throughout the first few weeks of training. She was also nursing at the time, so when she could not feed her kids, she developed mastitis. She also missed her children who were at home with their father. Her rivals thought that she was past her peak. When she ended up with a silver at the Asian Women's Championships, her father told her off: 'See, this time you got only a silver. Do you want to end your career in disgrace? Do you want people to backbite and criticise your performance? You should have stopped when you were at the top.' His words enraged Mary, who decided to better her performance and prove them wrong. Eventually, Mary won the fourth World Championship title.

Success in the boxing ring brought several accolades to Mary: Arjuna award (for Outstanding Performance in Sports and Games), Padma Shri (fourth-highest civilian award in the country), and Khel Ratna award (for spectacular and most outstanding sports performance over a period of four years at the international level). Corporates came forward to sponsor her, bringing additional resources for equipment and travel to Mary. Yet, one award was missing in Mary's portfolio: Olympics, the biggest sporting arena in the world. Her dream of the long-desired Olympic podium finally came to fruition at the 2012 London Olympics, when Mary won the bronze. Mary's winning streak continued, and in 2018 she became the first female boxer to win six world championships.

As Mary climbed the ladder of success, she did not forget to give back to her community and society. Her giving back took the form of the M C Mary Kom Boxing Academy, where aspiring boxers were trained free of charge. Here too Mary dreams big: she wants to create a world-class boxing academy with top-of-the-line facilities for young people who dream of bringing medals for the country.

Pullela Gopichand
A Beacon of Excellence in India's Sporting Legacy

Pullela Gopichand was born on 16 November 1973 in Prakasam district of Andhra Pradesh. His parents, Pullela Subash Chandra and Pullela Subbaravamma, were both interested in sports and this love for sports rubbed onto Gopichand. Growing up, Gopichand wanted to play cricket. However, his brother encouraged him to play badminton instead. His family settled in Hyderabad from where he completed his schooling and graduation. At college, he led the badminton team in the years 1990 and 1991.

Gopichand started training under Prakash Padukone[1] and it was due to his hard work, dedication and commitment towards badminton that he went on to create magic on the court and registered many firsts to his name. He won his first national Badminton Championship in 1996 and went on to defend the title five times in a row, till 2000. In 2001, he became only the second Indian to win the All England Open Badminton Champion[2] (Prakash Padukone first won the title in 1980).

Gopichand's story is also that of courage and determination. He was unfortunately injured in 1986, when he experienced a multiple ligament rupture. However, young Gopichand who was only 13 years of age overcame the injury and reached the finals of the Andhra Pradesh State Junior Badminton tournament in 1987.[3] Though, he lost the finals to his elder brother, Rajashekar, he impressed one and all with his dedication and determination. His badminton skills were the centre of attraction and conversation at St. Paul's School in Hyderabad, from where he completed his schooling.

Gopichand completed his graduation in Economics from the AV College in Hyderabad. He won his first singles title at the National Championships held in Goa in the year 1989. He also went on to win the doubles title in the tournament. By 1999, Gopichand was seeded 26 after winning the Indian International, Scottish and French titles, among many others. He won the SAARC gold medal that very year.

Continuously a warrior, Gopichand remained undeterred by his loss in the 2000 Sydney Olympics and consistent with his reputation outplayed the Olympics champions to arrive at the finals of the All England Badminton Championship. He comfortably defeated Olympic Gold medalist Anders Boeson in the Quarterfinals of this competition. In the elimination rounds, he defeated world number 1 Peter Gade of Denmark, and in the finals defeated Chen Hong of China. He was ranked fifth, his best, in April 2001.

A student of Prakash Padukone, Gopichand is a reserved individual who is extremely sharp in net play. He is an officer at the Indian Oil Corporation in Hyderabad, but the corporation has allowed him to spend most of his time training at the Sports Authority of India (SAI) facilities in Bangalore. Gopichand is a combination of mental resilience and concentration who is continuously working towards improving the quality of badminton in the county.

Subsequent to retiring from active playing, Gopichand decided to set up a badminton academy in Hyderabad. With the support of Nimmagadda Prasad, an industrialist from Andhra Pradesh and his Olympian wife, P V V Lakshmi, and funds obtained from mortgaging his own house, Gopichand started the Gopichand Badminton Academy in 2008. The academy has eight badminton courts of international standards, a swimming pool, rooms for players, gym and a cafeteria. The academy has become one of the best training facilities in the country and is producing world class players. The Government of India sent the 2010 Commonwealth games team to train at the academy.

The Gopichand Badminton Academy has contributed immensely to the growth of badminton in India. The academy has produced India's top badminton players including Saina Nehwal, P V Sindhu and Srikanth Kadambi, among many others.[4] Saina Nehwal won the bronze medal at the 2012 Olympics at London and went on to become world number one. P V Sindhu is one of India's most successful sportspersons and won the silver medal at the 2016 summer Olympics held in Rio and the bronze medal at the 2020 summer Olympics held in Tokyo. She also became the first Indian to win the Badminton World Federation (BWF) World Championships in 2019. Srikant Kadambi is a former world number 1 badminton player who became the first Indian ever to reach the finals of the men's BWF World Championships. Gopichand also served as the official Indian Olympic Badminton Team coach at the 2016 Rio Olympics held in Brazil.

Himself an adherent of the Art of Living philosophy propounded by Sri Sri Ravishankar, Gopichand is now working on the mental health of athletes. In 2020, he launched the *Dhyana* app that provides carefully curated meditation sessions for athletes. All sessions on the app are in Gopichand's voice and are inspired by his own personal experiences. The sessions touch upon topics such as gratitude, forgiveness, uniting your inner self, stillness, visualisation, discipline, pre-workout and post-workout exercises. Commenting on this initiative, Gopichand reflects,

'The ability to stay positive and focus-driven is a quality that one needs to cultivate, particularly in these trying times when most of our goals for the year have been waylaid by the pandemic. We designed *Dhyana* for sports to help athletes and others alike to achieve a strong emotional wellbeing and motivate and enable themselves to focus on the road to excellence. Victory doesn't always go to the stronger or the faster person. It ultimately goes to the stronger mind, the tougher spirit. I am certain that these guided sessions will prove to be fruitful to anyone wanting to become the best version of themselves.'[5]

Recognising his contributions to sports in India, the Government of India conferred on him the Arjuna Award, the second highest sporting honour in the country, in 1999, and the Major Dhyan Chand Khel Ratna award, the highest sporting honour in the county, in 2001. He was conferred the Padma Shri in 2005, and the Padma Bhushan in 2014. Gopichand is one of the rare sportspersons in India to have received the Dronacharya Award (in 2009), which recognises outstanding sports coaches. Gopichand has been recognised not just as a great sportsperson but also as a great coach and mentor.

ಠಠಠ

P V Sindhu
The Shuttle Queen

Pusarla Venkata (PV) Sindhu was born on 5 July 1995 in Hyderabad, India to PV Ramana and P Vijaya. For Sindhu, the love for sports came naturally as her mother and father had both played professional sports. They were members of the Indian volleyball team. Her father was part of the team that won a bronze medal in the 1986 Seoul Asian Games and had also been honoured with the Arjuna award[1] in 2000. However, growing up Sindhu chose badminton over volleyball as she was inspired by Pullela Gopichand who won the 2001 All England Open Badminton Championship (see the chapter on Pullela Gopichand for more details).

Sindhu grew up in Hyderabad and started playing badminton at the age of eight years. Reflecting on her initial days and her aspirations, Sindhu had observed in 2017, 'I used to play for fun initially but slowly the number of hours increased. I used to love playing badminton and that's how my parents came forward to support me... I definitely want to see myself at the top of the world'.[2] Soon, she joined the Pullela Gopichand Academy[3] in Hyderabad and started training under Gopichand, her inspiration. 'I would watch him (Gopichand) play and later shifted to his academy to get further training,' remembers Sindhu.[4]

Sindhu was a hard worker from the beginning. She would undertake an arduous journey to reach the training academy but never failed to be on time. While noting young Sindhu's dedication for the sport (when she was a student of class seven), a reporter with The Hindu observed: 'The fact that she reports on time at the coaching camps daily, travelling a distance of 56 km from her residence, is perhaps a reflection of her willingness to complete her desire to be a good badminton player with the required hard work and commitment. She hates to be away from sport.'[5]

Gopichand took personal care in fine-tuning Sindhu's game and helping her improve. He had noted that Sindhu had remarkable stamina and that, 'This is one of the most significant aspects of her game and should take her a long way'.[6] Sindhu's dedication, love for sport and physical as well as mental health soon started to show results.

At the domestic level, Sindhu won several medals in the under-10 category, such as the fifth Servo All India ranking championship, and the Ambuja Cement All India ranking. At the under-13 level, she won the singles title at the sub-juniors in Pondicherry, a doubles title at the Krishna Khaitan All India Tournament. In the under-14 category, Sindhu won the gold medal at the 51st National State Games in India.

Sindhu started playing at the international level from the age of fourteen. She won the silver medal at the Iran Fajr International Badminton Challenge. Her first major gold came at the Commonwealth Youth Games Badminton Championship held in Scotland in 2011. Delighted at the win, Sindhu had remarked, 'I am delighted to win this title. I dedicate this gold to you (parents) and my coach Gopi Sir'.[7] Seeing this as a precursor to many great things, Gopichand had observed, 'This shows her growing maturity in playing big events. No doubt, she is one of the favourites from India to emulate what Saina Nehwal has achieved in the big league.'[8]

Sindhu's watershed moment came in 2012 at the age of 17 when she defeated China's Li Xuerui at the quarter finals of the China Masters (but lost in the semi-finals) and won the silver medal at the Syed Modi international tournament. Next, in 2013 she had a semi-final run at the India Open and won gold at the Malaysian Grand Prix. She also won a bronze at the semi-finals of the BWF World Championships in 2013 making her the first Indian shuttler to win a BWF championship medal. All these events raised her ranking to among the ten best players in the world.

Winning bronze at the 2014 Commonwealth Games and 2014 BWF World Championships, Sindhu went on to become the first medal winner in badminton in the 2016 Rio Olympics.[9] The medal was only a stepping stone to becoming the star that Sindhu was destined to become. Sindhu never looked back thereafter. She beat Carolina Marin of Spain, the famed badminton player to whom she had lost in the 2016 Olympics, to win the Syed Modi and India Open titles. After winning successive medals at the BMW World Championships, Sindhu created history when she won gold at the prestigious Badminton World Championships in 2019. She became the first Indian to do so displacing Marin.[10]

At the 2020 Tokyo Olympics, Sindhu further consolidated her claim to greatness by winning a bronze medal in the women's singles and became the first Indian woman to ever win two Olympic medals.[11]

Today, Sindhu has become a brand to reckon with. She is the third highest paid endorser after cricketers Virat Kohli and MS Dhoni. She is the highest paid among women and among non-cricket sportspersons in the country. Commenting on Sindhu as an individual and as a brand, a brand manager commented, 'Sindhu is positioned as a player with grit, determination and doggedness. These are the qualities we, as marketers, position her around. Moreover, brands are now aware she is no longer playing for "a medal", but is playing for "the gold" having reached the final four in most of the tournaments."[12] She has also made it to the *Forbes* list of highest-paid female athletes in 2018, 2019 and 2021.[13]

For her contribution to sports and for inspiring the younger generation to take up sports as a vocation, Sindhu has been honoured with prestigious Indian awards such as Arjuna Award in 2013, Major Dhyan Chand Khel Ratna in 2016, as well as the Padma Shri in 2015, and the Padma Bhushan in 2020.

Bachendri Pal
Summit Conqueror

At a time when women had few career choices, Bachendri Pal decided to carve out her own path. Defying the social norms existing at her time about women, Pal decided to become a professional mountaineer rather than a school teacher as desired by her family. She was born to Hansa Devi and Kishan Singh Pal on 24 May 1954, in Uttarakhand. Her parents ran a grocery store at the Indo-Tibetan border.

Despite the challenges she faced, Pal was determined, focused, passionate and hard working. She was a bright student excelling in academics and sports. When she was still in school, Pal along with a few friends decided to have lunch on top of a mountain. At a school picnic, a 12-year-old Pal along with her friends scaled a height of 13,123 ft. This was her first successful ascent. She realised her true calling for adventure and mountaineering and decided to pursue her dream of becoming a professional mountaineer.

After finishing her schooling, Pal went on to do her graduation, post-graduation and B.Ed. from the Dayanand Anglo Vedic (DAV) Post Graduate College in Dehradun. Pal was not only a bright student but also an active participant in sports. She won prizes at shot-put, discuss throw and javelin among other sports events. To fulfill her dream of becoming a mountaineer and pursuing her passion, she joined the Nehru Institute of Mountaineering. Pal knew her financial status and also learnt stitching during her college years to finance her studies.

While attending the Nehru Institute of Mountaineering, Pal conquered a few smaller peaks like the Mt. Gangotri (21,900 ft high) and Mt. Rudragaria (19,091 ft high). Given her exceptional mountaineering skills, in 1983 Pal became an instructor at the National Adventure Foundation[1] (NAF). She became a symbol of grit, determination, motivation and being passionate for women at a time when pursuing mountaineering as a career was not an easy option for young girls and women.

Pal joined the sports department of Tata Steel in December 1983 and in the following month, Pal filled her candidature for the selection camp named 'Everest '84' to be held on the Mana Mountain, the fifth highest peak located in Uttarakhand. At the base camp of her expedition, fate had some other plans and Pal was down with fever. However, her zeal and enthusiasm to participate in the expedition led her to refuse to withdraw despite the hardships. Soon after recovering, Pal rejoined the training and made up for the lost sessions. She successfully ascended 7,500 metres on Mana, the highest climb of her life till then. She was still an amateur.

After the completion of her mountaineering course, Pal joined India's Mount Everest Mission—the Everest '84. This was a mixed mission comprising of eleven men and six women. The group was divided into two teams, forward and rear. Pal was in the forward team that set up its camp at 24,000 ft.

'On the night of May 15, when the team was resting, I remember hearing a loud sound and minutes later the camp was crushed under a huge mass of snow. At first, I thought my oxygen cylinder, that was kept outside the camp, had burst. Moments later something heavy fell on me and I was buried under it. My camp partner helped me out of the debris and with the help of the lower camp, we returned to the base camp', recalled Pal.[2]

The mission was threatened and members were injured and the team decided to abandon the mission. But Pal was determined to finish her mission. She believed that if she could survive the avalanche, she could finish her mission as well. Under the guidance of Ang Dorjee, a Nepali Sherpa, a new team was formed of which Pal was the only female member. The team began their ascent on 22 May 1984.

On 23 May 1984 at 1pm, Pal became the first ever Indian woman to successfully summit Mount Everest. 'My heart stood still. It dawned on me that success was within reach. And at 1.07 pm on 23 May 1984, I stood on top of Everest, and I was the first Indian woman to have done so', remembers Pal.[3]

Pal stood at the peak for 45 minutes, placed a small idol of Durga Maa, offered her prayers and thanked God, and remembered her family. At the summit of Mount Everest, Pal unfurled the Indian flag and the Tata flag. 'Thank god I took that decision because whatever I am today is all because of that decision', says Pal.[4]

Pal is very grateful to Tata Steel for their support. 'Tata Steel supported me when I was nothing. The company employed me in the sports department in December 1983. I was selected to be in the team that would scale Mount Everest, but being in the team is no guarantee that you will be able to reach the top. I never forgot that gesture. My parents taught me to appreciate those that reach out to help us when we have done nothing to deserve that help. I took their advice to heart.'[5]

Pal's expedition made her a symbol of women empowerment. In her honour, Tata Steel set up a full-fledged department, called the Tata Steel Adventure Foundation (TSAF), that conducts adventure and leadership programs for youth, women, corporates and organisations. Pal works as the Director of TSAF and is also the Chief of Adventure Programmes at Tata Steel, Jamshedpur.

Recognising her pioneering role in planning, organising and leading path breaking expeditions for women, Pal was conferred the Padma Shri in 1984, the Arjuna Award in 1986, the National Adventure Award in 1994, and the Padma Bhushan in 2019.

Bachendri Pal is a living example of grit, determination, courage and the 'live life to the full' motto. She is a name that figures in school textbooks and there are many who would wish to be like her.

❦❦❦

Viswanathan Anand
India's Grandmaster

When Vishwanathan 'Vishy' Anand was young, chess in India was in a dismal shape. India is the birthplace of chess, a game that has been called a gymnasium of the mind.[1] Yet, before Vishy came on the scene, India had not produced even one chess grandmaster, the highest title a player can attain globally. Chess had come to be dominated by Russians, followed by Germans and Americans. Before Anand, few Indian chess players had made a mark globally.[2]

Born in 1969 in a solid middle-class family, Vishy was the youngest of three children. His father worked for Southern Railways, and so the family got to travel around the country. He grew up watching his mother play chess at home. She taught Vishy how to play chess and encouraged him to join a local chess club.[3]

When Vishy was around nine, his father took a position with the Philippine National Railway and the family moved to Manila, the capital of Philippines. At that time, Philippines was a 'hotspot for chess'. The local TV station had a chess show from 1.00 – 2.00 PM in the afternoon when Vishy was still in school. His mother would take detailed notes to share with Vishy after he came back from school. The TV show also had a quiz at the end, where viewers were asked to send in their answers to win a small prize. Vishy's mother would encourage him to solve the quiz and mail his answers. Soon, Vishy was winning the quiz so often that the show hosts asked him not to participate any more. His frequent wins were discouraging others from participating.[4]

Vishy was barely thirteen when he won his first title, the Tamil Nadu State Junior Championship. He finished fifth at the National Sub Junior Championship later in the same year. In 1983, the Madras District Chess Association (MDCA) made an unprecedented effort to play a special team of teenagers in the National Team Chess Championship in Bombay. The intention was simply to provide talented youngsters valuable playing experience with the Big Guns of Indian Chess. With sponsorship from the famed playback singer and music director SP Balasubramaniam, the MDCA sent the Madras Colts team to the tournament.[5]

In a stunning upset, young Vishy defeated 9-time national champion Manuel Aaron. As India's first International Master (IM), which is a step below the more well-known Grandmaster title, Aaron was among the highest ranked chess players in the country at the time. Vishy was running a fever, but he insisted on playing. Where Manuel was a careful player taking his time before making a move, Vishy was the 'lightning kid' who seemed to barely give any thought to his moves.

In 1984, Vishy made his debut in India's FIDE *(Fédération Internationale des Échecs)* ratings, appearing at number seventeen. In the same year, he won the National Junior (U19) Championships and finished fourth in the National 'A' Championships, the premier national chess competition in the country. He competed in the World U16-Championship in Nice (France), finishing with a bronze. By some accounts, it was at this tournament that his parents first realised how much their son loved chess.

Vishy was not winning all his tournaments, finishing well in some and subpar in others. At the World Junior Championship in Finland, he finished tenth. He won the Lloyds Bank Junior Invitational Tournament in England, becoming the second Indian chess player to win a tournament in London. In 1984, he won the Asian Junior Championship in Coimbatore (Tamil Nadu), bringing him to global attention. The next year, the Asian Junior Championship was in Hong Kong and Vishy won there too, achieving the IM title. At the time, he was India's youngest IM. His success as a junior chess player earned Vishy the 'Arjuna Award' from the Indian government.

In 1987, he became the first Indian to win the World Junior Chess Championship in the Philippines. One impressive feature of Vishy's winning performances was that he barely took 30 minutes to win some of his games. Many dubbed him India's Bobby Fisher, after the American who had first challenged the Russian monopoly over the world title.

Despite his successes, Vishy had until then tried and failed several times to make it as a Grandmaster. Finally, in 1988 Vishy became India's first grandmaster at the Shakti Finance International Chess Tournament in Coimbatore. At 18, he was among the youngest Indians to have received the Padma Shri for excellence in sports.

When Vishy started playing at the international level, the upper echelons of global chess was a duopoly with two Russians—Anatoly Karpov and Garry Kasparov—at the top. For Vishy, the first World Chess Championship title came in 2000 when he won the FIDE tournament in Delhi (India). No Indian had ever been world chess champion before Vishy. In 2001, he received the Padma Bhushan from the Indian government.

Vishy won his second world champion title in 2007 at the World Chess Championship in Mexico. He then won the title three more times, back to back, in 2008, 2010 and 2012, until finally ceding the top position to a player half his age in 2013.

Vishy has said that he never really made a conscious decision about playing chess. He was playing from a young age, then began winning, and so his chess journey has been quite organic. As he explained in an interview:

> I drifted into chess as a career. It was an emotional decision based on what I love, and I realise I'm very lucky it was that smooth for me. In India, there's a couple of inflection points in 10th grade and then in 12th grade where people who compete at sports hesitate and think: Am I really getting anywhere? Should I look at options? But I won the national championships when I was in 10th grade, I became a GM in 12th, and when I finished university I was ranked five in the world. That was very nice because it meant that I never had this difficult conversation with myself. I wanted to do chess, and nobody ever showed me a reason why I shouldn't.

Vishy has played an important role in raising the profile of chess in the country, not just because of his success and fame, but also because of his efforts to promote chess and improve coaching camps.[6]

♛♛♛

Abhinav Bindra
Hitting Bull's Eye

Abhinav Bindra was the first individual Olympic gold medalist of independent India. He won the medal in 2008, more than sixty years after independence. His event was the men's 10 meter air rifle, where competitors stand side-by-side to shoot at a bullseye target over a distance of 10 meters. A year after he reached the top podium at the Beijing Olympics, Abhinav was conferred the Padma Bhushan. The road to success, Abhinav recalled years later, was long, sweaty, and painful with many twists and turns on the way.

As a sport, shooting is not widely practiced in India. When Abhinav came on the scene, shooting facilities were still quite primitive in the country. 'In the range in Tughlakabad in Delhi, prior to the 2010 Commonwealth Games renovation, there would be power cuts, airconditioners would stop functioning and targets would break down. You'd stand there sweating in your shooting jacket or trying to shoot with water dropping onto your head through a leaky roof', Abhinav explains. 'India in the 1990s and early 2000s especially, and even now, has few ranges. Fewer coaches. No sports shops selling world-class guns. No ammunition easily available. No culture of shooting competitions in small clubs on weekends', he elaborates.[1]

Born in 1982 in Dehradun in what was then the state

of Uttar Pradesh, Abhinav's initial interest in shooting came from his father, who was himself the son of an army officer. Abhinav's father wanted him to play, but he was fat and not very keen on physical activity. When Abhinav was about ten, he showed some interest in shooting with his father's guns. As Abhinav became better at shooting, he started target-practicing with bottles in the lawn of his parents' house. One day, a friend of his father saw Abhinav shooting at bottles and suggested professional training for the young boy.

His father's friend also knew a coach, a retired Lieutenant Colonel who trained at a range built in the backyard of his house in Chandigarh under the shade of a mango tree. There was, however, a problem. The coach they found did not want to train Abhinav. Rich kids do not like to sweat, the coach believed, and those who do not sweat cannot become good shooters. Family connections, and a personal appeal from Abhinav promising to 'make him proud one day', finally managed to convince the old Colonel, and he took the lad under his wings. Abhinav shares the training regimen in those early days:

> I trained every day with the Colonel. I returned from school at 2pm, had lunch and was in the Colonel's house, 10 minutes away, by 2.40 pm. Training continued till 5.30 pm, whereupon I returned home for schoolwork. On weekends I trained twice a day. And I was never late for practice. Never. The Colonel estimated later that I spent roughly 2000 hours under the mango tree.

Soon, Abhinav was winning at regional shooting competitions. With success, came naysayers. At a championship in Ahmedabad in 1996, when Abhinav was only fourteen, he recorded a perfect score. The officials had never seen such a performance and were not able to accept that a young Indian kid could shoot so well. The gold was given to the second-place shooter. Abhinav was asked to re-shoot to qualify for the nationals under the watchful eyes of the doubters.

Around this time, Abhinav and his coach agreed that more professional expertise was needed to take his performance to the next level. Abhinav and his mother moved to Germany. There, in an atmosphere of shooting excellence and under the watchful eyes of good coaches, Abhinav thrived. His scores improved. As Abhinav explained later:

> Watching top shooters produce phenomenal scores next to me produced an immediate impact. It's the way it is in sports. Play with someone better and it inspires you to match them. You look, you learn, you find a way to become better, so much better that you can beat this better person. The more we shot abroad, the clearer we saw that the best shooters were within our reach. Psychologically, this was a boon. If greatness looks intimidating close-up, paradoxically it also looks more human.

Encouraged by his new German coaches, Abhinav entered the World Championships in Barcelona. He finished forty-fourth in the junior category. Not an award-winning performance, but enough to get him selected for the next Commonwealth Games in Kuala Lumpur. There, he finished sixteenth. Once again, no medal. At the national trials, Abhinav dominated over his rivals with a 10-point lead. Playing against the best from around the globe, Abhinav finished 89th at the World Cup in Munich, 94th in Milan, and 69th in Atlanta. Finally, he won a bronze (team pairs) at the Commonwealth Shooting Championship in Auckland, New Zealand. Another bronze at the Asian Championship in Malaysia.

At the Sydney Olympics, Abhinav failed to reach the finals. He was disappointed and decided to make some changes. He started training with a German husband-and-wife coaching team, shooters themselves. Initially, they were hesitant to coach him. He won them over with his dedication and perseverance. 'You have to be crazy to be a shooter. But this crazy we've never seen. He could keep shooting all day, and I recognised something special in him. His motivation was fantastic. That was one thing with Abi, we never had to motivate him', his new coach observed about Abhinav.

Despite his motivation and the world-class training, Abhinav did not win a medal at the next Olympics in Athens, placing last in a field of eight. He was discouraged and frustrated, felt like a failure. A back injury incapacitated him, making matters worse. His coaches, however, did not lose confidence in him. More practice, more work, more training. Then, things turned around. Abhinav won the World Shooting Championship in Zagreb (Croatia), qualifying for the Beijing Olympics, where he placed first and made history.

When asked about his phenomenal success on the world stage, Abhinav likes to remind people that he is not a natural shooter and has bad eyesight. Practice and dedication, day after day, for years. '250 days a year. Six hours a day. Even on my rare days off, I'd go in and fiddle with equipment', is the recipe that made Abhinav successful.

🥇🥇🥇

Harry Boniface Prabhu
A Pioneer of the Sport in India

H. Boniface Prabhu is a quadriplegic wheelchair tennis player from Karnataka, one of the pioneers of the sport in India and a medalist at the World Championships. When he reached the podium in shotput, javelin, and discuss throw at the 1998 Paralympics World Championships, he became the first Indian to win a medal in Paralympics internationally. 'I am very proud of that win because until then independent India had never won a medal in world championships', Boni says.[1] In 2014, he received the Padma Shri award from the Government of India.

Boni was born in 1972, a normal child. When he was only four a doctor's medical negligence completely changed Boni's life, leaving him a quadriplegic for life. 'I used to often contract fever as a child. So, the specialist suggested that I go in for lumbar puncture. A wrong spinal tap by the doctor left me permanently disabled', he explains matter-of-factly.

Boni's parents were devastated by the shocking turn of events. They wanted to raise him as normally as possible, but there were no schools with facilities for disabled children like him. As a result, Boni was home-schooled. His parents and two brothers were fiercely supportive and protective of him. 'My parents never treated me differently and I think that gave me strength and determination', says Boni.

Neighbours and relatives rallied around young Boni, who says his childhood was as normal as it could have been in the circumstances. 'Frankly, there are no horror tales in my life. Sure, I could not go to a regular school as they did not have any facilities for people like me. So, I did my education privately. I grew up with my neighbours, who became my close friends', he recalls.

After passing his secondary school (Class X) exams, Boni got involved with sports. Many different sports attracted his interest. He liked shotput, javelin, discus-throw, badminton, and ping pong (table-tennis), playing at national and international events. He adored John McEnroe, Martina Navratilova, Steffi Graf, Kapil Dev, Sachin Tendulkar, and APJ Abdul Kalam.

The 1996 World Wheelchair Games in the United Kingdom was an eye-opening experience for Boni. He won two gold medals and a silver at the competition. In the U K, he participated in a workshop on archery and shooting, and saw a tennis match for disabled people. The range of sports played by disabled people and the facilities available to them there impressed him. After his return to India, he tried his hand at shooting. However, shooting was an expensive sports that needed sponsorship, which he was unable to obtain at the time. He then turned to tennis, one of the most popular and fastest growing wheelchair sports in the world. Wheelchair tennis is played in the same way as regular tennis, the only exception being that a tennis player on wheelchair is allowed two bounces of the ball.

Like many young people, Boni had been fascinated by tennis as a child. 'I must have been around seven, when I discovered my love for tennis. I was a huge fan of John McEnroe and Ivan Lendl those days.'[2]

Finding a sponsor is difficult for any sportsperson. As a disabled tennis player, Boni was initially supported by friends and philanthropists. 'There are many who start with a great zeal but quit midway because of lack of support. That way I was lucky to have some very good hearted people who supported me during my rough days', he admits.

For the next few years, Boni invested himself in tennis. He approached the Karnataka State Lawn Tennis Association for permission to use their courts. He reached out to a coach, who was initially hesitant to train a disabled player, but agreed when he saw Boni's interest and dedication. As he became better at playing tennis, he also needed a new wheelchair. He found a sponsor willing to help him buy a good wheelchair. 'It took me a while to find a sponsor (for a new wheelchair). Luckily, a good Samaritan came to my rescue. I flew to Australia in 1999 to buy a tennis chair, which cost INR 1.5 lakh. While there, I took part in the Sydney International Wheelchair Open Tennis, which I won', Boni says.[3]

Since then, Boni has won many international competitions. In 2001, he won the Japan Open Wheelchair Tennis Championship, and the Sydney International Wheelchair Tennis Championship in 2007. At the 2004 Florida Open Wheelchair Tennis, Harry won both the singles and doubles titles. At his peak, he was India's number one wheelchair tennis player, second in Asia, and number 24 in the world rankings.

In 2016, he led Thums Up Veer K2K Road Expedition, a 5000 kilometer journey from Kashmir to Kanyakumari, to support the government's Accessible India initiative, becoming the first quadriplegic athlete in India to lead such an initiative. 'We need to do a little more, so that's why I decided to drive from Kashmir to Kanyakumari. When I started my journey even my disabled friends said, "Boni, there are no toilets and this and that", but I said, "That's why I am doing it". If everything is there then why do I need to educate people, why do I need to fight and teach people', he explained.[4]

Boni also founded the Bengaluru-based Boniface Prabhu Wheelchair Tennis Academy to support physically and intellectually challenged people and provide them with opportunities to nurture their talents. The Academy provides free sports training for disabled people. 'We need courtesy and opportunity, not favours', Boni observes. 'Every disabled person has potential and all we need to do is unleash that.'

Boni sees the 2016 Right of Persons with Disabilities Act as 'one of the most optimistic things to have happened for the country'. The 'country is progressing', he says. 'I think disabled people should come out from under their shells. Disabled people have too much insecurity. You have to create things for yourself.'[5]

Love Raj Singh Dharmshaktu
Summiteer Extraordinary

Climbing Mount Everest is very difficult. It is one of only fourteen mountains over 8,000 meters above sea level—known as 'Eight-thousanders'. Climbing at this level is incredibly strenuous on the body—especially on the heart and lungs. Mountaineers must be in peak physical and mental condition to even attempt getting to base camp.

Everest presents an intense challenge of icy temperatures and altitudes where oxygen is limited. As you get closer to the summit, the winds sound like a 747 jet taking off endlessly. It is not a hospitable place for any living thing, and people's bodies begin to shut down as they get closer to the summit. On average, around five climbers die every year trying to summit Everest. The majority of the dead are still on the mountain. Some of the bodies have never been found, some serve as grim 'markers' along the route, and some are only exposed years later when the weather changes.[1]

Yet, some people do summit the world's highest mountain, and a few have reached the top many times. Among these serial Everest climbers, there are at least 11 from India. The Indian record-holder for the maximum successful ascents up the Everest is Love Raj Singh Dharmshaktu, who has reached the top seven times.

Dharmshaktu, employed with the Border Security Force in India, summited Everest for the seventh time in 2018. He was breaking his own national record of six successful climbs to the top of the world. 'I have seen strong, physically fit, financially stable people failing in the expedition and not so physically fit people scaling Everest. The feeling of standing on the top of Everest is like magic. It can't be described in words. I consider myself fortunate for having scaled Everest so many times', he says.[2] In 2014, Dharmshaktu received the Padma Shri from the Indian government.

Dharmshaktu hails from the small village of Bona in Pithoragarh district of the Indian state of Uttarakhand. With only about 85 families living there, the village is considered mid-sized by the Indian census. To this day, the village lacks basic infrastructure like proper roads, electricity, and telephone. When Dharmshaktu was growing up there in the 1970s and 1980s, life was simple with few modern amenities and comforts. As a child, he was part of the annual upward migration into the mountains to take sheep and goats to summer pastures.

Dharmshaktu got his early education in the village school. For higher education, he went to the city of Lucknow in Uttar Pradesh where he was associated with an adventure club. His aim in becoming associated with the adventure club was to earn some spending money. When he was about 17, the adventure club arranged an expedition to Nanda Kot (6861-metre high), a mountain peak in the Himalayas located in his home district of Pithoragarh. The expedition was led by Chandraprabha Aitwal, a pioneer of women's mountaineering in India.

A couple of the high-altitude porters fell ill, and Dharmshaktu was asked to help out. Although Dharmshaktu had been approved to climb only upto base camp, Aitwal allowed him to go all the way to the top as he had the fitness and skills needed to make the arduous trek. When Dharmshaktu successfully scaled the mountain with other members of the expedition, he felt a sense of achievement he had not experienced before.[3]

'It was my first time. It was just being on top of a peak. There was nothing to say. What I remember most is not the summit. At one point on the way down I was alone and there was this huge crevasse, and I was too scared to cross it and had no skills. I could see the camp below, and when somebody came out to pee, I hailed them and they helped me over.'

The Nanda Kot expedition gave Dharmshaktu exposure to mountaineering. He loved the fitness, discipline, and punctuality needed to climb mountains safely.

In 1998, an expedition to Mount Everest was organised as part of the Indian Independence Golden Jubilee celebration. Eight members of the expedition, including Dharmshaktu, successfully climbed Everest.[4] Before this expedition, all successful Indian climbs of Everest had been limited to the armed forces. The 1998 expedition became the first successful civilian expedition of Everest in India. The expedition was sponsored by the Tata Group.

In 2000, Dharmshaktu joined BSF, which sent regular expeditions to peaks above 7000 feet. With support from the BSF, he scaled Everest a second time in 2006. Then, again in 2009, 2012, 2013, 2017, and 2018. The 2017 expedition was sponsored by the Oil and Natural Gas Corporation, partly with the goal of bringing back some of the garbage that had accumulated on the mountain over the years. The 2018 expedition put 15 members of the climbing team on top, which was a world record for the highest number of climbers in an ascending team.

Over the years, Dharmshaktu had several close brushes with death while climbing Everest. He barely escaped some snowstorms on the mountains, including the deadly avalanche in 2015 and another big avalanche that hit the base camp in 2019.

For Dharmshaktu, there 'is no short cut to success. Hard physical work and diet control have become a lifestyle.' He thinks that one should not be discouraged when things seem difficult and others do not believe in you. 'When anyone starts discouraging you, don't take them to heart. Take it as a challenge and achieve it because discouragements make life more interesting and challenges push us to do better', he shares.[5]

Arunima Sinha
Conquering the Mountain

Before losing her leg on a railway track in Uttar Pradesh, Arunima had never climbed mountains. As she lay recuperating in the hospital bed, with rods in her right leg and fractures in the spinal cord, Arunima decided she wanted to do something meaningful with the rest of her life. An easy option, she thought, was to return and play volleyball again. She had played volleyball for her college before the accident as well as dabbled in soccer and field hockey. A far more challenging path, she felt, was to climb Mount Everest, the highest peak in the world. Had she chosen to return to playing volleyball again, Arunima would still have had to overcome many odds. By choosing mountaineering, Arunima was setting her sights on the unthinkable.[1]

Born in 1989 to a father in the army and a mother who worked as a health supervisor in a government health center, Arunima had a difficult childhood. When she was just six, her father was found dead in a pond outside the government accommodations where the family lived. The family had barely recovered from the aftermath of her father's mysterious death when her older brother was murdered, betrayed by friends with whom he had set up a small business. After much upheaval, her family found happiness when the elder sister married an employee working for the Central Reserve Police Force (CRPF). Her brother-in-law, who the family affectionately called Sahib, encouraged Arunima to apply for a head-constable position at the CRPF.

When Arunima got the interview letter from CRPF, it had the wrong date of birth on it. As she really needed the job, she decided to get the mistake corrected before the interview, which involved a quick trip to the CRPF office in Greater Noida near Delhi. The train journey from Lucknow to Delhi is routine, thousands of people do it daily without incident. For Arunima, the train ride that fateful day changed her life. Within a few hours of boarding the train, Arunima was permanently disabled, bleeding heavily on a railway track with no one to help her for hours.

As Arunima lay in the hospital recuperating, Sahib asked her if she wanted to climb Everest. She recalls:

> He had just read an interesting piece of information in the newspaper. While many had scaled the Everest, no female amputee had ever done so. I wasn't amused. 'I have lost a leg. And you talk of Mt Everest!' Sahib smiled. 'That is precisely why I am talking of Everest,' he said. By now even I was beginning to see what Sahib was trying to get at. If I could take a shot at the Everest and succeed, I would become the first female amputee ever to have done so. Of course, it was a very tough task. Even inside my ward I had to walk with the support of my family. To even think of conquering the Everest appeared a distant dream. Sahib insisted that if I agreed and kept faith, I could make 'history'.

After her release from the hospital, before leaving for home, Arunima reached out to Bachendri Pal — the first Indian woman to successfully climb Everest. She wanted to train under Pal to learn how to conquer Everest. Pal was supportive and encouraging. 'Arunima, in this state, you thought about such a difficult challenge like the Everest, it means you have already conquered it in your heart. Now, you just have to show it to the world', Pal told her.

Arunima joined the Nehru Institute of Mountaineering, India's premier institution for training aspiring mountaineers. Pal was one of its alumni. Training to climb mountains is difficult for anyone. For Arunima, it was even more difficult as her wounds were still healing. It takes an experienced climber several months of intensive workout and hike-training regimen to attempt the climb. Getting to Everest Base Camp, where the trek ostensibly starts, is itself a 10-day, 17,000-plus-foot affair. Climbs last an average of about two months, including acclimatising to the high altitudes that few people have experience traversing with heavy gear.

Before Arunima could start her climb up towards the Everest, she ran into her first hurdle. The designated sherpa refused to accompany her up the mountain when he found out that she had a prosthetic leg. Bachendri's personal intervention and Arunima's insistence finally convinced the sherpa. When she got to the death zone, the 26,000-ft mark where there is virtually no oxygen in the atmosphere, Arunima found out she was short of oxygen; there might not be enough left for the climb down. Many climbers turn back at this point, before they get to Hilary's steps, a nearly vertical rock face with a height of around 40-ft located near the summit. She decided to continue anyway. As she got closer to the summit, Arunima saw many dead bodies, a reminder that climbing Everest is not to be under-estimated.

After successfully summitting, and getting her picture taken at the highest point on Earth, Arunima started climbing down. She had come down only a short distance when her oxygen cylinder showed empty. Fortunately for Arunima, another climber who was turning back without summiting, was getting ready to jettison his extra oxygen. He gave his spare oxygen cylinder to Arunima, which she was able to use. Shortly thereafter, Arunima's prosthetic leg began giving her trouble. By the time Arunima got back to camp, many people had given up on seeing her alive again.

On 21 May 2013, Arunima became the first female amputee globally, and the first Indian amputee ever, to summit Everest. After Everest, Arunima decided she was going to climb the highest peaks on every continent. Over the next few years, she scaled mountain peaks on different continents: Mt. Kilimanjaro in Tanzania, Mt. Elbrus in Russia, Mt. Kosciuszko in Australia, Mt. Aconcagua in South America, Mt. Denali in North America, and Mt. Vinson in Antarctica.

Her advice for young people is simple: 'Failure is not when we fall short of achieving our goals. It is when we don't have goals worthy enough.' In 2015, the Indian government recognised Arunima's achievements with the Padma Shri.

Deepika Kumari
Bowstring of Ambition

When Deepika Kumari told her father, she would be a top archer one day, he did not believe her. Archery had been part of life for their tribe for centuries, but few people—men or women—had taken it up seriously. Years later, when Deepika became a national champion, her father admitted she had proved him wrong. He told the media, 'I was wrong. I underestimated her. She has proved her point.'[1]

Deepika grew up in a small village near Ranchi, now the capital of the Indian state of Jharkhand. The village had no running water or electricity. She was not a good student in school. Her talent, if one could call it that, was throwing stones to bring down mangoes from the trees.

One of Deepika's cousins, who was also her best friend, was an archer, and she encouraged her to try archery. 'You have a good aim. Try archery', she was advised. Deepika started with traditional handmade wooden bows, not much different from the kind that is ubiquitous in India's heartland around the festival of Dussehra.

Jharkhand is a tribal state, with a long tradition of shooting with bows and arrows. By the time Deepika started showing an interest in archery, Jharkhand had been carved out of Bihar to become an independent state. Meera Munda, the wife of

Jharkhand's second chief minister, ran an archery training school in her husband's constituency. Deepika's parents took the 12-year-old there to enroll her for archery training. 'You can't do this! Even the bow looks heavier than you', Meera told the frail girl. When her parents insisted, Meera asked the coaches to set up a trial for Deepika. The coaches were not impressed. They rejected her.[2]

Deepika went back to Meera Munda and convinced her to enroll her in the training academy to prove her talent. For the next three months, Deepika was the first to get to the training ground in the morning and start her drills. 'She would always do two times of what she was told during the drills. With her frail structure, her body would easily give up, but she would keep running, doing other drills, double than others', a colleague from her training days at the Academy revealed. What she lacked in physical prowess, she made up with hard-work and persistence. When she could not get the anchor-position of the hand underneath the face with a full drawn bow right, she stayed up all night to practice with a tube in front of the mirror. By morning, she was holding the posture correctly.

Within a few weeks at the training academy, Deepika was beating boys of her own age at archery. Yet, when she made her debut at the sub-junior nationals in Jabalpur, she came back empty-handed. Unfazed by this setback, Deepika kept practicing. 'You need strength and stamina for archery. She looked a complete misfit but there was determination in her eyes and she worked really, really hard to prove all of us wrong', her coach recalled. Soon, Deepika won her first gold.[3]

When it was time to get better training, Deepika moved to the Tata Archery Academy (TAA) at Jamshedpur.[4] Since its inception in 1996, the TAA has been a training ground for hundreds of sports-persons in the country, many of whom had won medals nationally and internationally. At TAA, for the first time, she got to practice with professional sports gear. She also earned a stipend of INR 500 per month, which was a big help for her poor family.

Deepika's family had never been rich, even by the standards of their community. Things had become more difficult after the small shop that her father ran closed, and her mother's salary as a nurse in a government hospital became increasingly erratic. 'There would be problems at home and the situation became such that there wasn't enough to eat. To tide over, papa drove an autorickshaw in Ranchi', remembers Deepika.

Deepika stayed at the TAA for eleven years. Although the TAA was the first place where Deepika was able to train with proper gear, it was also further away from her family. Determined to return to her home only after she had succeeded, she barely got to see her parents and siblings. The next three years were filled with rigorous training for Deepika. In 2009, she became India's first Archery World Champion in the cadet (U-16) section in Utah (USA), returning home to a warm reception. The next year, she won two gold medals at the Commonwealth Games in Delhi. She was only 16. At an age where most girls are still trying to figure out what they want to do in life, Deepika had become the pride of her state and country. In 2012, Deepika became the best female archer in the world.

A documentary on her life, *Ladies First*, was produced by Netflix in 2017. When she was approached for a movie role, she turned down the offer because it would clash with her archery plans. 'I realised if I plunged into the world of celluloid, I would lose focus on archery. It was an important year and I desperately wanted to turn around my fortunes in the sport. So, I finally rejected the offer', she said. Three gold medals in the 2021 archery world cup—in the women's individual, team, and mixed pair events—helped her regain the top position in global rankings.[5]

Deepika's life is an example of how someone achieves success with hard work and determination, regardless of their station in life. In 2012, she received the Arjuna Award, India's second highest sporting award. She was the FICCI Sportsperson of the Year in 2014. She was honored with the Padma Shri in 2016.

☫☫☫

Devendra Jhajharia
Paralympic Legend

Devendra Jhajharia was born on 10 June 1981 to Jevani Devi and Ram Singh Jhajharia in a small village in the Churu district of Rajasthan. His father was a farmer and mother, a housewife. When he was eight-year-old and playing with his friends in his village, he climbed up a tree and touched a live electricity transmission wire. The wire was entwined in the branches of the tree and was not visible. Jhajharia was immediately electrocuted and rushed to the hospital. Unfortunately, it was too late and his left hand had to be amputated.[1]

'I didn't know what electricity was at the time. There was no electricity in the village, but it was travelling on a cable that ran through there...I had climbed up the tree to break a branch and I happened to touch the line, which had 11,000 volts. I was alone at the time and stuck on the tree. It was close to the village. There was a lot of smoke, so villagers rushed to it. When they got me down from the tree, they had declared me dead. My left arm was all burnt. But slowly, I regained consciousness. When they took me to the doctor, he said I will never be strong in my life. But God had a different plan', remembers Jhajharia describing the freak accident.[2]

True to his words, God had a different plan and Jhajharia realised that he should not let this incident break his morale.

Other children would tell him that they would not play with him as he was not strong. Jhajharia was not the kind who would take such behaviour lightly. "After I lost my left hand, when I used to play with my friends, they used to tell me you have become weak. They would not want me to be a part of their team. That's when I started playing sports seriously, to prove I was not weak', recollects Jhajharia.[3]

Jhajharia studied at a school that had basic sporting facilities and the track-and-field events included javelin as a sport. Jhajharia took a liking to javelin as it could be thrown with one hand and with his thin and frail body. Sports like discuss or shot-put needed a lot of strength. His family supported him and encouraged him to take sports seriously. His first javelin was a self-designed javelin made out of bamboo and he would use it to compete at sports events at the school-level.[4]

At the age of fourteen, Jhajharia won the javelin competition at the district-level competing against regular athletes. In 1997, his talent was recognised by the renowned athletics coach and Dronacharya awardee[5] Ripudaman Singh Aulakh while he was competing at a school event. Jhajharia qualified for the 2004 Athens Paralympics[6] by winning a gold at the 8th FESPIC Games[7] in South Korea in 2002.[8] Jhajharia took the world by storm by setting a world record of 62.15 metres at the Athens Olympics. By winning the gold medal, he became only the second Indian to win a gold medal in the Paralympics after Murlikant Petkar, who won a gold in the 50m freestyle swimming at the 1972 Summer Paralympics held at Heidelberg, Germany.[9]

Remembering the night, Jhajharia comments, 'I didn't sleep that whole night... At 11.30pm, I sat up thinking, is this a dream? Did I actually do that? The Indian national anthem was played at the Games for the first time, the Indian tricolour was fluttering. That day was for India, and there can't be a better feeling'.[10] Jhajharia was only twenty-three years old at that time.

While his career was off to a great start, the F46 category[11] in which Jhajharia competes was not included in the 2008 and 2012 Paralympics. This was a difficult period for him and he was not sure what to do. In order to remain injury-free and fit during this period, he trained regularly and intensively. His family, parents and wife, stood by him during this time and ensured he did all that was necessary to stay competitive.

The F46 category games were included in the 2016 Rio Paralympics and Jhajharia did not let go of the opportunity. He trained hard and spent a few months in Kuortane, Finland training. Jhajharia broke his own record at the 2016 Rio Paralympics and set a new world record of 63.97 meters. By winning gold at the games, he went on to become the only Indian athlete to win two gold medals at the Olympics or Paralympics.[12] He was 35 years of age at the time. Defying age, Jhajharia competed again at the 2021 Tokyo Paralympics and won a silver medal.

Jhajharia's family has been a source of strength and support for him over the years. 'Since my childhood days, my mother kept me focused and told me: "You concentrate on your sport. Rest, we will look after". She would not even phone me thinking that I would get disturbed. She has so far kept on fulfilling my need but never took anything in return… My wife on the other hand left kabaddi[13] so that she could take care of the family as I mostly stayed away. My father ensured that I get farm fresh lentils and wheat even when I'm away', mentions Jhajharia with a lot of gratitude.[14]

Recognising Jhajharia's achievements and contributions to sports in the country, the Government of India conferred on him the Arjuna Award, India's second-highest sporting honour in 2004, and the Padma Shri in 2012. He was the first para-athlete to be conferred the Padma Shri. In 2017, he became the first para-athlete to be conferred the Major Dhyan Chand Khel Ratna award, India's highest sporting honour. In 2022, he was conferred the Padma Bhushan.

In an interview after receiving the Major Dhyan Chand Khel Ratna award, Jhajharia mentioned, 'The challenge for me began even before I stepped on to the playing field. My fight has been of changing mindsets, of proving people wrong. I began with a small dream of representing my country and look where that persistence has brought me. This Khel Ratna is not just mine, it belongs to all para-athletes in India, who overcome big challenges to bring themselves to the field and perform for the country. I hope this honour inspires more and more athletes from the small towns of our country to chase their dreams. This award shows that you can achieve what many believe is unachievable'.[15]

🏅🏅🏅

Social Work

Saalumarda Thimmakka
Padma Shri 2019

Hari Pal Singh Ahluwalia
Padma Bhushan 2002
Padma Shri 1965

Anil Prakash Joshi
Padma Bhushan 2020
Padma Shri 2006

Arunachalam Murugantham
Padma Shri 2016

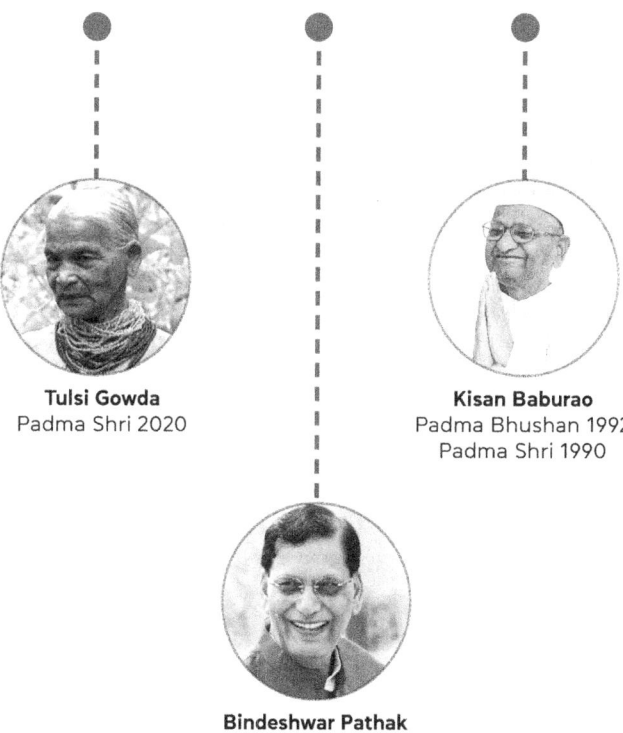

Tulsi Gowda
Padma Shri 2020

Kisan Baburao
Padma Bhushan 1992
Padma Shri 1990

Bindeshwar Pathak
Padma Bhushan 1991

Saalumarada Thimmakka
Compassionate Environmentalist

What does one do when faced with a series of difficulties from which there is no respite? Karnataka-based Saalumarada Thimmakka turned her attention to solving an unrelated problem that few would have dared to take on even in the best of circumstances. A four-kilometer road between her village and the nearest town of Kudur had no shade. 'It was a dry, hot road. Our villagers had to go to Kudur frequently—and dreaded it. So, we thought it would be nice if trees came up and shaded the way', she says.[1]

She was born at a time when few records of birth and death were kept in rural India. She thinks it was around 1910 in a small village where she got little formal education. At a young age, she does not really know when, she was married to Chikkanna of Hulikal village in Karnataka. Chikkanna, who herded cattle, had a stammer, earning him the nickname, *Bikkulu*. She worked as a casual labourer, sometimes there was work, mostly there was none. As time passed, it became clear that parenthood was unlikely. There seemed to be no end to her misfortune. At one point, she considered ending her life, but better sense prevailed.[2]

One day, Chikkanna and Thimmakka decided to plant trees. 'We thought why not plant trees and tend to them like we would our children', Thimmakka reminisced years later.[3] They started small, grafting ten saplings in the first year from trees on a lush green plot given to them as landless labourers. In the second year, there were fifteen saplings, and twenty saplings in the third year. They erected thorn guards around the plants, which had to be watered. Every morning the couple would set out, Chikkanna's load of two pots hanging from the ends of a pole over his shoulder and Thimmakka with a pot on her head and another on a hip. The pots had to be refilled from wells and ponds along the way—about forty to fifty pots a day. It was tiring work, but Thimmakka and Chikkanna were determined and focused.

The saplings were planted only during the monsoons. Post-monsoon, the couple watered each sapling once or twice a week till the end of summer next year. By the time the monsoons came again, says Thimmakka, the saplings had taken root. 'I do not recall any sapling perishing. Perhaps a couple of them did not survive, but my husband was very particular that we replant those that had perished. In all, we planted about 284 trees. I should not take credit for more than what I have done', she says in earnest.

Some villagers in Kudur wanted to cut the trees, which led Thimmakka—with support from a few alert citizens—to file a complaint with the police. A local journalist covered the story, which brought Thimmakka to the notice of then Prime Minister HD Deve Gowda, who hailed from the state. The Prime Minister recognised her selfless act, honoured her with the National Citizens Award, changing her life forever.[4] She was now in the limelight. By then, Chikkanna had passed away, but their children—the trees lining the road from Hulikal to Kudur—flourished and thrived.

Since the award from the prime minister, Thimmakka has received scores of awards, honoured on various occasions, lauded by various governments, environmental activists and grassroots organisations, from all sides of the political spectrum. A short documentary film *Thimmakka Mathu 284 Makkalu* was made about her, which was screened at the International Film Festival of India in 2000. The state government donated some land and built a house for her to live. Many rooms in the small house are filled with the various awards and honours that Thimmakka received over the years.

In 2019, she was given the Padma Shri by the Government of India. By then, Thimmakka had reportedly planted more than 8000 trees. The award ceremony, marked by strict protocol, saw a deviation that made national news: Thimmakka blessed the President, 33 years her junior, by touching his forehead. President Kovind later tweeted that he was 'deeply touched' when Thimmakka 'thought it fit to bless me'.

Neither awards nor age have diminished Thimmakka's love for her children, the hundreds of trees she and her husband planted along the highway from her village. When she was 107 years of age, she learned that the trees were at risk of being felled due to a proposed road-widening project. Thimmakka met with the chief minister and deputy chief minister of the state to request them not to chop the trees, receiving their assurance that the project would be reviewed to avoid cutting down the trees.

Thimmakka can neither read nor write. Yet, she dreams of doing more for her village. She wants to start a hospital. She knows she will likely not be alive to benefit from a new hospital in the village, but that does not stop her from dreaming about new ways to make the village better.

Thimmakka has become a sort of role model for environmentalists and conservationists. She gets invited to almost every tree planting initiative in the state. 'Even one sapling each can make a better place for our children', is her simple message.[5]

Anil Prakash Joshi
Making Rural India Economically Independent

Anil Prakash Joshi was born on 6 April 1955 in a family of farmers in Kotdwar, Uttarakhand. He is a post-graduate in Botany and has a doctorate in Ecology. He started to work as a faculty member at the Kotdwar Government PG College but in 1979 he resigned to set out on a journey to help the deprived.

The sense that managers who have nothing to do with the production of resources are richer than the actual producers troubled Joshi. Moreover, his students were unable to justify their work in rural areas due to lack of representational platforms. Hence in 1979, Joshi founded the Himalayan Environmental Studies and Conservation Organisation (HESCO), a non-profit organisation which is a core support group of SEED,[1] Department of Science and Technology, that carries out research and development activities in various sectors such as agriculture, horticulture and energy. HESCO was established with the aim of boosting the local resource economy and helping the producers.

Joshi was inclined towards social service since the beginning of his career as a teacher. With HESCO, he concentrated on need-based technology development and science and their application in mountain-based areas.

Also referred to as the 'Mountain Man' he committed his life to resource-based rural development and achieving economic independence for rural India through community empowerment.

The turning point in his life came when he saw that the deprived in the villages had nothing of what people in cities had. He observed that though villagers were poor, they were rich in resources. He thought that being a teacher would not create the impact that setting an example for the underprivileged would. 'It was my compassion for the underprivileged and my will to help that drove me, not inspiration', mentioned Joshi.[2]

The will to work for the people motivated him to initiate an Open Scholars program through which people who had acquired knowledge from the environment and had created their own education could share their knowledge and experiences with the world. This could also help the poorest of the poor to imbibe and grow with the world, and to put forth their thoughts and ideas. 'What I aim via this program is to promote the innovations that they think of, but are not given an outlet for promotion or scientific validation', shared Joshi.[3]

Over the years, Joshi has played a pivotal role in motivating villagers to tap their local resources to not only generate their economy but also contribute towards ecological economy. He started key projects and programs such as the Women's Technology Park and the Technology Intervention for Mountain EcoSystem. Joshi also initiated the Women's Initiative for Self-Employment (WISE). Since 1979, Joshi has also worked towards exploring botanical methods to stop landslides in the hilly areas. The Border Roads Organisation has taken his advice multiple times to check soil erosion from landslides in the region.

To offer tribute to the majestic Himalayas, in 2010 Joshi designated September 9 as the Himalaya Day. This initiative has not only been accepted widely but also appreciated by various government and non-government organisations. The Himalaya Day has helped attract attention of policy-makers and planners towards issues of people living in the Himalayan region.[4]

Joshi is also known as a green activist and has criticised governments for promoting industrial development in Uttarakhand, an ecologically sensitive state. In June 2013, a cloudburst shook the entire state of Uttarakhand leading to huge loss of life and property. It was then that the government of Uttarakhand decided to introduce the notion of the Gross Environmental Product (GEP), a metric started by Joshi that indicates the overall health of the environment.

'It is high time that along with Gross Domestic Product (GDP), which indicates economic health, the country and the states collected data on forests, water sources, quality of air and soil and measured the GEP to know the health of our ecosystem', said Joshi in an interview.[5] The then Chief Minister of Uttarakhand, Shri Vijay Bahuguna said that Uttarakhand will become the first state to adopt the metric GEP, and accept the proposal to form a committee to assess the same. Joshi was made a part of the proposed committee.

Keeping in mind the acute water shortages that the mountain states have to go through, Joshi feels deeply saddened that while half of the population of India gets its water needs from the Himalayas, the Himalayan states face water shortages during summers. He believes that it is high time Himalayan states got to voice their environmental concerns and opinions. He mentions that there is an urgent need for consumers who live in the plains to realise that the eco-services they use are provided by the Himalayas. They must understand the significance of mountain states, forests, environment, water and air as a whole.

Joshi, in his more than forty-year-long career, has not

only provided a platform to Himalayan states but also fought for the environment and worked out initiatives for the people and the environment of the Himalayan region. He has over 100 research papers and 10 books on various topics related to sustainable development of the Himalayas to his credit. He has guided around 20 PhD students and has inspired and motivated many people to take up work in the villages of the Himalayan region and to use science and technology to solve the basic needs of the mountain community. He also publishes a children's newspaper titled *Bachcho Ka Akhbar* with an aim to bring awareness to village-children about science and the local natural resources. The paper is distributed locally in 2600 villages.

Joshi was conferred the Padma Shri in 2006 and Padma Bhushan in 2020. His contributions in promoting indigenous technologies, uplifting the environment with the help of rural communities have been unmatched. The 'Mountain Man' has inspired many to become the voice of the Himalayan states. His *Gaon Bachao Andolan* (save the village) and celebration of 'Himalaya Day' every year has helped many people know more about the pivotal role Himalayan states play in our daily lives.

☘☘☘

Hari Pal Singh Ahluwalia
The Summit of the Mind

29 May 1965. Major Hari Pal Singh Ahluwalia, or Hari as people often called him, was part of the three-member Indian team to successfully summit Mount Everest.[1] It was the first time in history that three people were standing together on top of the world. All three men were part of India's first successful attempt to climb the highest peak in the world, the Third Indian Everest Expedition. The first two attempts, in 1960 and 1962 respectively, had been unsuccessful. The third attempt had turned out to be more successful than expected, placing a total of nine men on *Chomolungma*— the Goddess Mother of the World, the traditional name of the Everest. The British had been the first to summit Everest when Edmund Hillary and Tenzing Norgay reached the top. The Swiss followed, putting four men on the summit. The Americans were third, placing six mountaineers on Everest. The Indians, after two failed attempts, had become the fourth, and the largest, contingent ever to reach the summit.

30 Sept 1965. Hari, and some officers, were returning from a forest near their camp in Sonmarg in Kashmir, after clearing it of infiltrators. The 1965 war with Pakistan had begun unexpectedly in August, when Pakistani soldiers crossed the border in disguise. By the time cease-fire was

declared on September 23, the Indian Army had reached the outskirts of Lahore. Despite the official ceasefire, the activities of the Pakistani infiltrators continued in border areas. Hari's unit, along with many other Indian army formations, were conducting operations to track down the infiltrators. On that fateful day, more than a week after the official declaration of the ceasefire, just as Hari was entering the base area, a bullet shot rang out from close quarters. Hari fell and lost consciousness. When he regained his senses after a fortnight, he learned that the bullet had hit him in the spine, paralyzing him and confining him to a wheelchair.[2]

Born on 6 November 1936 in the Sialkot district of undivided Punjab, Hari grew up in the city of Simla, where his father worked as a civil engineer in the Central Public Works Department. It was here that Hari first fell in love with the mountains. Later when his family—parents, three siblings (two sisters and a brother)—moved to Dehradun, Hari cultivated several hobbies, including photography, hiking, and trekking.

When Hari joined the Indian Military Academy (IMA) in 1956, no one could have predicted that he would literally stand on top of the world in a few short years. He had previously failed to make the merit list for the Navy, which was a disappointment for his parents. At the IMA, Hari did well in the academic courses, but was found to be deficient in outdoor activities, resulting in a 'warning' from his instructor. To address this problem, Hari doubled down on physical training, and started spending all his free time on the fields. He also got more involved in sports such as tennis, hockey, and football among others. Hari recalls:

> I sincerely felt that my outdoor performance did not call for a 'warning' but I was determined to remove my Assessing Officer's doubts about my ability in this regard. I made sure that I was in the fields when my Assessing

Officer was on a round in that area. It was an extra effort to show him how keen I was on outdoors. My efforts were rewarded when I was taken off the warning…In a way, my Assessing Officer's warning had done a lot of good to me. Even though I was no more on warning, my interest in outdoor activities had grown tremendously. I would now take part in all the games. I also picked up a good bit of tennis.[3]

Hari was 26 when he completed his Basic and Advance Courses at the Himalayan Mountaineering Institute. At 29, he successfully summited the highest mountain in the world. Just five months later, before the celebrations of his mountaineering achievements had finished, Hari had become disabled for life, the victim of an insurgent's bullet that should never have been fired. The Padma Shri (Sports) for Hari, and others in the Third Indian Expedition, had been announced even before the group had returned to the plains. When Hari went to receive the award, he was already in a wheelchair.

For most people, going from being a globally acclaimed mountaineer to being confined to a wheelchair would be a tragic turn in their life that would have ended their aspirations. Hari was not one of them. At the time, India did not have the facilities to help Hari recover. Determined to rebuild his life, he traveled to Stoke Mandeville Hospital in the United Kingdom, where he stayed for five months, to undergo intensive rehabilitation. Hari later said:

> While a handicapped person has to be rehabilitated physically by means of exercises, his mental rehabilitation is even more important. Just after the accident and before coming to England, I had become afraid of people and places. I had become extremely shy and had started getting an inferiority complex. It was here

in Britain that this barrier was broken and I once again started meeting people, going to parties and giving talks on mountaineering which I would never have done otherwise. This restoration of self-confidence was the most important element in my rehabilitation through the methods adopted at the hospital.

When Hari returned to India, he wanted to set up a similar hospital in India to support others who had been injured like him. He went on to help establish the Indian Spinal Injuries Centre (ISIC) in Delhi, a collaborative venture between the Government of India and the Italian government.[4] ISIC is a 178-bed super specialty hospital on a sprawling campus of 15 acres. In 2002, Hari's achievements were recognised with the Padma Bhushan (Social Work) by the Indian government.

Hari's friends describe him as jovial, friendly, and cheerful. Hari's own motto for living: 'life is all about conquering the other summit—the summit of the mind'. His experience as an Everester provided the inspiration to resolutely face the unexpected twists and turns of life.[5] He successfully adapted to the new conditions of life imposed by his life-altering disability that destiny had in store for him. He not only remained active throughout his life, but also scaled great heights in other areas.

888

Arunachalam Muruganantham
The Pad Man

Before Arunachalam Muruganantham married, he had never noticed the women around him dealing with monthly periods. One day, soon after his wedding, he noticed his wife trying to sneak something into their room, hoping to hide it from him. When he asked her what it was, she was evasive.[1] When he insisted on knowing, her response was clear and direct: 'None of your business'.

As she would find out, Arun was not someone to give up so easily. Arun did not know what to think of her behavior. When he found out she was hiding a rag – an old cloth worth nothing – he was even more puzzled. Why was his wife so possessive about a rag that should have already been thrown away in the garbage.

'I don't even use that cloth to clean my two-wheeler. Then I understood she is adopting that unhygienic method to manage her period days', he says.[2]

When he went to the neighbourhood store to buy the pad for his wife, he was in for a shock. First, he learned that men rarely bought sanitary pads. Apparently, it was common for men to sell pads, but rarely did men go to buy them, at least in his small town. Second, the pad was expensive. His wife told him that if she and his sisters all started using the 'fancy' hygiene products available in the market, the family would have little left for groceries and other necessary purchases. It was simply unaffordable for low-income families like theirs, especially when one considers that it is a regular purchase.[3]

Arun had always been a hustler. His father, a handloom weaver, had died in an accident when Arun was just fourteen.[4] His mother worked on a farm to support the family and Arun dropped out of school to support his mother. For the next few years, he took up all sorts of odd jobs to make money for the family, working on farms, operating machines, and selling yams. By the time of his marriage, he owned a small welding workshop. He was not rich, but he had hustled his way to knock at the doors of India's growing middle class. Or he thought he did.

The price of the sanitary pad posed a problem for Arun. Pad or milk, his wife told him, meaning that they could afford either new pads or daily milk, not both. Arun decided to make pads himself. What he had seen at the store did not seem very complicated to him. He bought cotton rolls, cut them into rectangles and felt he had a good solution. He convinced his wife to try it. She was not happy with his creation, telling him she preferred the rag over what he had made for her.

Arun began experimenting with milled cotton, using cloth from a different mill for each effort. None worked. Tired of being a guinea pig for his monthly creations, his wife declined to try out his products anymore. So, he turned to his sisters. When things did not work out as hoped, the sisters too told him they did not want to continue their involvement with his project.

Arun reached out to girls at the local medical college. They declined. Arun then did the unthinkable. He decided to try out the pad on himself, tying a bottle filled with animal blood around his waist and connecting it using a tube to the pad he wore. Pressure on the bottle—as he went about his daily activities, walking and cycling around town—imitated the menstrual process.

When his wife found out what he was doing, she left him.[5] After two-and-a-half year of experimenting, he really had nothing to show for it. All his money had already been spent. His neighbours thought he was crazy and wanted him to get treated for the demons that had possessed him. They did not want him anywhere near the women of the neighbourhood. Arun promised to move elsewhere. Things got so bad for Arun that even his mother disowned him.

Most people would have given up by now. Arun was not among them. He knew something was not right with his products. When he reached out to a few manufacturers of pads, he learned that he had been missing a key ingredient. Good pads needed a special cellulose made of pine wood pulp. The problem was one needed to import a multi-million dollar plant to make the cellulose fibers. Unfazed, Arun decided to use his welding shop to make a machine that would grind and defibrate locally sourced pulp, then press and sterilise the pad under ultra-violet light.

The cost of the machine Arun made was less than one percent of the imported machine. Professors at the Indian Institute of Technology in Madras helped him get a patent for it. The media started talking about his low-cost solution for the masses. When his wife saw him felicitated on TV and read about him in the paper, she returned to him. They had been separated for five years. The growing fame came with seed funding to set up his own manufacturing unit for making pads. He worked with NGOs and self-help women's groups to help them set up their own sanitary pad manufacturing units in villages.[6]

Arun decided to publicly share the know-how to make the pad manufacturing machine, giving away the knowledge for free. His machines are now installed in almost all Indian states and territories, as well as countries in Africa and Asia. In countries such as the US and Germany Arun's machines are being used to produce pads without chemicals and for women with sensitive skin. The pads made on his machines are also biodegradable. 'They can be buried in the ground after use', he says.[7] Arun's machines are so easy to operate that in many places school children are using them to make pads for free distribution in under-privileged areas.

People who once ostracised Arun now want to take selfies with him. His story is featured in textbooks in his home state of Tamil Nadu. His hard work once got him on *Time* magazine's list of 100 Most Influential People in the World. In 2016, he was awarded the Padma Shri by the Indian government.

❦❦❦

Tulsi Gowda
Cultivating Trees

It is not common to see someone walk up barefoot to the President of India to receive an award. But then, Tulsi Gowda—a 2020 Padma Shri awardee—is no ordinary Indian. She says she has walked barefoot all her life and never worn footwear.

Tulsi does not know the year of her birth but believes she may have been born sometime in the 1940s. She belongs to the Halakki Vokkaliga tribe, an indigenous group with a population close to 200,000 (per the 2011 census) living at the base of the Western Ghats. The tribe is often described as the 'Aboriginals of Uttara Kannada'.[1] The Uttara Kannada is one of the largest districts of Karnataka, with a forest cover of over eighty per cent and a long coastal line of around 140 km. Yet, the roads in the district are unpaved, schools are largely nonfunctional, and there are no emergency hospitals for the sick and the injured.

The Halakki Vokkaliga tribe is quite patriarchal, with only male members of the family inheriting ancestral property. If there is no male in the household, the property goes to the nearest male member in the clan. The women of the Halakki Vokkaliga have a distinctive attire, with saris tied like a sarong. They wear layers of beads around their neck and adorn their hair with bright coloured buds and flowers.[2] This was the attire that Tulsi was wearing when she received her award from the Indian President, the same attire she wears in her daily life.

Tulsi's early life resembled that of the countless women of her tribe before her and since then. She was born in a poor family, and her father passed away when she was around two years old. She received no formal education. As was common for the girls in her tribe, Tulsi was married in her early teens (she does not know exactly when).

As a teenager, Tulsi joined her mother in working at the local nursery. For thirty-three years, she laboured as a daily wage worker before she was given a permanent position. She worked for another fifteen years, finally retiring at the age of 70. Even after retirement, she remains emotionally attached to her work. 'I'm retired, so I don't go to the nursery unless I find a rare seed or a sapling. Then, I take it there', she said in an interview.[3]

During her time at the nursery, she helped with afforestation efforts by leveraging her traditional knowledge of the local plants and trees. The Halakki tribe is known for their knowledge of medicinal plants which they mostly utilise to prevent and treat diseases. This knowledge and tradition has been passed down through generations and Tulsi, like many members of her tribe, learned without any formal instruction.

As a child, Tulsi would take daylong trips with her mother deep into the forests to collect firewood for the family. It was from her mother's side that Tulsi learned how regeneration is best done with seeds from big, healthy trees. When she was a teenager she is reported to have transformed a gutted landscape near her family's small house into a dense forest. 'Since her childhood, she spoke to trees like a mother would speak to her infant children', shares a local woman who worked with Tulsi for decades.

Tulsi has lost count of the number of trees and plants

she has cultivated over the years. 'Lakhs, maybe crores', she noted. She knows so much about trees that she is referred to as the 'Encyclopedia of Forest'.[4] Her tribe refer to her as 'vruksha devata' (or 'goddess of trees').

Tulsi's work would have gone unnoticed by the world at large had it not been for the then conservator of forests AN Yellappa Reddy who was impressed with her dedication and knowledge of the wild flora. Reddy noticed her potential and brought attention to her work. 'I met Tulsi Gowda after putting in more than twenty-eight years of service as an Indian forest service official trained at the Indian Forest Academy. My favorite subject during that period was the silviculture of Indian trees that includes everything involved in the growing and cultivation of trees, its ecological and economic value, its utility, etc. I had noticed that more than ninety percent of native Indian trees have regeneration problems despite much research being conducted on them. Gowda could identify a mother tree of any species anywhere in the forest. Regeneration is best done with the seeds from the mother tree. She knew the timing of its flowering, germination and the best time to collect the seeds from the mother tree of a plant, like say, *Hopea parviflora (Bogi Mara* in Kannada)', he recalls.[5]

The national award has brought Tulsi unexpected attention. Villagers bow when they cross her on the road and children stop her to take selfies. Busloads of students arrive at her home, where she lives with 10 members of her family, including her great-grandchildren. Some want to talk about climate change with her, a topic about which she knows nothing. All she knows, she says, is that people have encroached on the space of trees and animals, destroying the forest and its ecosystem. The stripped land can be regreened, she thinks, but it will take a lot of time.

Despite her age and frail health, trees remain Tulsi's first love. 'I wish to plant more trees. Trees help to improve and maintain the quality of air, water and soil and remove pollutants from the air. Trees enrich people's lives and beautify landscapes. We need to grow more trees since we destroy hundreds every day for developmental activities', she says.⁶

❦❦❦

Bindeshwar Pathak
The Man behind Sulabh Shauchalaya

Bindeshwar Pathak, social reformer turned entrepreneur, is the head of an international company that manufactures flush-style private and public toilets. He has also built four clinics across India to teach scavengers—tasked with hand-sweeping the contents of often-dry latrines into bamboo baskets and then carting away the results on their heads—basic hygiene, literacy and job skills, to improve their lives. He also helms a popular toilet museum in New Delhi.

Born in rural Bihar in 1943, Pathak had an ordinary childhood. His parents believed in the value of education, and young Pathak went to the school in the village, after which he moved to Patna for a degree in sociology. When Pathak graduated in 1964, he got hired as a teacher.

A major turning point in Pathak's life was his decision to study criminology at Sagar University in Madhya Pradesh. On route to Sagar in the train, Pathak met an elderly family friend who encouraged him to join the Gandhi Centenary Committee, promising him good compensation for his work.[1] Bihar was where Gandhi had first become the Mahatma, so the centennial of his birth was expected to be observed in the state in a big way.

Lured by the promise of good pay, Pathak changed his

travel plans and went to the Committee office. On reaching there, he found that there was no job. Having missed the Sagar deadline for applying as well, Pathak decided to stay on with the Committee in a temporary position.[2] The pay was meager, but he hoped the job would become permanent one day. Survival was difficult as by then Pathak was a married man. 'We got by, selling trinkets from my wife's jewel box', he remembers.[3]

Pathak soon found himself working with the *bhangi-mukti* (scavenger liberation) cell of the Committee in Bihar.[4] He even went to live in a bhangi cluster in the town of Bettiah and witnessed their life up-close. During his stay there, Pathak decided that a possible solution to the bhangi's plight was the simple toilet Gandhi had championed: dig a pit, put a toilet pan over it, and use it layering faeces with soil. When it fills up, dig a new hole, and start all over again.

By then the Centennial Committee was winding up. The Chief Minister of Bihar wanted the sanitation cell to be institutionalised, formalising it under the name of *Sulabh Sauchalaya Sansthan* (Simple Toilet Institution). Pathak was appointed Secretary of the new organisation. Soon after, the state government collapsed, a new Chief Minister came in, and toilets were no longer a priority. Officers promised funds for Sulabh, but nothing really materialised. At one point, after much pleading and cajoling, Pathak convinced a local politician to take the matter to then Prime Minister Indira Gandhi. She wrote a letter to the Chief Minister of Bihar asking him to take personal interest in the matter. Nothing changed for Pathak and Sulabh.

As Pathak waited for funds, the technology for dry latrines was improving considerably. The Planning Research and Action Institute in Lucknow (Uttar Pradesh) developed a pour-flush toilet system wherein the user pours water to flush the toilet. Pathak decided to adapt this system to replace dry latrines as well as to offer houses with no toilets a viable solution for their daily need. 'My idea was not just to provide a solution but to liberate the society that remained imprisoned in formulaic traditions. I was determined to restore the dignity of manual scavengers that they were deprived of. By virtue of their birth, they worked as manual scavengers, and faced severe discrimination', Pathak observed.[5]

Despite the lofty ideals and the best intentions, Pathak's plans failed. Years went by with no help for the toilet project. By then, Pathak had a family to feed. Desperate, he took to selling his grandfather's home-cure remedies to provide for his wife and children. One day, in the small town of Arrah in Bihar, Pathak walked into the small office of the 'Municipal Officer' and tried to sell the idea of a toilet for the masses. Within minutes, the officer gave him an advance payment of INR 500 for two public toilets.

India's first two-pit, maintenance free public toilet was built in 1973 in Arrah with the help of local masons. An officer had advised Pathak to charge for the use of toilets, so the toilets could be self-sustaining. Many people around him believed paid toilets for poor people to be a non-starter. The poor, they argued, would not want to pay for using a toilet. Arrah proved them wrong. People were willing to pay a small amount of money to use a clean toilet. The Arrah model—advance payment for toilets, no subsidies, donations, loans, or grants, and a small charge to use the toilet—became the Sulabh model.

After Arrah, a Sulabh toilet came up in Buxar, part of the eponymous district famous for the two historic battles that changed the course of Indian history (in 1539 between Sher Shah and Humayun and in 1764 between the British East India Company and Mughal king Shah Alam II). The Patna toilet was next, with 48-seats, ten urinals, and twenty baths. The grand toilet became the talk of the town. Politicians visited the site to witness the social miracle: poor people paying to use a private toilet!

Over the next few years, Sulabh began to spread around Bihar and in other states. The rest, to use a cliché, is history. The company, Sulabh International, runs numerous public pay toilets in India, as well as in Ethiopia, Madagascar, and Afghanistan. The for-profit, private-sector solution to a complex social problem Pathak pioneered with Sulabh has been widely praised.

Pathak was the recipient of the Padma Bhushan in 1991 from the Indian government. Often referred to as 'The Toilet Man', he likes to make the point that 'unless the last person is brought to the mainstream of development, it is not true development'.

♉♉♉

Baburao Hazare
Campaigning for Mankind

Anna Hazare, a retired soldier from the Indian Army, shot into the national limelight in 2011 when he threatened to go on a hunger strike unless the Indian government enacted a stringent anti-corruption law. His fight against corruption, which most Indians consider among the biggest challenges facing the country today, attracted support from various segments of society, including film stars, politicians, lawyers, and taxi-drivers. Following a practice popularised by Mahatma Gandhi, his ideal and India's conscience, Hazare threatened to starve himself to death if the government failed to enact the anti-corruption reforms he sought.[1]

When Hazare was born in 1937 to uneducated parents barely able to make ends meet, few could have guessed that he would one day be considered a modern-day Gandhi and take on the national government using Gandhian practices. His grandfather had been a constable in the British army and his father was an unskilled labourer. His family moved to the small non-descript village of Ralegan Siddhi in Maharashtra state soon after his siblings—two brothers and three sisters—were born.

Hazare studied only until seventh grade, then took a job selling flowers to make ends meet. He actually did quite well as a florist, making enough money to spend his free time going to the movies and hanging out with friends at street corners.

China's unprovoked incursion into India in 1962 provoked him into joining the army. He trained as a truck driver and was sent to the frontline. During the 1965 war with Pakistan he was the only member of his unit to survive an attack. His miraculous escape from certain death led Hazare to introspect. 'That incident set me thinking. I felt that God wanted me to stay alive for some reason. I was reborn in the battlefield of Khem Karan. I decided to dedicate my new life to serving people', Hazare said.[2]

Passing through the Delhi railway station, Hazare was attracted to a poster of Swami Vivekananda, the nineteenth century Indian Hindu monk and philosopher, widely considered one of the most influential social leaders of modern India. 'I bought a book on his ideas. After reading it, I realised that serving the poor means serving God. After that, I understood the meaning of life', says Hazare.[3] He decided to renounce material pleasures and follow in Vivekananda's footsteps by dedicating his life to the service of others.

Hazare retired from the army and returned to Ralegan Siddhi in 1975. At the time, the village, like many others in the Indian countryside, was a textbook case of rural dysfunction. No schools or medical care, open defecation, tons of garbage, and lots of alcohol. Children died early in the village, domestic violence was endemic, and disease ran rampant. Even the woodwork in the village temple had been ripped out to feed the local liquor stills. Hazare started by using his army savings to repair the dilapidated temple. Some villagers contributed financially to the temple renovation, others in kind (such as wood), and yet others donated their labour. 'This taught me one thing', Hazare says. 'If people are convinced that you are not selfish, they're on your side.' A few young men joined Hazare, calling him Anna—big brother in Marathi, the local language. As more youngsters joined, Anna organised them into a youth club.

After a villager was beaten up by some drunks from a neighbouring village, Anna warned the distillers to close shop. Not content with merely shutting down illegal distilling, Anna prohibited drinking in the village. 'You can drink elsewhere', he told villagers. 'But if anyone here is found drunk, he'd better watch out.'[4] When three men returned drunk from another village, Hazare had them tied to a pole and whipped them with his army belt. The public floggings have long stopped, but the pole stands as a reminder to wayward villagers.

Over time, Ralegan became a model village, one that attracted the attention of development experts from around the world. Two of Anna's transformative projects are particularly noteworthy for their impact on the village. First, Anna took leadership of a watershed restoration project that made the arid hillsides bloom. The villagers, following Anna's initiative, constructed several small dams of cement or soil called *bunds* that eventually raised the groundwater level manifold. 'Water should not be seen on the surface', Hazare observed, 'it should be caught, held and kept below.'[5] Second, Anna led a campaign to get a high school in the village. The literacy rate in the village is now nearly 100 percent, with girls and boys receiving the same education.

In 1991, Anna launched an anti-corruption movement to fight against corruption in Ralegan village. In early 2000, Anna started a movement to get the Maharashtra state government to introduce a Right to Information (RTI) Act, which later became the basis for the RTI Act at the Center.

With about two decades of experience staging hunger strikes in Maharashtra to pressure state officials linked to corruption, Anna came to Delhi to demand that the government enact a bill to create a powerful anti-corruption agency. Surprised by the public support for Anna, the government invited him to join a special committee charged with drafting the bill. When committee negotiations broke down over the scope of the bill (Team Anna wanted the prime minister to be covered by the bill, the government refused), Anna threatened to fast until his demands were met. The panicked government arrested him, which led to more outpouring of support for Anna. When the government offered to release him from jail, Anna declined to accept the terms and vowed to stay in prison unless the release was unconditional. Anna's reputation as a social activist soared. People wore caps that declared 'I am Anna'.

After the 2011 protests, Anna went back to his native village in Maharashtra, where he continues to work for local development and against corruption. His advice to his followers and fellow citizens is simple, but profound: 'If wealth is lost, nothing is lost. If health is lost, something is lost. But if character is lost, all is lost.'[6]

AWARDS

Literature & Education

Sitakant Mahapatra
Padma Vibhushan 2011
Padma Bhushan 2002

Ruskin Bond
Padma Bhushan 2014
Padma Shri 1999

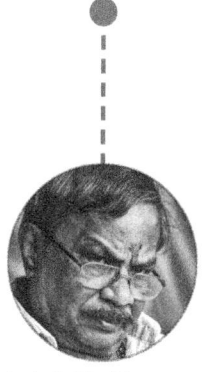

Madath Thekkepaattu Vasudevan Nair
Padma Bhushan 2005

Shekhar Gupta
Padma Bhushan 2009

Sitakant Mahapatra
Weaving Words into Timeless Tapestries

Sketching the Odishan ethos and bringing the tradition of Odisha to the world, Sitakant Mahapatra is one of the top names of Indian literature. Born on 17 September 1937 in Mahange village located on the banks of the Chitrotpala in Odisha, Mahapatra grew up reciting the Bhagavad Gita in Oriya. He completed his schooling from the Korua Government High School in Odisha and then finished his graduation in history in the year 1957. From there, he moved on to pursue post-graduation in political science from Allahabad University.

Mahapatra became the editor of the university journal of Allahabad University and started writing in English and Oriya. He joined the Indian Administrative Service (IAS) in 1961 and went on to hold important positions in the government such as the post of the Secretary to the Ministry of Culture, the office of the president of UNESCO's World Decade for Cultural Development, a senior fellow of Harvard University, and an honorary fellow of the International Academy of Poets, Cambridge University.[1] He also completed a diploma in Overseas Development Studies from Cambridge University.

Mahapatra is a prolific writer and poet. He has written more than 300 poems in Oriya and has 28 publications in English. Back in those days one could have seen this as a courageous move since writing only in a regional language restricted his readership. Mahapatra made a promise to himself in university that he would write poetry only in Oriya. His work in Oriya has won accolades and resonated with the lives of tribals, bringing a freshness and innovation through the use of a vernacular.

Mahapatra's fondness for primitive poetry[2] has impacted his works making them unique. He recalls his work in primitive poetry as a love at first sight. 'When I was a deputy commissioner in the Sundergarh district, I got the opportunity to listen to Munda songs and see the accompanying dance numbers. I was charmed by the simplicity and freshness of the songs and their haunting music', mentions Mahapatra.[3] Not just poetry, but his works on social anthropology portray the relation between traditional tribal society and new government sponsored policies and programs.

Mahapatra believed in the power of tribal poetry and folklore. Time spent with the tribals of Odisha made him realise the importance and the richness of Indian folklore. In his poetry one can point out and feel the emotions with which he draws parallels between the traditional tribal world and the modern world. His unique combination of living and experiencing tribal life has made him understand that tribal poetry carries with it the zest for life which is both personal and universal. His writings have been inspired by the Santhal tribe with whom he had lived, experienced and witnessed the tribal life and noted its cultural ethos and traditions meticulously. 'In fact, I used to converse with them in my broken Santhali without hesitation', recalls Mahapatra.[4]

Despite writing poems and books, travelogues in various languages, his heart still beats for Oriya language. He is of the thought that the mother tongue is as intimate as a mother and hence the poetry that comes from the soul is well expressed in mother tongue.

Mahapatra's love for his native language and the zeal to work for it has not gone unrecognised. He has won plenty of accolades for his work. In 1974, he was awarded the 'Sahitya Akademi Award'[5] for his collection of poems named *Sabdar Akash*. In 1993, he received the Jnanpith[6] Award for his contribution to Indian literature. The citation of the Jnanpith award noted the following about Mahapatra: 'Deeply steeped in western literature his pen has the rare rapturous fragrance of native soil.'[7] He also bagged the Award of the Highest Honour by Soka University of Tokyo in 2001 and the Padma Bhushan and Padma Vibhushan in 2002 and 2011 respectively.[8] In 2016, he was selected for the Tagore Peace Award which is given to a person who has contributed towards promoting global peace based on the ideals of humanism and pacifism dear to Rabindranath Tagore.[9] His work has been translated in not only Indian languages but also in thirteen foreign languages including Chinese, Hebrew, Arabic and some European languages among others.[10]

'I am very happy for the recognition of my work. More so because there is a noticeable trend of Oriyas being overlooked in such awards', said Mahapatra when he received the Padma Vibhushan for his contribution to literature.[11] Mahapatra portrays the people of Odisha in his poetry as a loving, simple and innocent community. He has made a great contribution in taking the 'little traditions' of tribal societies to mainstream literature, and to the masses who had hitherto not known or understood tribal culture. He credits the widespread reach of his work to his translators who have helped the world know a little more about the people of Odisha through his eyes.

Ruskin Bond
Crafting Tales of Charm and Nostalgia

Ruskin Bond was born on 19 May 1934 in Kasauli, in present-day Himachal Pradesh. His father, Aubrey Alexander Bond, used to teach English to the princesses of Jamnagar in Gujarat. Later, during World War II, his father joined the Royal Air Force.[1] Bond spent the first six years in Jamnagar and later moved to Dehradun, now capital of Uttarakhand, when the war began. When he was eight, his father and mother, Edith Clerke, separated and he started living with his father in Delhi. However, in 1944, at the age of 10 years his father died in the war and he was orphaned.

Bond was raised in Dehradun and studied at the Bishop Cotton School in Shimla. He graduated in 1951 and developed a flair for writing. His first short story *Untouchable* was written when he was sixteen years old. Reflecting on his love for writing, Bond recollects, 'As a boy and right from my childhood, I was interested in reading. Charles Dickens was one of my all-time favourites. By the age of fourteen or fifteen years, I wanted to become an author and before leaving the school, I was clear that I wanted to tread on this path. My first work was published when I was seventeen or eighteen years old.[2]

After the completion of his schooling, Bond went to the UK to live with his aunt. He stayed there for two years and at the age of 17 years started writing his first novel, *The Room on the Roof.* The novel depicts the story of an Anglo-Indian boy named Rusty who is an orphan and lives with a strict guardian Mr Harrison. Rusty runs away from Harrison and starts living with his friends in Dehradun. The novel won the John Llewellyn Rhys Prize[3] in 1957.[4] Commenting on the book, *The New York Times* observed, 'Like an Indian bazaar itself, the book is filled with the smells, sights, sounds, confusion and subtle organisation of ordinary Indian life.'[5] *The Hindu* said, 'Bond so picturesquely draws the contrast from the stark and claustrophobic English part of town with the noise, colour and vibrancy of the Indian quarter. This is a touching story of love and friendship.'[6]

Post the publishing of the novel, Bond returned to India and settled in Dehradun. He started freelance work from Delhi and Dehradun and sustained himself writing short stories and poems in magazines and newspapers. He wrote *Vagrants in the Valley* in 1956 as a sequel to *The Room on the Roof* and settled in Landour, Mussoorie in 1963.[7]

It was perhaps because of his encounters with life and tragedy at an early age that he developed a keen interest in supernatural fiction and wrote several novels such as *A Face in the Dark and other Hauntings, Ghost Stories from the Raj* and *A Season of Ghosts* in which the supernatural figured prominently. Reflecting on his writings on ghosts, Bond mentions 'I have been writing for all ages. And whenever I ran out of topics, ideas, content or people, ghosts came in handy and I could easily bank on them, although ideally there is nothing called ghosts'.[8]

Bond became best known for his short stories for children. He wrote more than 500 short stories, essays and novels for children. Some of his famous writings for children include *The Blue Umbrella, Funny Side Up,* and *A Flight of Pigeons*. There have been movies, made by Bollywood directors, based on 'The Blue Umbrella and *A Flight of Pigeons*'. He has written over 50 children books. 'I have always written a lot about the past. I go back into my life. So, in a way the older I get the more I have to write about because you have more people to remember—friends, family, incidents and events. Many people ask me why I write so much about children which I started doing in my 40s. Before that I was writing more or less about adults. I had a pretty lonely childhood and it helps me to understand a child better', Bond once said.[9]

Bond lives in Landour, Mussoorie with a *pahari* couple, whose family he has adopted as his own.[10]

He has written his own autobiography in two volumes, entitled, *Scenes from a Writer's Life* and *Lone Fox Dancing* respectively. He describes his Indian identity in the book *Scenes from a Writer's Life* where he writes, 'Race did not make me one. Religion did not make me one. But history did. And in the long run, it's history that counts.'[11] Bond had two siblings. His sister Ellen lived in Ludhiana, Punjab till her death in 2014 and his brother William lives in Canada.

Recognising his contributions to children literature, he was conferred the Padma Shri in 1999 and the Padma Bhushan in 2014. He was also awarded the Sahitya Akademi Award[12] in 1992 for his novel *Our Trees Still Grow in Dehra*.

Bond has touched innumerable individuals, especially children, through his writings. One of his fans mentions that, 'My heart is filled with gratitude for Ruskin for expanding our limits of imagination and for finding something extraordinary in the ordinary. Sometimes, we don't even notice the simple yet most special things in life which he has the knack of immortalising through his pen.'[13]

Asked what he likes the most about his life, he said, 'That I have been able to write for so long. I started at the age of 17 or 18 and I am still writing. If I were not a professional writer who was getting published, I would still write.'[14]

MT Vasudevan Nair
Doyen of Malayalam Literature

Madath Thekkepaattu Vasudevan Nair—Vasu to his friends, MT to others—is considered one of the doyens of post-independence Indian literature, writing in Malayalam. In 1995, he received India's highest literary award, *Jnanpith*, for his novel *Randamoozham* (The Second Turn), widely regarded as his masterpiece. He also writes scripts for Malayalam films, winning the National Film Award for Best Screenplay four times, the most by anyone in the screenplay category. In 2005, he was recognised with the Padma Bhushan by the Indian government.

MT was born on 15 July 1933 in the scenic village of Kudallur, which is now part of the Indian state of Kerala. The youngest of four children, MT spent his early years in Kudallur with his mother's family and his father's house in the village of Punnayurkulam, which has become famous as the birthplace of many award-winning Indian writers. Describing his childhood, MT says, 'As a young boy, I had to tend cattle, and help out elders in farming. There was always that inherent danger of being branded as a "good farm hand and a cattle tender" if you did a good job...I was also an introvert child. I did not mingle much with other children or played with them. Fortunately, I had great love for books from a young age and read all the publications and books brought home by my brothers.'[1]

After high school, MT was advised to take up science in college as it offered better prospects in the job market. As an undergraduate student in Chemistry, MT participated in the World Short Story Competition co-organised by *The New York Herald Tribune*, *Hindustan Times*, and the Malayalam-language newspaper *Matrubhumi*.[2] By this time, he had already published several short stories, inspired by his elder brothers who also wrote for literary magazines. The short story he submitted to the competition, *Valarthumrigangal* (domesticated animals — a story of the silent sobs of the circus artistes), won the first prize.

Winning an international writing competition may bring you critical attention and the envy of your friends but does not always result in job offers. After finishing his chemistry degree, MT struggled to find a job. To make ends meet, he taught mathematics in some schools and also in a tutorial college for a couple of years. In 1957, he joined *Matrubhumi* as a sub-editor, which brought some stability to his career. The *Matrubhumi* Weekly, a general interest magazine, also serialised his debut novel *Pathiravum Pakalvelichavum* (Midnight and Daylight).

At the age of 23, MT published his first major novel, *Naalukettu* (The House Around the Courtyard—translated into English as *The Legacy*), which won the Kerala Sahitya Akademi Award in 1959.[3] The novel tells the story of a boy from a matrilineal clan who lives in a society struggling to adapt to modern practices. The *Naalukettu* was a typical feature of the Kerala joint family system, where several generations of the family lived together in a multi-block house with a patriarch and matriarch overseeing all important matters. The novel has become a classic of Malayalam literature, with translations into several languages and lakhs of copies sold.

In 1965, MT wrote his first screenplay based on his short story *Snehathinte Mukhangal*, portraying the decline and fall of a joint Hindu family living on the banks of the river Bharathapuzha in Kerala. It focused on the tensions within traditional family structures in a crumbling feudal system. The film's depiction of traditional rituals like *Sarpapattu* (sarpa means snake and pattu means song; a ritual performance dedicated to snakes), traditional sports like *Kaalapoottu* (bullock race) and the festival of *Thiruvathira* (a 10-day festival dedicated to Shiva) were received well by critics and lay audience alike. MT made use of the Valluvanadan dialect from central Kerala in the film, which brought a new authenticity to the story. The movie received a Certificate of Merit at the national film awards in 1965. It also marked the beginning of his collaboration with the director A. Vincent, forming a powerful team that was to give many super hit films in the future.

Over the next few years, MT wrote the scripts for many films, but it was not until 1989 that MT won his first National Award for Best Screenplay for *Oru Vadakkan Veeragatha* (A Northern Ballad of Valour). Based on a folk song from North Malabar, the film reinterprets the life of a sixteenth century warrior. Three other national awards for best screenplay followed, in 1991 (for *Kadavu, The Ferry Slip*), 1992 (*Sadayam: Mercifully*), and 1994 (*Parinayam: Wedding*).

MT directed his first film *Nirmalyam* (*Yesterday's Offerings*) in 1973, which won the National Film Award for Best Feature Film the next year. It is a story of a neglected temple and the caretaker's family that depends on the temple for their livelihood. MT went on to direct seven other films, including two documentaries (one on the classical Indian dance form *Mohiniyattam* and another on the renowned Malayalam writer Thakazi Sivasankaran Pillai).

At the core of MT's varied work is the notion of self-suffering, which is presented with an emotional intensity that captivates the audience. His books and films often bring up the story of Kudallur village and the Bharathapuzha river. He takes a critical look at changing lifestyles and mores in his own community, reimagining folk tales of forgotten heroes and legends of warriors from epics. 'An original narrative structure, the ability to fuse the traditional with the contemporary and the celebration of humanity make MT the master he is', observed an eminent Malayalam literary critic.[4]

MT has been honoured with three doctorates by Indian universities and has been the recipient of several awards, including literary and film awards. 'I am conscious of the problems of our times', he says. 'Through my writings I put questions to society, to our times, to God and to myself.'[5]

Shekhar Gupta
Shaping Discourse in Indian Media Landscape

When Shekhar Gupta was honoured with the Padma Bhushan in 2009 for contributions to journalism, he was Chief Executive Officer and Editor-In-Chief of *The Indian Express*, one of the top daily Indian newspapers, and long known for its anti-establishment stance. During much of his time at the helm of *Indian Express*, he also hosted *'Walk the Talk with Shekhar Gupta'* for NDTV in which he interviewed an eclectic mix of more than 600 guests on his show, including heads of states, top politicians, celebrities from films and sports, beauty queens and scientists, and Nobel laureates from different fields.[1] The show brought him face-to-face with the Who's Who of the world and gave him the kind of fame most journalists see only in their dreams.[2]

Shekhar was born in 1957 in Punjab in independent India to Vishambar Dayal Gupta, a low-ranking government employee, and a housewife mother. After the state was reorganised on linguistic basis, Shekhar's family found themselves in the new state of Haryana, where they lived in Palwal. Growing up, Shekhar studied at the Saraswati Shishu Mandir, a chain of junior schools run across the country by the Rashtriya Swayamsewak Sangh.[3]

Shekhar was an average student doing his Bachelors

degree in Science from Punjab University in Rohtak. He was visiting the university campus in Chandigarh when he learned about the journalism program there and decided to appear for the entrance exam. He got in, and was only 19 years old, when he graduated with a journalism degree. His first real job was at the sports desk of Indian Express in 1977. Despite the journalistic heights he scaled later in life, the Haryana-Punjab background remained central to Shekhar's identity. He sees his own speaking style as 'hopelessly *desi*, non-convent accent and delivery', which is an oddity in the English-language media landscape of the country. He considers himself an 'HMT,' or a 'Hindi Medium Type', which he once described as 'new, small town, modestly brought up but ambitious, hard-as-nails Indian…anybody who could have been considered an outsider in the upper-crust power structure till the other day'.[4]

From his earliest days, Shekhar was ambitious and worked hard to rise in the media business. After *Indian Express*, Shekhar's next stop was *India Today*. It was here that Shekhar had his first brush with TV, which at the time was still a new medium with limited reach. He found an early mentor in Madhu Trehan, who had founded Newstrack, India's first video news magazine. Although Madhu's upbringing was very different from Shekhar's, she saw the hard-working, upcoming journalist as someone with potential. She asked him to be a substitute co-anchor with her when the regular host had to take time off. She also sent him (and a small team) to Afghanistan as the Najibullah government was entering its endgame with the Mujahideen, which was notable because Indian news cameras had never been in Afghanistan before.

As things went downhill in Afghanistan, Shekhar's career was on an upward trajectory. Enthused by his experience with TV, Shekhar went to Prannoy and Radhika Roy of NDTV to ask if he could do something for them. The Roys were also running Star News at the time. Shekhar's estimate of his ability was not shared by the Roys. 'Look, we do not think you are ready for TV yet', they told him. Like a good student, Shekhar asked 'what do I do to get ready?' Pat came the response: 'Nothing, we will know when you are ready and let you know.'[5]

Shekhar was discouraged by the unfavourable response from the Roys, and decided to pursue other initiatives. He started writing a weekly (mostly Saturday) column for Indian Express. A few months later, he received a call from Prannoy Roy to host a news-show where the anchor read the news and an expert rendered judgment. Roy, one of India's foremost media personalities, had seen Shekhar's fledgling column and felt that the young journalist had gained the gravitas to host his own show on national TV.

Shekhar had been told the new show was formal in look. As was general practice among young male journalists of his time, Shekhar bought some ties to get the formal look on screen. There was only one problem: He had rarely worn a tie until then and did not know how to tie a knot. He managed to tie a single knot, but the camera caught him looking suffocated and distracted with the albatross around his neck. Prannoy was unforgiving, telling Shekhar how he should conduct himself on camera: 'You may be feeling awful about something, you may be sick, uncomfortable, irritated by the anchor's questions—the viewer does not know or care. So, do not display any of this on your face. Never.'

While Roy's sermon had the desired effect on Shekhar's camera appearances, the young man from Palwal never got comfortable with wearing a tie. When the Roys invited him to do a weekly show for NDTV, he laid down two conditions: 'Outdoors and without a tie, probably even with my sleeves rolled up.' His idea was of an informal well-informed conversation between grown-ups, the host and the guest, which eventually became the longest running interview-based show on Indian TV.

As a talk-show host, Shekhar knew ratings were important, but there were some red lines he was not willing to cross. When one of his guests, the famous filmmaker Ram Gopal Verma, expressed shockingly sexist views, the interview was not aired. Another guest Ashwini Akkunji, who had won golds at Commonwealth and Asiad Games, was dropped when she was reported for doping (she was later banned for two years from athletics competition).

Shekhar's ability to maintain relationships over time, and with people from varied backgrounds has played an important role in his success. 'People are the capital of our lives', he says, 'each person you come across is a relationship, because they keep resurfacing in a reporter's life.'

Medicine

Neelam Kler
Padma Bhushan 2014

Devi Prasad Shetty
Padma Bhushan 2012
Padma Shri 2004

Tsering Landol
Padma Bhushan 2020
Padma Shri 2006

Suresh Hariram Advani
Padma Bhushan 2012
Padma Shri 2002

Neelam Kler
Nurturing Health and Hope for infants

Neelam Kler is a famous neonatologist[1] working at the Ganga Ram Hospital in Delhi where she is Professor and Chairperson of the Neonatology and Paediatrics Department. She has set up a state-of-the-art intensive care and ventilation unit at the hospital where she and her team of doctors tend to young children. She has been able to save several pre-term babies[2] and the department today boasts of survival rate of children upwards of 90 percent.[3]

Kler was born in Srinagar, in present-day Jammu and Kashmir. After completing her schooling from the Presentation Convent school in Srinagar, Kler pursed Paediatrics from the Postgraduate Institute of Medical Sciences and Research, (PGIMER) Chandigarh, one of the most reputed medical colleges in India. She then went on to pursue an advanced degree in neonatology. She obtained a further degree in neonatology from the Copenhagen University in Denmark.[4]

After returning from Denmark, Kler joined the Sir Ganga Ram Hospital, New Delhi in May 1988 and started working on ensuring the most advanced care to babies. She has dedicated her life to saving the lives of preterm babies. She set up the Department of Neonatology at the Ganga Ram hospital and ensured that the centre would grow into one of the best and largest in the country, giving care on par with world standards.[5]

Reflecting on her decision to take up neonatology as her specialisation, Kler mentions; 'My resolve to become a neonatologist is related to a story which happened when I was in medical school in Kashmir. I was at the Community Hospital in Doda (a remote hilly area in Jammu & Kashmir) for my rural posting. One day, I was asked by the Chief Medical Officer to accompany the head nurse to visit a woman in advanced labour. After reaching there, we found the young woman experiencing great pain. We assisted her in delivering a baby boy who underwent asphyxia, i.e., could not breathe at birth because of a long and difficult labour. Despite all my efforts to revive the baby, he did not survive. As a young medical student, that was my first experience of trying to resuscitate an asphyxiated baby and I failed. This made me decide that I want to save babies and become a neonatologist.'[6]

The Neonatal Intensive Care Unit at the Ganga Ram hospital has grown to become a centre of excellence today, equipped with the latest equipment. The centre has been able to save pre-term babies even below 1000 grams. The success rate of the centre today is about 90 percent and the infection rate is below 9.8 per 1000 admissions.[7]

Not only saving lives, Kler has been instrumental in promoting neonatology as a field of study in the country. She was the first to start the three-year post-graduate program on neonatology in India under the aegis of the National Board of Examinations.[8] She worked as the Secretary and later as the President (2009-10) of the National Neonatology Forum in India. She also served as member of the 'newborn and child health strategy' panel of the Ministry of Health and Family Welfare during 2012-15. As a member she was instrumental in setting standards and designing policy frameworks for the promotion of the science and education of neonatology.[9]

Kler has worked on various global committees as well such as the World Health Organization expert committee on the prevention of birth defects in South-East Asia. She is a member of the Global Neonatal Nutrition Consensus Group and also is master trainer for helping baby's breath (affiliated to the American Academy of Paediatrics).[10] This has enabled her to contribute to developing international guidelines on the care and feeding of pre-term babies.

Reflecting on the state of neonatal care in India, Kler states, 'As a neonatologist who has worked for a quarter of a century towards a relentless pursuit of making the best neonatal care and technology available in India, the still high neonatal mortality rates in the country makes me immensely sad. As a community of healthcare providers we should make collective efforts to improve healthcare delivery and make available better life-saving technology across every nook and corner of the country.'[11] She is an advocate for changes in India's healthcare policies. She advocates, 'Universal health coverage–health insurance for all, with access to both private and public sectors and nationwide integration of health data as also the setting up of a system like the UK's National Health Service, where every morbidity and mortality is accounted for.[12]

According to Kler, 'Three leading causes of neonatal deaths in India are premature births, neonatal infections, and birth asphyxia. Although Neonatal Mortality Rate (NMR) in India has decreased from 52/1000 in 1990 to 25/1000 at present, the decline has been rather slow. Neonatal mortality is hugely dependent on socio-economic factors such as education, women's empowerment, availability of health infrastructure, which is why we find disparities in neonatal deaths among rich and poor and urban and rural populations. While there are no easy solutions, I firmly believe that strengthening the public health infrastructure for even the most marginalised population with available and accountable health personnel at all levels is the long-term sustainable solution.'[13]

Recognising her services in the field of medicine and neonatology, the government of India conferred on her the Padma Bhushan in 2014. She was also conferred an honorary fellowship of the Punjab Academy of Sciences in 2015 for her contributions to her field.

Devi Prasad Shetty
Revolutionising Medical Care

Dr Devi Prasad Shetty is an Indian cardiac surgeon, an entrepreneur, a social reformer and the Founder and Chairman of Narayana Health, a chain of multi-specialty hospitals headquartered at Bangalore, Karnataka. He was born on 8 May 1953 in the Kinnigoli village of Dakshina Kannada district in Karnataka. He was the eighth of nine children and was inspired to become a cardiac surgeon at a very young age after hearing from his teacher in his fifth-grade class that Christian Barnard, a South African doctor had performed the first successful heart transplant in the world. Also, Shetty's father suffered from severe diabetes and had gone into a diabetic coma multiple times while he was young. Growing up, he saw doctors treating his father. To the young Devi, doctors seemed God-like. These experiences strengthened his resolve to become a doctor.[1]

After completing his schooling from St. Aloysius School in Mangalore, Shetty enrolled for an MBBS at the University of Mysore. He completed his MBBS in 1979 and then went in for a post-graduate degree in surgery from the college in 1982.[2] From 1983-1989, he trained as a cardio-thoracic surgeon under the National Health Service, UK at the Brompton Hospital, and then at the West Midlands Cardio

Thoracic Rotation program, and Guys Hospital in London.[3] In 2009, he was received as a Fellow of the Royal College of Surgeons (FRCS).[4]

Shetty started his practice in India in 1989 after returning from London. He was offered a job at the B. M. Birla Hospital in Kolkata. Shetty made a name for himself by performing heart surgeries even when there was lack of proper hospital support structure to perform complex surgeries. He remembers that his stint at the B. M. Birla Hospital prepared him for the future. He says, 'I completed 100 heart operations without a single fatality. It was the happiest day of my life and I knew that it was possible to start a revolution in cardiac surgery in the country.'[5]

Another turning point in Shetty's life came when he got a chance to serve as personal physician for Mother Teresa.[6] On one of Shetty's rounds when she saw him examining a boy who had a hole in his heart and whom he had successfully operated, she had remarked, 'When children suffer from heart problems at birth, God thought, okay, there is a problem and someone has to fix it. He thought he would send people like you to do so.'[7] Shetty remembers getting very emotional on hearing those words. He said, 'It was the best job description of a heart surgeon I had heard. I was really touched. When somebody like her says there is a higher purpose, your whole approach to work changes.'[8]

Shetty returned to Bangalore and set up Narayana Health (then called Narayana Hrudayalaya) in 2010 with an aim to provide low-cost cardiac surgeries to people who could not afford expensive treatment. By cutting cost on multiple things such as the energy bill (only the ICUs and operation theatres are air-conditioned in order to bring down the cost), doctor gowns, sutures, reducing unnecessary tests and using relatively cheaper India-made equipment, he has been able to perform an artery-cleaning coronary bypass surgery for USD

1,583. The same surgery at the Cleveland Clinic in Ohio, US costs USD 106,385.[9]

Also, Shetty uses his machines and time far more efficiently than hospitals in the West. Each of the machines operate 15 to 20 times a day, at least five times more than that in the hospitals in the US. His surgeons perform 2 to 3 procedures in a day and work 60 to 70 hours in a week, compared to one to two surgeries, five days a week in the US.[10] In spite of this, the success rates of his hospitals are better than that of the hospitals in the US. The Narayana Health hospitals report 1.4 percent mortality rate within a month of a coronary artery bypass graft surgery as compared to an average of 1.9% in the US. Also, the hospitals earn a profit-after-tax of 8 percent compared to 6.9 percent in the US.[11]

The fees from the rich and affluent are used to subsidise surgeries for the poor. In addition, the hospital is particularly careful in the case of a girl child. A girl in India is much more likely to die due to lack of medical care than a boy. 'They will never raise the money for a girl child. So, if it is a girl child we talk to them very politely and the moment they start asking tough questions, we tell them, "Don't bother, you don't pay anything; we'll take care of the child"', says Shetty.[12]

Today, Narayana Health has expanded to 18 cities in India having 21 hospitals and one in the Cayman Islands, US with six exclusive heart centres. In 2003, Shetty started a low-cost medical insurance scheme for rural farmers named 'Yeshasvini scheme' in association with the Government of Karnataka where they pay a sum of INR 250 to get insurance cover for their families for medical emergencies. The insurance scheme covers 823 surgical procedures at around 572 network hospitals in various districts of Karnataka.[13]

Recognising his service to the country and to the medical field, the Government of India conferred on Shetty the Padma Shri in 2004 and the Padma Bhushan in 2012. He is also popularly known as a 'philanthropist-surgeon', *(bypasswale baba)[14]* who delivers cardiac care 'Henry Ford-style[15]'.[16] He is best known for making healthcare accessible for the common Indian. He believes India will become the first country in the world to 'dissociate health care from affluence', and will prove to the world that quality healthcare is possible at an affordable cost, and at scale.[17]

Tsering Landol
An Advocate for Women's Health

The snow land of India, Ladakh, is home to Tsering Landol, who has not only been the first female gynecologist of Ladakh but has also transformed the traditional childbirth systems in Ladakh. The state of Ladakh had no female gynecologist until she decided to become one. Born in Leh's Changspa locality, Landol was the first of five siblings to have completed her formal education.

Landol recalls that her father was a farsighted man and had played a major role in helping her become a doctor. She managed to score good grades and made her way to the Government Medical College in Srinagar specialising in obstetrics and gynecology. The British Council sponsored her to further train herself for four months in London. She later worked in Singapore and Delhi.

'There was a doctor, an assistant surgeon, who had come to Leh when I was a child. He always had a stethoscope around his neck wherever he went. After this caught my attention, there was no looking back. I wanted to become a doctor', Landol states.[1] Her hard work and dedication to provide a better life for pregnant women paid off. Today women in arid areas like that of Ladakh are well prepared and aware about their health especially during pregnancy.

While growing up she was perturbed by how women were treated post-delivery. 'I innately felt there was something wrong with that, but couldn't say anything. As I grew up, I understood things better.' Since there were no female gynecologists, women talked less about their health. It was in college that Landol had decided to lend ears to women of Leh-Ladakh and help them combat urinary tract infection, anemia etc. Gradually more women started coming to her for consultations.

In 1979, Landol decided to join the Sonam Norboo Memorial Hospital in Leh after getting some experience from Srinagar. It was a district hospital with bare minimum facilities. Everything had to be restarted, right from re-examination tables to operation theatres. 'I was the first gynecologist posted in that area and there was no "readymade" thing for me. We had to put a demand for everything right from the start.'[2]

Remembering her initial years, Landol said that people did not like to consult a doctor, especially for gynecology-related problems. She had started with five patients, then slowly people started coming to her. They talked amongst each other and suggested that one must take a doctor's consultation in case of any difficulty.

Apart from fighting social stigmas and inhibitions that prevented women from consulting a doctor, Landol also had to face the rough climatic conditions of Leh-Ladakh. During winters the temperature drop led to high mortality rates, making it difficult for doctors to deliver babies professionally. A cold environment and toxic gases from traditional coal heaters added to the challenges. But thanks to Landol's Srinagar experience, she demanded the replacement of traditional coal heaters with Kashmiri *Hamam*[3] systems and proper labour rooms. The installation of *Hamams* improved room temperature and helped reduce delivery death rates during winters. After many months of delays and indecisiveness the government finally gave approval to an air conditioning plant at the hospital's operation theatres.

In 1980, a year after her joining, Landol's efforts were rewarded with success. That year Leh recorded 114 births and this kept on increasing in the coming years. Landol is a firm believer in communication in the medical field. In order to make people understand the importance of healthcare in addition to fighting the social inhibitions, she not only had to communicate but also had to have honest and dedicated talks with the people. She was a pioneer in raising awareness about adolescent health, and convinced people not to produce more babies.

In her career spanning four decades, Landol had not restricted herself merely to hospitals. She used to set up camps and awareness programs where she not only guided the people but also raised awareness. 'I knew the vernacular and social conventions, the traditions, I knew the diet and climatic conditions and geography, I was the right person to understand my people. I could speak their language and had gone through their lifestyle', recalls Landol.[4]

She believes that in order to reach out to the masses, it is important to train local doctors. The reason why she could reach out to people was because she is a Ladakhi and she could identify their issues, encourage them to open up and convince them with solutions, all this in their local language that made her even more trustworthy. Her field emergencies further helped her interact with women in remote areas where she could advise them on diet and hygiene.

Today at the age of 76, she conducts seminars and visits camps raising awareness and guiding women about maternal health. Every Thursday, she provides free counseling and guidance to women patients. She also visits the foundation in Delhi where she examines pregnant women with heart issues.

Landol credits her success to her friends who stood by her.

Her foreign expeditions helped her make new friends, who were ready to support Landol to improve and uplift medical facilities in India. On knowing the scarcity of resources, her friends helped raise money for the same with the help of NGOs. Currently she is working towards bringing cervical scan technologies to the SNM Hospital. Landol, along with her team, now also educates schoolgirls about puberty and other hormonal changes.

Landol's altruism and zeal to bring change in women's healthcare in Ladakh brought her the Padma Shri in 2006 and the Padma Bhushan in 2020. She also features on 'Ladakh's Wall of Fame' for her contributions and groundbreaking work towards women's healthcare in Ladakh.

Suresh Hariram Advani
Defeating Illness to Become Hope for Millions

Dr Suresh Hariram Advani, India's leading and best-known oncologist, was born in Karachi in present-day Pakistan on 1 August 1947. Two weeks later India gained its independence and the partition caused a bedlam. His family relocated to India. Eight years later, Advani witnessed yet another fatal blow in his life when he was struck with polio confining him to a wheelchair. Back in those days the vaccination for polio was not available in India.

With eighty per cent locomotor disability, he did not give up on his dreams. Advani received treatment for his ailment and was truly inspired by how doctors play a pivotal role not only in society but also in the lives of the people. That is when he decided to become a doctor and help improve the lives of the people.

Indomitable and determined, Advani went on to become a doctor. His journey had its fair share of fluctuations. On applying to Grant Medical College to pursue his ambition, Advani was rejected by the college which told him, 'They didn't want a crippled person.'[1] Advani, a spirited man, did not give up on his dreams and wrote a letter to the Mumbai University Chancellor and the government describing the injustice and discrimination he faced. His efforts made the authorities at the Grant Medical College admit him to medical programme after receiving a letter from the state's health minister.

The road ahead was not smooth. In his final year of MBBS, he was denied a 'house job'[2] by five out of six sections. It was Dr RD Lele, a renowned physician, who eventually offered him the house job. Advani then went on to pursue his MD in general medicine under Dr Lele's guidance. 'See he has succeeded in life despite all the odds', Dr Lele had said in an interview.[3]

Advani decided to become an oncologist while completing his MD. At that time oncology was not considered an appealing field. But his interest, research and dedication in the field took him places. In 1974, he started working at the Tata Memorial Hospital (TMH) as an Assistant Medical Oncologist. After a few years, he moved to London for three years to work there. On returning to India, he joined TMH again but this time with enriched knowledge and experience.

Few years later, he was fortunate to travel to Seattle and work at the Fred Hutchinson Cancer Research Centre. He got to work with Dr E Donnall Thomas[4] who is known as the father of bone marrow transplants. It was there that Advani learned the art of bone marrow transplant. He also travelled to different parts of the world to learn refined methods of treating the disease. In 1983, Advani successfully transplanted bone marrow into a nine-year old girl suffering from myeloid leukaemia.[5] Her brother was the donor. This was the first successful bone marrow transplantation in India.

Advani's peers hold him in high regard. 'He is a healer. He is a role model for us', mentions Dr Mehboob Basade, a stem-cell specialist at a Mumbai hospital.[6] 'He is a role model for aspiring medical students and also for those who are physically challenged. He not only sailed through all difficulties but also excelled in his field', mentions Dr Gurmukh Sainani, a veteran physician who had taught Advani. A colleague of Dr Advani, Dr Boman Dhabhar, an oncologist said, 'Because of the training we received from Advani who makes hard work look easy, we (oncologists) have a bent for working hard.'[7]

Working for about fourteen to fifteen hours every day, Advani attends to over 100 cancer patients, many being from out of the country. He is an ocean of knowledge and his expertise in the field of oncology inspires many. He has authored and co-authored around 648 national and international publications. He is a consulting doctor at many leading hospitals treating patients as well as imparting his knowledge and expertise to young minds. He is involved in developing the syllabus along with the teaching manual for the DM, Medical Oncology Course, in association with the Indian Medical and Paediatric Oncology Association. 'We learn as we teach',[8] is what he believes and what better learning than from the future doctors while also training them.

With changing times, Advani is concerned about the changing lifestyles especially in urban cities that have become one of the principal causes for rise in cancer cases. Unhealthy food habits, late pregnancies, increasing pollution are some of the reasons for this rise.

Furthermore, an acute shortage of specialists in the country is an issue of critical importance. Hence it is important to create awareness amongst people.[9] He is also a part of an NGO named 'Helping Hand' that offers assistance to cancer patients and helps them deal with the psychological and financial impact of the disease.

Advani was the first Indian oncologist to have done a successful bone marrow transplantation. In 2012, he was conferred the Padma Bhushan for his exemplary contribution to cancer treatment. His zeal for his work, patience, dedication towards his patients as well as his never-say-die spirit have made him an inspiration. Despite being confined to a wheelchair due to polio, he never stopped chasing his dreams. No matter what the difficulties, Advani's life shows that one must neither stop dreaming nor stop chasing and achieving their dreams.

888

Arts

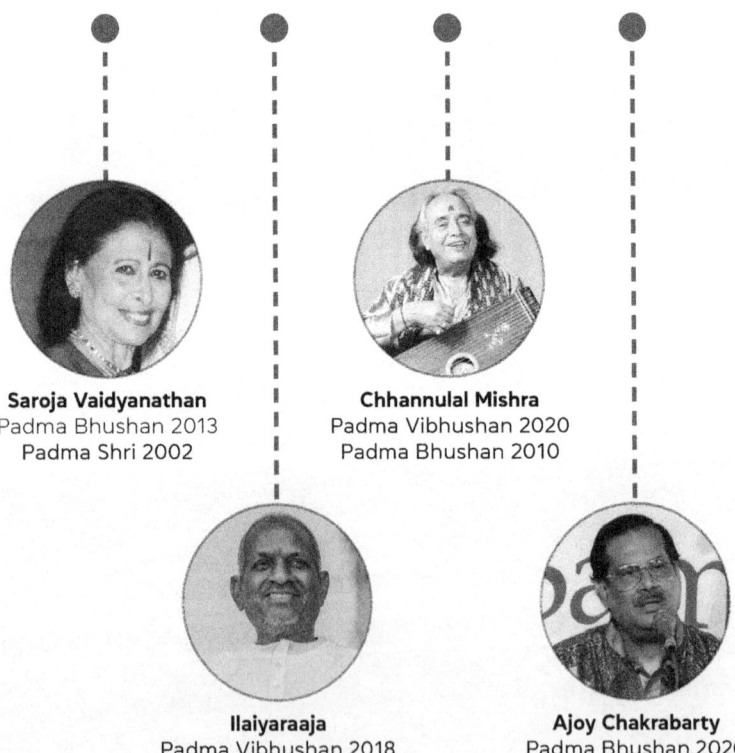

Saroja Vaidyanathan
Padma Bhushan 2013
Padma Shri 2002

Chhannulal Mishra
Padma Vibhushan 2020
Padma Bhushan 2010

Ilaiyaraaja
Padma Vibhushan 2018
Padma Bhushan 2010

Ajoy Chakrabarty
Padma Bhushan 2020

Hari Prasad Chaurasia
Padma Vibhushan 2000
Padma Bhushan 1992

A R Rahman
Padma Bhushan 2010
Padma Shri 2000

Zakir Hussain
Padma Vibhushan 2023
Padma Bhushan 2002
Padma Shri 1988

Sudarsan Pattnaik
Padma Shri 2014

Arts

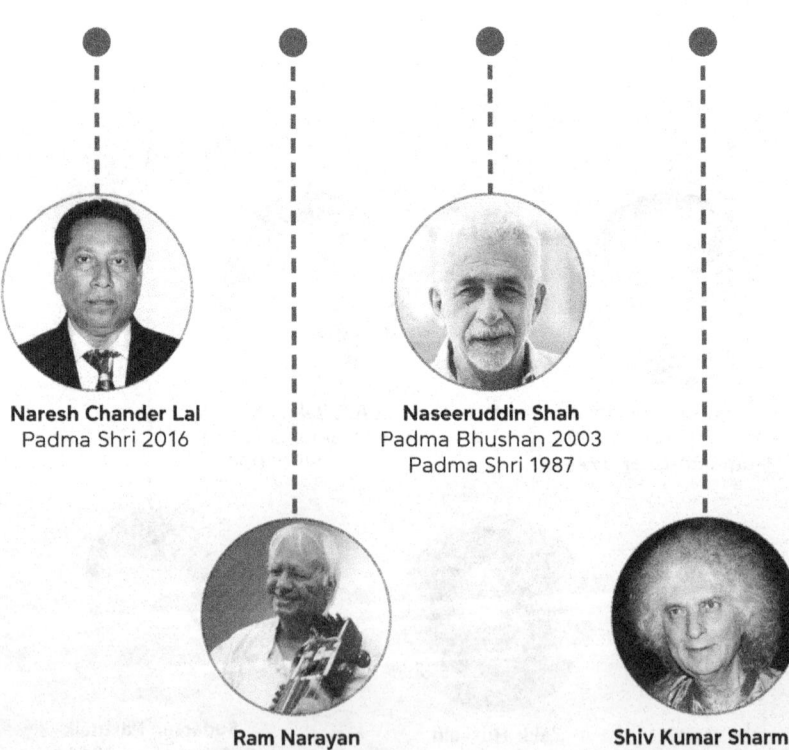

Naresh Chander Lal
Padma Shri 2016

Naseeruddin Shah
Padma Bhushan 2003
Padma Shri 1987

Ram Narayan
Padma Vibhushan 2005
Padma Bhushan 1991
Padma Shri 1976

Shiv Kumar Sharma
Padma Vibhushan 2001
Padma Shri 1991

Amitabh Bachchan
Padma Vibhushan 2015
Padma Bhushan 2001
Padma Shri 1984

Teejan Bai
Padma Vibhushan 2019
Padma Bhushan 2003
Padma Shri 1988

Kattassery Joseph Yesudas
Padma Vibhushan 2017
Padma Bhushan 2002
Padma Shri 1975

Manoj Bajpayee
Padma Shri 2019

Saroja Vaidyanathan
Keeping Bharatanatyam Alive

Bharatanatyam, considered among the most geometrically multidirectional of the Indian dance styles, often conveys Hindu religious stories, in part through an intricate lexicon of hand positions known as *mudras*. With a history of more than 2000 years, Bharatanatyam may be the oldest classical dance style worldwide. For Saroja Vaidyanathan, a noted performer, guru, and choreographer, Bharatanatyam is not just a dance form, it is also a powerful medium to share India's rich culture and traditions with the world. 'I feel proud and happy that I am an Indian and God has given me the opportunity to present our country's heritage and history to the world', she shares.

For centuries, Bharatanatyam was associated most closely with female courtesans *(devadasis)* accompanied by male musicians and dance-masters *(nattuvanars)*, who performed in social venues such as salons, royal courts, marriages, and temples. It was not until the 1930s that the traditional dance form was stripped off its erotic aspects that were a legacy of its association with the devadasis and repackaged as Bharatanatyam (the dance of *Bharat*). It was in this milieu that Saroja was born in 1937 in the Bellary district of Karnataka. Her parents were educated and passionate about art, yet traditional and orthodox.[1] Music was encouraged at home, but dance was not considered appropriate. Young Saroja was interested in sports and the arts. Her parents provided the resources for her to pursue her interests. 'I joined a nearby school under Guru Lalita at the age of seven in Chennai. I am so glad that my parents supported me', she recollects.

Saroja flourished under the tutelage of Guru Lalithamma, who had made tremendous personal sacrifices to completely devote her life towards art. When Saroja was 16, she performed at the Gokhale Hall in Chennai. Seeing her performance, a producer offered her a role in a film. Her family was outraged at the prospect of their daughter entering films. She was told to stop training. It was time to get married.

Her marriage to C R Vaidyanathan, an officer in the Indian Administrative Services, was a turning point in her life. When her husband was posted as a District Commissioner in Bihar, she started teaching dance to children. 'I created, composed and choreographed numerous dance dramas for children and made them perform at various places', she states proudly.[2] She then also started performing, sometimes with the children, at venues considered 'decent', such as the local Rotary Club and other social gatherings. Her husband had one condition for her teaching and dancing: she could not charge money as it would not be commensurate with the status of the commissioner's wife. 'I agreed to it because I was not keen on earning money, it was more to satisfy my soul', she shares.

Saroja had just begun to find her rhythm in Bihar when her husband was transferred to Delhi in 1972. She started using the bungalow they had been provided to teach dance, beginning with just four female students. This time Saroja institutionalised her teaching by founding Ganesa Natyalaya, a school for learning dance. She also began to look for an independent place in which to set up a dance school, outside the boundaries of her house. She found a suitable place in the Qutub Institutional Area, which was in the very early stages of development at the time.

Her husband was himself a trained singer, but he had given up his interest in music for his IAS career. Seeing his wife's passion for dance, he wanted to support her. Yet, he was also concerned about his reputation as a senior government officer. Nor could he imagine his wife being able to realise her ambitious dreams, and at the same time run the household, and take care of their two children. When her husband told her that she should not expect any help from him to raise funds for the land and construct the building, she was not discouraged. She managed to collect the money without involving him.

For the next few years, Saroja led a regimented daily life. Early in the morning, when her husband and children were still asleep, she practiced dance. After getting the family ready for their day, she went to the construction site to oversee the work and manage the workers. Post lunch, she taught dance till the evening before rejoining the family for dinner. Her mother-in-law, who was skilled at playing the harmonium, proved very helpful at this time as Saroja balanced the demands of building a new institution and managing the family. By 1988, the building for the Natyalaya was ready. 'I knew the value of time and knowledge and developed a belief that hard work would surely take you to the top', she says about her struggles.

Soon, the Natyalaya took off, attracting students and fame. It has a paid staff of dance teachers, many of them Saroja's own disciples, as well as teachers for Carnatic vocal music, mridangam, Hindi, and Tamil. Many of her students receive scholarships from the Indian Council for Cultural Relations (ICCR) or from the Council for Cultural Resources and Training (CCRT). Students can take classes part-time or full-time, which allows them to learn at their own pace.

When her husband retired, the Vaidyanathans moved into the cosy residential apartment on the Natyalaya premises to be closer to her work. Saroja had been allotted an apartment in the

Asiad Village Complex under the artist scheme, but she did not consider it appropriate to accept it. Over the years, she received many awards for her work, including the Padma Shri in 2002 and Padma Bhushan in 2013.

Saroja finds the young generation of Indian dancers smart, quick and focused, yet impatient. She advises youngsters, who train under her, to be patient, practice constantly and focus on the subject. Hard work, she believes, will eventually bring success and recognition.

Ilaiyaraaja
Creating Timeless Melodies that Transcend Generations

Born as Gananthesikan on 3 June 1943, in a Dalit[1] family in a village in Pannaipuram, located in the Theni district of Tamil Nadu. He changed his name to 'Rajaiya' in school and when he joined his guru, Dhanraj master, he was given the name of 'Raaja'. While working on his first (Tamil) film, *Annakili*, the film maker Panchu Arunachalam added 'Ilaiya' ('Ilaiya' in Tamil means 'youthful') as a prefix to his name. Raaja was thus renamed 'Ilaiyaraaja'.

Ilaiyaraaja was once told by an astrologer that he will not be able to get educated post class eight. To prove the astrologer wrong and fund his education, he started working at the Vaigai dam.[2] At the dam, his job was to pour water on the concrete through a hose pipe to fortify it. While he worked seven days a week on the dam, he also used to entertain his fellow workers with melodies and tunes that merged with the noise at work—stones being blended for concrete at the site. Thus, he proceeded to join class nine.[3]

In the meantime, Ilaiyaraaja's elder brother, Pavalar Varadarajan, a communist supporter had set up a troupe to promote communist ideals through his songs. His brother had become quite famous and required a hand for a *kutcheri*[4] in Thiruverumbur. His mother advised him to join his sibling in the *kutcheri* to sing tunes and play music with him. That was the beginning of his music career and the end of his formal education. His brother used to take them to different political and social events where their program followed after the speeches were over. The busy travel schedule did not hamper his energy. He used to play the harmonium for the troupe and kept learning from the mistakes he made in his performances.

Ilaiyaraaja's brother also trained him to bring innovation into the songs and the method of capturing audiences' attention. His brother used to write songs for tunes that had been composed by M S Viswanathan.[5] While playing songs with his brother, Ilaiyaraaja realised the power of cinema and that the applause his troupe would receive was more due to the tunes composed by M S Viswanathan. It was at that point that he made up his mind to become a composer of songs himself. He started attempting to make new tunes for songs written by his younger brother.

Until 1967, Ilaiyaraaja continued to play with his brother. However, he recognised that he wanted to do more than just be part of the propaganda machinery for the communists. His mother gave him and his other brother INR 400 (at that point, an enormous amount of cash for them) and he left with his siblings for Chennai to further his music instruction.

In Chennai, his music coach Dhanraj master recognised that Ilaiyaraaja had a knack for remembering tunes and encouraged him to pursue western classical music. Later, he completed a course in western classical music and turned into a guitarist for Salil Chowdhury[6] and following that, he took up the role of an assistant to G K Venkatesh.[7]

Generally viewed as one of the best Indian music composers, Ilaiyaraaja's most admired skill was his ability to fuse different genres of music. He had the ability to bring together different traditions and instruments of music and play them in harmony. He is regularly credited with catering to western musical sensibilities in South Indian films' mainstream music. As of 2020, he had composed over 7,000 tunes, film songs for more than 1,000 films and has performed in excess of 20,000 shows. Ilaiyaraaja is also nicknamed 'Isaignani' (saint musician), Ragadevan (Lord of the ragas) and is frequently alluded to as 'Maestro', among others by the Royal Philharmonic Orchestra of London.[8]

Ilaiyaraaja's other contribution comes from breaking the hegemony and the stronghold of brahmins on the Tamil film music. While the music was said to be composed for the masses, before Ilaiyaraaja the music industry in Tamil Nadu was dominated by brahmins. Ilaiyaraaja changed all this. In 1979, one of his songs *Oram Po* was even banned from being aired by the brahmin-dominated All India Radio.[9] In an interview on his 75th birthday, Ilaiyaraaja explained his ideas of spiritualism by stating that, 'Spiritualism itself is simplified… everything is equal and same!'

Ilaiyaraaja believes that music is a must for a peaceful society. He explains, 'I believe that people exposed to music and who are taught music will not commit violent crimes. Music and greater exposure to it will help bring peace to society.'[10] Also, to him music is universal and undifferentiated. While people accuse him of fusion, to him it is natural and all-pervasive. He mentions, 'I always felt music to be universal and undifferentiated—Western classical, folk, Carnatic or Hindustani and so on… People call this "fusion" but these are not two different things that are fused together. Music is universal and undifferentiated in my view.'[11]

In 2012, he received the Sangeet Natak Akademi Award, the highest Indian recognition given to practicing artists, for his creative and experimental works in the music field. In 2010, he was awarded the Padma Bhushan, and the Padma Vibhushan in 2018. In a 2013 poll conducted by CNN-IBN celebrating 100 years of Indian cinema, Ilaiyaraaja was voted as the all-time greatest film-music director of India. In 2014, American world cinema portal 'Taste of Cinema' placed him at the 9th position in its list of 25 greatest film composers in the history of cinema. Ilaiyaraaja was the only Indian in the list.[12]

☙❧☙

Channulal Mishra
Maestro of Hindustani Classical Music

From the ancient city of Varanasi comes one of the most gifted, celebrated and renowned vocalist Pandit Channulal Mishra. He was born on 3 August 1936 in the Hariharpur village of Azamgarh district in Uttar Pradesh and went on to become a noted promoter of the *Kirana Gharana*[1] of Indian Classical Music. He is a versatile performer who captivates the audiences' attention with his voice and 'Swarmandal',[2] leaving the attendees spell bound.

Mishra learnt music from various gurus. His father has been his constant source of inspiration and motivation since childhood. For him, his father was an epitome of classical music who despite financial problems pushed his son to learn music under Ustad Abdul Ghani Khan. 'As for my mother, she taught me religious Hindu *granths* like the *Ramayana* and *Sunder Kand* which helped me grasp deep knowledge about literature. Today I can sing more than 150 ghazals without even glancing at a book', says Mishra.[3]

Mishra's journey has helped him in creating his own distinct style of music that reflects the amalgamation of different gharanas whose styles he learned from his gurus over the years. Though he has been emphasising on preserving the Banaras gharana and Varanasi's vanishing musical heritage, he has also been advocating the setting up of a culture ministry-run music academy in Varanasi.

Mishra's expertise and rich knowledge about the literature of music has helped him transcend the peripheries of gharana styles to bring a streak of spiritualism into his singing thereby making his performances aesthetic.

For over 30 years, Mishra has been celebrating his guru Ustad Abdul Ghani Khan and paying tribute to him by showing the world the different dimensions of the Kirana Gharana which has flourished under this living exponent of semi-classical music forms whose voice leaves the audience speechless from. His music has often been described as rich in *bhakti gyan*, intensely peopled and invokes a sense of stillness along with continual movement just like the city of Kashi. His music calls for longing, desire, changing seasons and God.

He was unknown to the world until he was fifty years old. His first commercial recording came when he got an opportunity to sing on Krishna and he decided to name it 'The Heart of Varanasi'. In an interview he had once said, *Aadhi roti chain se khaate the, riyaaz karte the* (I used to eat half bread and then practice). I have seen a lot of hardship. I have struggled a lot all my life. I was noticed only after the age of 50 years. It's all fate. *Bank balance se kya karna, bus roti nahin rukni chahiye* (What will I do with money? I should have enough to eat and fill my stomach)."[4]

Also, Mishra's short stint of singing in films gained him popularity. While he has been offered the opportunity to sing in multiple films, he has always refused to do so. He believed that at his age he should sing songs that are appropriate. Even though the famous singer Shankar Mahadevan considers Pandit Mishra as his guru, Mishra has never had time for film music. 'I have never actually taught Shankar Mahadevan. I just indicated one or two things to him, *jaise swar ko kaise lagaana hai, meru khand mein antar kya hai* (How do you sing? What is the difference in the meru khand). But yes, he considers me his guru, and does *pranam*.'

Mishra calls today's music 'confused music' as it is different from classical music due to the involvement of fusion. Fusion is gaining popularity amongst youngsters who must understand that respecting and maintaining our tradition, heritage and classical music is important. Patience is the key element to learning music and one must be determined to excel. Music is the only means by which one can connect with God, believes Mishra.

Mishra firmly believes that classical music must be included in school curriculum so as to keep the classical tradition alive in the future. Today music is not looked at as a means of *sadhana* (prayer), rather it is seen as a means of entertainment. Earlier music was considered equivalent to penance where one not only devoted but also surrendered themselves to music. *Khele masane me holi* is one of Mishra's signature songs which was written by Mangal Baba. The song is about death, the ultimate truth of life, and describes how Lord Shiva is playing Holi on the cremation ghat of Varanasi, and how euphoric and celebratory is the environment of the place. Songs like these are gradually disappearing as people are becoming less interested in classical music.

Mishra was conferred many awards that include the Sangeet Natak Akademi Award in 2000 and the Padma Bhushan in 2010 for his contribution in music. 'It (Padma Bhushan) is not a recognition of my work as it is too late and too little but still you feel better when you get something from the society and the government', said Mishra in an interview.[5] In 2020, Mishra was bestowed the Padma Vibhushan.

'One needs to do something to fill the stomach and we as a family didn't have a family business to run',[6] remarks Mishra. Had it not been for music and his father's determination to teach his son classical music, Channulal Mishra would have been driving a rickshaw or would have been a poor farmer. Mishra's keen interest in music, devotion and dedication led him to open the doors of Indian classical music, more specifically the Kirana Gharana, to the world.

Ajoy Chakrabarty
Weaving Harmonic Tapestries with Emotion

A renowned and poised singer and a cult vocalist in Hindustani classical music, Pandit Ajoy Chakrabarty was born on 25 December 1953 in Kolkata, West Bengal. His father, late Ajit Kumar Chakrabarty, had relocated to India from Bangladesh during partition and became his first guru. Growing up, Chakrabarty learned music from his father and mothers late Smt Mahamaya Devi and Smt Jayanti Chakrabarty.

Learning under various gurus, Chakrabarty eventually got the opportunity to train under Ustad Munawar Ali Khan[1] of the *Patiala Kasoor Gharana*. His dedication and passion for music led him to do his graduation and post-graduation in music from the renowned Rabindra Bharati University, Kolkata. When Chakrabarty topped his class in music, he got an opportunity to join the ITC Sangeet Research Academy (SRA) in 1977. As a fellow of the Academy with a gold medal, he became a member of the Experts' Committee of the Academy.

Chakrabarty is a scion and a doyen of the Patiala Kasoor Gharana but during his time with ITC Sangeet Research Academy, he had the opportunity to assimilate knowledge from gurus who belonged to gharanas other than his own, such as Ustad Latafat Hussain Khan, a pioneer of the Agra Gharana, Pandit Nivruttibua Sarnaik of the Alladiya Jaipur Gharana, all of whom helped him incorporate the subtle features of their paramount gharanas into his singing.

Chakrabarty also explored the Carnatic music tradition under the guidance of Dr M. Balamuralikrishna, a legend in his own right. Learning from distinct gurus elevated his musical expression and enriched his repertoire. His hunger for knowledge and the quest to learn sharpened his awareness and he never shied away from learning. He believes that, 'Whatever touches the mind and the heart and if one yearns for it, never mind what word you use, it is still learning', says the maestro.[2]

Chakrabarty is a trendsetter who can modify different forms of music like *Thumri, Tappa, Geet, Bhajan,* Folk, Filmy, non-filmy and many other forms into their lighter version. Today, he is a distinguished one-of-a-kind musical personality in the field of music in India. Moreover, acknowledging his musical brilliance, not only musicians but legends from other fields such as filmmakers Satyajit Ray and Tapan Sinha, all-time great writer Premendra Mitra, internationally recognised sports personalities like Saurav Ganguly have also appreciated his genius.

'Indian music is known the world over for its intrinsic spiritualism. It demands *nishtha* (dedication), *chintan* (reflection), *parishram* (toil) and *aahuti* (surrender). These have no colours of isms', believes Chakrabarty.[3] He believes that music must be made compulsory in schools. Music can not only help people connect to their heritage and culture but also be of service in curbing the criminal mindset. Additionally, he believes that classical music enthusiasts should be policy makers and more institutions with enthusiastic and passionate faculty must be established in the country to impart the knowledge of music.[4]

Chakrabarty is of the opinion that music can bring normalcy in society and help youngsters value their culture and heritage. Music has a lasting and universal impact on the soul that also helps develop one's character and personality. On this thought, he conceived the project called *Shrutinandan*—music classes that recognise the musical nature in a student. The motive behind *Shrutinandan* is that the music teacher must be able to unleash the flow of music within the student to make them realise their full musical potential, by living and breathing it, in every single aspect of their lives. *Shruti* means auditory perception and *Nandan* is what is aesthetically pleasing in nature. The organisation is working towards imbibing the very essence of creating and nurturing beautiful musical minds.[5]

Pandit Ajoy Chakrabarty - The Seeker of Music Within is a book written by David Lagercrantz, translated by Shyam Banerji and Published by Niyogi Books. The book pays homage to Chakrabarty's contribution in the field of music.[6] Chakrabarty has won many awards including the Padma Shri in 2011 and the Padma Bhushan in 2020 for his contributions in the field of music and classical music. 'I am happy and feel this is a result of the blessings of my guru, Pt Gnan Prakash Ghosh. I hope I can carry on with the work that I want to do', said Chakrabarty after receiving a Padma award.[7]

The torchbearer of the Patiala Gharana was also bestowed a doctorate from Indian Institute of Technology (IIT) Kanpur in the presence of Honourable Prime Minister Shri Narendra Modi.[8] He was also awarded the Sangeet Natak Akademi Award (1999-2000), the Kumar Gandharva Samman (1993), and the Best Male Playback Singer (Bengali Film *Chhandaneer* in 1990).[9] Recently, on the occasion of Sheikh Mujibur Rahman's birth centenary and Bangladesh's 50th Independence Day, Chakrabarty composed and dedicated a song titled *Maitree* that celebrates the friendship of India and Bangladesh and their shared heritage.[10]

No matter how successful Chakrabarty becomes, he will always be an eternal student, ready to learn. In his years of learning music from geniuses, he considers Guru Gnan Prakash Ghosh and Baba Alauddin Khan as unique for their contribution in educating humanity. He firmly believes that one must listen to the great masters and absorb from them, while having one's own style of singing. 'Even if you become a lion or a tiger, you will still not get a place at Saraswati's feet. You have to be a swan to be at her feet: drink the milk like a swan and leave the water out.'[11]

Hariprasad Chaurasia
Reawakening the Bansuri

Pandit Hariprasad Chaurasia, an Indian classical flautist who brought global recognition to the simplest and most natural musical instrument—the *Bansuri* also known as the flute. Born in a family of non-musicians in Allahabad, Uttar Pradesh on 1 July, 1938. Chaurasia was surrounded by wrestlers. His father ran an *Akhara*[1] and wanted his son to follow in his footsteps, but the son's heart was somewhere else.

Chaurasia was extremely passionate about music and was ready to utilise his lung power after undergoing rigorous training as a wrestler. 'I wasn't very good at wrestling. After those sessions, I would go and learn music at a friend's house.'[2] He used to learn music secretly from a noted vocalist of Varanasi, Raja Ram. One day in his early teens, Chaurasia was transfixed as he heard, on the radio, the notes of a flute played by Pandit Bholanath, a staff artiste with the All India Radio (AIR). This small incident changed his entire life.

Chaurasia was now enthusiastic about the flute and went to meet Pandit Bholanath. He requested him to be his guru and Pandit Bholanath gladly accepted him as his student in exchange for running errands, cooking and cleaning. For around eight years he was under the tutelage of Pandit Bholanath until he received an offer from the Cuttack station of AIR. 'When the offer came, I had to finally tell my father, as I had to shift to a different city. He was shocked. But it was a government job, and he saw how happy I was, so he reluctantly agreed', recalls Chaurasia.[3] Finally in 1957 he joined the Cuttack station of AIR, performing and composing songs.

In Cuttack, Chaurasia found like-minded people and started enjoying their company. Odissi dancers used to ask him to accompany them as their musician, while some called him for films. Chaurasia later got transferred to Mumbai and while the salary he was getting was barely sufficient to live in a city like Mumbai, after a month's struggle he got a job as a Sessions Artist in Bollywood.[4] In the industry he got the opportunity to collaborate with great musicians and composers like Madan Mohan, S D Burman and Naushad.

Sometime later, Chaurasia visited Delhi to attend a youth festival where he was introduced to a noted santoor[5] player called Pandit Shiv Kumar Sharma. The two became extremely close friends over time and collaborated for films under the pseudonym Shiv-Hari. One day, the famous actor Sanjeev Kumar provoked them into getting back to classical music and to the instruments they were born to play.

Subsequently, in the 1980s, Chaurasia was determined to relearn classical music under the guidance of an eminent surbahar[6] player Annapurna Devi, daughter of late Ustad Allaudin Khan and sister of Ustad Ali Akbar Khan. Chaurasia had to earn her guidance after three years of persuasion. In an interview, he reminisced, 'She would say that she played the surbahar and couldn't teach the flute. I told her I was there to learn music. Then she told me I'll have to forgo all the learning I have. I told her if she'd teach me, I'll change my original flute position.'[7]

Chaurasia credits achievements to his guru Annapurna Devi who taught him the solemnity of depth in music and gave a new dimension to his talent. He believes that she was the catalyst and all of this was possible only because he had surrendered himself to her and had accepted her as his guru. With his passion, determination and hard work, Panditji once again started off on his career as a performing artist.

Chaurasia is known as an innovator and a traditionalist who has brought the bamboo flute to the attention of the world. His one-of-a-kind flute adaptations of raga forms demonstrate his thorough knowledge of the language. His control over his instrument is a result of his wrestling days that gave him immense stamina and strength giving rise to an eccentric blowing technique.

Chaurasia's love for music and for teaching music led him to set up the Vrindaban Gurukul in Mumbai in 2002 and in Bhubaneswar, Orissa in 2010. It is built around the Guru-Shishya parampara that is deeply embedded in India. The gurukul was built under the patronage of Sir Ratan Tata Trust, where underprivileged kids live for free and learn with full concentration and dedication.

Chaurasia devotes much of his time to his students as he wants them to learn as much as possible from him. 'I want my students to grow the music they are learning here. They should uphold the tradition, the gharana and teach others. I want them to be better than me. When they outdo me, I am their best teacher. Else, I have not succeeded.'[8]

Chaurasia has won accolades over the years for his grit, hard work, zeal and passion towards music. He was conferred the Sangeet Natak Akademi Award in 1984, the Padma Bhushan in 1992, the Padma Vibhushan in 2000 and the NALCO (National Aluminum Company) Sangeet Sudha Award in 2018 among many others for his contributions towards music.

Chaurasia's message to his students is to live carefree, devote more time to music, approach it with an attitude of prayer. Not only will they gain knowledge, but they will also gain as musicians.

Chaurasia has juggled between the west and India, performing, learning and teaching music throughout his life. His ultimate goal is to play the bamboo flute as long as he can and reach out to as wide an audience as possible. One of his students believes, 'Guruji is not only the best artist today, I think he's the best of the millennium.'[9]

ooo

Zakir Hussain
Taking the Tabla to the World

Zakir Hussain is often described as the world's greatest living *tabla* player. The tabla is a centuries-old instrument dating back to the Mughal era. Zakir helped lift it from its second-class role to the starring act in concerts. The tabla, which has a range of about an octave, is actually a collective term for two drums: the smaller being the right-hand tabla proper, and the larger being the bass drum called the *banya* and played with the left hand.[1]

How did a boy who lived the first few years of his life in a one-room apartment *(chawl)* with no indoor plumbing come to rank among the world's most famous and respected musicians? The credit goes to his father Ustad Allah Rakha Khan Qureshi and his mother Bavi Begum.

Allah Rakha was himself a world-renowned musician, credited with having introduced the tabla to the global audience. He played the tabla in some of the world's grandest concert halls, often with the renowned sitar player Ravi Shankar. Alla Rakha was bestowed the honorific Ustad, which means teacher or guru, because, for years, he taught his disciples the mathematically complex rhythms of the tabla (Zakir also teaches tabla, though primarily in the US).[2] As a child, Zakir Hussain was up at 3 am, practiced rhythms with his father until six in the morning, then went off to a madrasa to study the Quran, and from there to St. Michael's High School. If Allah Rakha had his way, Zakir would just practice tabla the whole day. 'Practice the tabla, what will you do in school?' the father would often tell his son. But, Zakir's mother would have none of it. 'Enough practice, let him study', his mother would say and then send him off to school. At one stage, she even sent him to stay with a very close friend of hers, so that he would be away from his father's influence and study instead of playing the tabla.

His father's passion for the tabla and his mother's enthusiasm for his education worked well for Zakir's development. From the age of seven, Zakir would sit on the stage when his father was playing with other famous musicians, absorbing and learning from the greats.

As Zakir became better at playing the tabla, his father encouraged him, as he did all his students, to develop his own style. When Zakir was about 13, a letter came to the house offering a concert date to his father. Zakir wrote back saying that Allah Rakha would not be able to accept the engagement but that his son was available. Zakir did not mention his age. It worked, and his musical career was under way. Soon, and still in his teens, Zakir was already composing for films and performing on stage. In Zakir's own words:

> When I was thirteen or fourteen, I got to travel, nobody was watching over me, I did what I wanted, ate what I liked, and when we went on tour, I slept in a room of my own and didn't have to share it with four others. I had a radio and all that stuff. It was luxury. I was as content as I am now.[3]

Although Zakir was making a name for himself from a young age, there was still the practical challenge of balancing the life of a musician with the demands of student life.

Seeing his dedication to music, the school allowed him to keep up with the studies at his own pace. Someone would drop off the homework at his place, and when Zakir came back from the recording studio, his mother would give it to him to finish. If Zakir travelled for concerts, he would study and do his homework on the train under the reading light.

Zakir was born on 9 March 1951 in a nursing home in Mahim in the city then known as Bombay. Soon after, a holy man appeared at their house and called his mother by her name. When she went out to greet the holy man, he told her to name the son Zakir Hussain in celebration of Hazrat Imam Hussain, the grandson of the Prophet. While Zakir is Muslim, his wife is Catholic, the two daughters are baptised, and some members of his family are Hindu (such as his brother's wife). Zakir describes his family as a 'beautiful mix of universal oneness'.[4]

As a young boy, Zakir considered swapping the tabla for a drum set. He was working on a record with George Harrison and told him about his dream to get into rock. Reminding Zakir that the rock world was very competitive, Harrison offered some advice to the young boy. 'If you want to be just one of the thousands and be somebody that you are not, that's entirely up to you. But if you want to take all these incredible (drummers)—Elvin Jones or Tony Williams or Ringo and everybody—and make that part of your music, just imagine how unique your music will be.' 'And it made total sense', Zakir recalls.[5]

Zakir stuck with the tabla, built his reputation as a world-class player by touring widely, playing the classical music he had learned from his father, but also experimenting and partnering with other musicians, Indian and foreign. His solo performances, brilliant accompaniments, and genre-defying collaborations, including his efforts to combine Indian and Western music and bring together Hindustani and Carnatic

Indian musicians, helped make him 'a living genius' both in India and globally, and elevate the tabla to historic renown and appreciation worldwide.

His contribution to music was recognised with the Padma Shri in 1988 and the Padma Bhushan in 2002.

A R Rahman
Musical Genius and Oscar-Winning Composer

When a son was born to Malayalam film composer R K Shekhar and his wife Kasthuri Shekhar in 1967, they named him A S Dileep Kumar. He was a frail sickly child who suffered from stomach issues for the first few years of his life. Because his father was a popular musician, the young child was exposed to music from a young age. He began learning the piano when he was four and the harmonium soon thereafter. 'My mother told me that I was a loner child growing up. I would lock myself into a room and play the harmonium for hours', he says.

Few could have predicted then that this quiet child would grow up to be A R Rahman, one of the most famous musicians in the world. By some estimates, Rahman's music has sold more than 100 million records and over 200 million cassettes, making him the only Asian in the list of the world's top 25 bestselling recording artists. Some believe that global sales of his music rival that of Elvis Presley and the Beatles. In the Indian music business, many call him 'the phenomenon that changed the face of the industry'.[1]

Rahman's happy childhood ended abruptly when he was just nine years old. His father died suddenly, leaving Rahman's mother to take care of four children. The family had a nice house, and Rahman's maternal grandparents lived with them. However, except for the money that came from renting out his father's musical instruments, the large family had no source of income.[2]

Despite the strained family finances, Rahman's mother wanted him to continue his musical training. She pushed him into remaining in touch with his father's friends. It helped that young Rahman was not content to simply coast on the fame of his father. By age 11, he was already playing in an orchestra. While he could play the piano, harmonium and guitar, he was especially attracted to the synthesizer. Still in his teens, he accompanied tabla maestro Zakir Hussain, a friend of his father, and others on a world tour. Impressed with his talent, dedication, and hard work, Hussain and some of his father's other friends helped him get a scholarship to Trinity College, Oxford, where he earned a degree in Western classical music.

After returning to India with his undergraduate degree, Rahman became a jingle writer. He was also playing in an orchestra helmed by Ilaiyarajaa, his father's contemporary and one of the greatest Indian music composers of his generation. Ilaiyarajaa is famous for introducing Western musical sensibilities in South Indian film music, the kind of fusion that Rahman was to take to a new level in his career.

Rahman got his break when director Mani Ratnam first noticed him playing keyboard in Ilaiyarajaa's orchestra. Ratnam was looking for new music for his upcoming film, and Rahman seemed promising.[3] What perhaps helped tilt the scale in favour of Rahman was the speed at which he delivered. Most music directors take a few days to compose a rough tune after a scene has been explained to them. Rahman was not one of them. Minutes after the director explained the scene, Rahman had a tune for the song.

The Tamil-language film *'Roja'* (1992) was released eight

months after Rahman recorded his first song for movies. The music was an instant hit. The album was well-received by the critics and the masses. It was later listed in the '10 Best Soundtracks' of all time by *Time* magazine. The film was later released in Hindi, once again to box-office success. The Tamil version of the music album sold more than 200,000 units and the Hindi version more than 2.8 million units, making it one of the most successful debut film soundtracks in India. Rahman was just 26 at the time.

Nothing, they say, succeeds like success. The popularity of *Roja*'s music brought more work to Rahman from established directors. Ratnam signed him for *Bombay* (1995) and *Dil Se* (1998). In *Taal* (1999), he created raga-based music for a song *(Taal se taal milaao)*, and then remixed it with a fast-paced hip-hop beat to produce two distinct versions for the same lyrics. When *Lagaan: Once Upon a Time in India* (2001) did well, the world took notice of Rahman's music.

The English composer Andrew Lloyd Webber had seen the song *Chaiya Chaiya* from *Dil Se* on TV. He found the bhangra song filmed on the roof of a speeding train irresistible and refreshing. 'Musical theatre had become very predictable', Rahman says. 'I think Andrew felt that Bollywood musicals could be a new treat for the Western audience.'[4] Andrew signed up Rahman for *Bombay Dreams,* a musical which first released in London and then on Broadway. The musical was a success in the West End, but on Broadway it closed in eight months and failed to recoup its investment.

When the director Danny Boyle met Rahman for scoring music for a film based on the improbable story of a young man's journey from poverty to stardom, none of them could have predicted that they were going to make history together. Rahman liked the story Boyle told him and moved to London for six weeks to work on the music.[5] One of Boyle's parameters for the soundtrack was 'loud', put-on-your seat-belt kind of music (another was 'no cello'). The film went on to win eight of the ten Academy awards, including two for Rahman. He received the award for the Best Original Score and shared the award for the Best Original Song for the song *Jai Ho* from the film. The song raced up pop charts worldwide as its catchy dance beat shimmied across borders with ease, winning a Grammy for Rahman.

Despite his global fame and incredible popularity, Rahman remains humble and grounded. 'I don't need to be in the tabloids', he says. 'All I need is my music and my following where people listen to my music. They don't want to see my face. They just want to listen to my music.'[6] In 2010, he was honored with the Padma Bhushan.

ॐॐॐ

Sudarsan Pattnaik
Building Castles on Sand

When criticising China became fashionable during the global onslaught of Covid-19, the beach of Puri in the Indian state of Odisha hosted a beautiful sand sculpture expressing solidarity with China. 'Fight against coronavirus. We stand with China', the sculpture read.[1] Photographs of the sculpture appeared in newspapers around the world. Prominent people tweeted messages of appreciation, such as one from the Director-General of the World Health Organisation: 'Such a beautiful way to express solidarity to the people of #China during this challenging #2019nCoV outbreak. Thank you, @sudarsansand.' The thought-provoking sculpture was the handiwork of Sudarsan Pattnaik, an award-winning sand artist from India.

Sudarsan grew up very poor, fatherless. The family barely had enough to eat; school and education were luxuries they could not afford. No one talked about art or hobbies. 'My father had abandoned us and the little money that came into the house was from my grandmother's pension', Pattnaik said.[2]

At age nine, he went to work in a neighbour's house. This solved his food crisis, but the hours were long and the work tiring. One day, he went to the beach, and started playing with the sand. Like many kids, he made castles in the sand.

He enjoyed the castle-making, finding it cathartic. He may not have been able to live in a nice house and sleep in a nice bed, but at least he could make castles, even if only in the sand, to be washed away later when the tide came in.

He started making frequent visits to the beach, before and after his shift as a domestic worker. Some days he was on the beach as early as 4 am, so as not to upset his employer. No one stopped him. Sand was free and available in plenty. One does not need much to make things with sand. 'The beach was my canvas and my fingers, the brush. Water gave shape to my sculpture and the only colour needed was that of sand', he said.[3]

The sandcastles gradually became larger and more nuanced. People began to take notice. Some offered feedback and suggestions. The free advice and comments encouraged Sudarsan. 'I remember once being told by a tourist that the nose of a figure I sculpted was abnormally large. I went back to the beach for the next few days and made that figure over and over again till I got to hear that the nose was perfect' he shared.[4]

The local media began to highlight his art. A picture, they say, is worth a thousand words. Photos and images of Sudarsan's art on the beach resonated with people. The national media picked up on his story. Fortunately for him, the town of Puri, nearly 60 km from Bhubaneswar the capital city of Odisha, is a popular destination for Indian pilgrims, with tens of thousands of Indians visiting the Jagannath Temple annually. Sudarsan's artwork on the beach was available free on the beach for everyone to see and enjoy.

Sudarsan's growing popularity attracted other artists to him. He was able to buy his own place. He stopped working at the neighbour's house. Whenever there was a major event in the world, Sudarsan used his extraordinary creativity to sculpt it in the form of amazing sand art. Whether it was the assassination of Shinzo Abe of Japan, the presidentship of Barack Obama in the United States, World Water Day (March 22) or International Women's Day (March 8) Sudarsan would work his magic on the beach. On Christmas one year, he crafted a Santa Claus, fifty feet long and twenty-eight feet wide, with sand and 5400 roses. His sculpture of a thousand Santa Clauses on the Puri beach was titled, 'Bring Happiness to the World'. Considering his very limited schooling, his ability to make his art relevant and timely to global events is quite impressive.

When he made the world's largest sandcastle on Puri beach, Sudarsan made it to the Guinness Book of World Records. His work has got him into the Limca Book of World Records on several occasions. His sculpture highlighting the issue of drugs in sports, aptly titled 'Drugs Killed Sports', won him the gold medal at the World Sand Art Championship. He frequently represents India at global sand art competitions, winning many prizes over the years. The distinguishing feature of Sudarsan's sand sculptures is the use of creative expression to highlight a social message.

Sudarsan is a pioneer of sand art in India. What is even more amazing is that he did it on his own, without any formal training or guidance. As his fame grew, Sudarsan also started the Sand Art Institute of Puri to teach young men and women about sand art. His students often help him with crafting the sculptures on Puri beach, and some of them have gone on to have productive careers of their own.

Few people in India had heard of sand art before the media started covering Sudarsan's work. Legend has it that the tradition of sand art may go back hundreds of years in Odisha. Because sand art, by its very nature, is temporary, there are no records of beach sculptures in Odisha's history. There are some stories passed down generations about beautiful sand art depicting religious figures and themes. It was, however, not until Sudarsan Pattnaik came on the scene that sand sculptures began getting national attention and fame. 'For about sixteen to seventeen years', Sudarsan says, 'I worked hard to make sand sculpting popular because this was an art form that was hardly known in those days.'[5] When asked for advice for the next generation, Sudarsan offers: 'Whatever you do in life, do it with passion and dedication. Never underestimate yourselves or what you can achieve if you set your heart to it.'[6] In 2014, Sudarsan was honoured with the Padma Shri.

Naresh Chander Lal
Theater Wunderkind

The Andaman and Nicobar Islands have the enviable honour of being the first Indian territory to gain independence from British occupation. Naresh Chander Lal became the first—and only—person from the islands to graduate from the National School of Drama (NSD), the foremost school for theatre training in India. Born into a family of performers (his grandfather was a folk singer and his father was a street performer), Naresh is a film-maker and theatre personality born and raised on the islands.

Naresh gained critical acclaim with his film *Gandhi: The Mahatma*.[1] Mahatma Gandhi never visited the Andaman and Nicobar Islands. Naresh's film is a fictitious story about what happens when four students from a local Andamanese school decide to skip the scheduled visit to the Cellular Jail (the infamous prison where the British occupiers held the most dangerous freedom fighters) for a walk on the beach only to cross paths with Gandhi. The young students think that the Gandhi they are meeting is an impersonator dressed for a 'fancy dress' competition in their school. Gandhi then takes them on a trip around the islands, to show them that wherever there is truth, non-violence, and honesty, they will find Gandhi. The movie was received well by the audience, bringing much acclaim to Naresh.

From a young age, Naresh was worked with his father in local plays on the islands. Impressed with the work of young Naresh, someone told him about the NSD and the possibility of studying there. Naresh and his father had never before heard of the NSD. Encouraged by the possibility of learning theatre professionally, Naresh applied to the NSD and was accepted. However, his father had second thoughts about sending Naresh to study there. Concerned about limited career opportunities for professional theatre artists, his father felt that studying at the NSD would not be very useful for Naresh. Father and son decided to decline the NSD admission.

Naresh spent the next few years working in the local theatre on the islands. He also held a full-time job with the island government. While Naresh enjoyed theatre, the earnings were not enough to provide for a family. After a decade-and-a-half, Naresh again applied to the NSD. By now, he had understood that professional training was needed if he wanted to do well in theatre. Once again, he got in, but life had other plans for him. Three months into his first year at the NSD, Naresh was told that his scholarship from the state government was not enough to keep him at the institution, and so he had to leave. Naresh was disappointed, to say the least.

Having seen the financial hardships of his father in local theatre on the islands, Naresh was discouraged. 'By now I was determined to get into the NSD and learn there', he said in an interview.[2] He reached out to many influential people, including the then Minister of State for Human Resources. She advised him to apply for a special scheme run by the Government of India called the 'Scholarship to Young Workers in Different Cultural Fields'. After Naresh received the scholarship, he applied again to the NSD. Finally, more than 17 years after his first brush with the NSD, Naresh was studying at India's premier training institute.

The first six months at the NSD were difficult for him.

Many times during that period he wanted to quit and go back to the islands. However, the embarrassment he would have to face if he went back without completing the program was a deterrent. So, Naresh decided to stay and put his heart and soul into the program. 'I very much enjoyed the NSD program. To be honest, I think no one else enjoyed NSD as much as I did.' He learned all aspects of theatre at the NSD, specialising in direction. When many of his colleagues were opting for acting, Naresh preferred direction as he thought it would help him contribute to developing theatre on the islands. 'I had only Andaman in my mind when I decided to focus on direction at the NSD. As someone from an economically challenged area, I thought direction would help me contribute to highlighting and addressing the issues of Andaman.'

After completing the programme at the NSD, Naresh went back to the islands where he did several plays for which he received several awards and much recognition. Naresh then decided to learn the art of film making under the renowned director Umesh Mehra. 'I see Umesh Mehra as my guru. If he had not taken me as an assistant director in his company, I would not be able to get to this stage in life. I learned a lot from him', Naresh said years later. Naresh had a chance to work with many stalwarts of the Indian film industry, including directors shooting their films on the island. 'I learned all aspects of film making during this time, working from production manager to assistant manager. I believe a director needs to also learn about production. If a director understands the production side, he will be able to keep his own film within budget. This is something I didn't know then, but I understood this later when I tried to make my own film.'[3]

Naresh's work in theatre and films brought positive attention to the islands he calls home. He also founded the Andaman People Theatre Association to nurture and promote local talent.[4] In 2016, the Government of India conferred upon him the Padma Shri award for his contribution to theatre and film. 'My works were always based on the islands' culture and I tried my best to project the islands' unity amidst diversity through my films and dramas. It is the love of the people that I have been chosen for this award and I dedicate this to the islanders', Naresh said.[5]

☙❧☙

Ram Narayan
Shaping the Soulful Resonance of Classical Indian Music

By the time he stepped onto the stage of Jehangir Hall in Mumbai (then Bombay) at the age of 27, Ram Narayan had been playing the *sarangi* – known as the bowed fiddle of India – for more than 20 years. It was his first solo recital for a large audience. The main performance at the concert was a *jugalbandi* (duet), and Ram Narayan was playing before it. The audience, looking forward to the jugalbandi, hissed and booed Ram Narayan off the stage.

The experience at Jehangir Hall devastated Ram Narayan. For days, he could not eat or sleep. He wanted to quit playing the instrument that had been his life for over two decades. After much contemplation, he decided to persevere and continue. It was another two years before he could get back on the stage, but this time the audience responded favourably. From there, Ram Narayan never looked back, earning the respect of listeners and critics alike. In the early 60s, he gave up accompanying other performers and did only solo shows. Following the famous sitar player Pandit Ravi Shankar, who had performed successfully in the West, Ram Narayan also toured Europe and North America for concerts where he was the main act. He emancipated the sarangi from its confined environment, turned it into a solo instrument, and made it known to the world at large.

Ram Narayan was born on 25 December 1927 in a small village near the city of Udaipur in the northwestern state of Rajasthan. His forefathers were singers at the royal court of Udaipur. His father, who was a farmer by profession, knew how to play the *dilruba*, a relatively unknown Indian musical instrument that is reputed to have been invented by Guru Gobind Singh, the tenth and last guru of Sikhism. When Ram Narayan was around five, he found a sarangi that had been left at their house by a holy man. His father repaired the sarangi and gave him a few lessons.[1] At the time, Udaipur had many sarangi players, so Ram Narayan had seen people play the instrument. Within a fortnight, he could play in tune.[2]

'My father, Nathuji Biawat, was not a professional musician. He played a little *dilruba*, but somehow taught me the correct fingering technique for sarangi. This was a unique gift, and, thanks to this, I progressed as fast as I did...I could play things with ease, which other sarangi players, using different fingering systems, were unable to produce. For that, I give all credit to my father', Ram Narayan reminisces.

A critical turning point in Ram Narayan's life came when he was about 15 years old. By then, he had trained under a well-respected sarangi player of Udaipur and with a wandering singer travelled around the countryside. He was teaching music in a school, earning INR 50 monthly. It may not seem much today, but in the 1940s, it was enough to give Ram Narayan a decent life in Udaipur. One day, the wandering singer—his former teacher—Madhav Prasad turned up in Udaipur. 'What are you upto these days?' asked Prasad. 'I am teaching music and earning a lot of money', Ram Narayan responded. 'Well, if you go on like this, every year your salary will increase by five or ten rupees, and after a few years you will earn Rupees 75. Then you will get married, and ultimately when you retire, you will perhaps earn Rupees 300. But as a musician you will be somebody!' Prasad told him. The truth of this statement resonated with Ram Narayan. When he resigned the teaching job to leave with Prasad to perform around the country as a wandering musician, Ram Narayan made an unconventional decision that was to change the course of his life.

Another turning point for Ram Narayan came in 1948 when he was accompanying Ustad Amir Khan, one of the most influential Indian vocalists in the Hindustani classical tradition. Classical music in India is divided into two main traditions: Hindustani in North India and Carnatic in southern India. At some point during the performance, Ram Narayan decided to switch from being an accompanist to leading the performance, forcing the famed vocalist to adapt to his playing. Most musicians applauded his effort, but the singers demanded that the accompanist be subdued. Years later, Ram Narayan looked back at that performance and explained, 'I thought if there is so much music in me, why should I stay in the background?' It would be several years – and many rejections – before Ram Narayan was accepted as the main player in a concert.

Ram Narayan was also way ahead of his time in terms of the place of women in classical music. Women were historically absent from Indian classical music, and the sarangi's association with courtesans and nautch-girls made it a taboo instrument for women from good families. Nevertheless, Ram Narayan trained his daughter to play the instrument that had historically been the domain of men. She in turn credits her father's open-mindedness and systematic teaching technique for her learning to play the sarangi.[3]

Sarangi, which means the instrument of 'a hundred singing colours', is the only bowed instrument in the Hindustani tradition of Indian classical music. It is played upright (like a cello) with a heavy, arched bow as the fingertips of the left-hand slide along the sides of strings made of gut. With three melody strings and 33 sympathetic strings, the sarangi is a difficult instrument; instead of choosing notes by pressing down the strings on the neck, as on a violin, the player presses upward with a fingernail.[4] The consensus among musicians is that playing the sarangi is technically and musically demanding, more so for those like Ram Narayan who choose to play solo. Despite his impressive success, Ram Narayan remains humble as he advises the next generation seeking to make a name in this profession: 'One who thinks he is great, who thinks he has nothing more to learn, is no good.'[5]

Ram Narayan was recognised with the Padma Shri (1976), Padma Bhushan (1991), and Padma Vibhushan (2005). Neither age nor success has dimmed his passion for the sarangi. The eponymous Pandit Ram Narayan Foundation which he started in order to promote the instrument—often referred to as the 'queen of all musical instruments'—awards scholarships to young and upcoming sarangi players.

Naseeruddin Shah
Masterful Actor of Film and Theater

His parents thought he was going to end up a complete failure, perhaps become a struggling cricketer. For a long time, it seemed he was going to prove them right, until he began to realise he loved acting on the stage and the audience seemed to respond well when he performed.[1] Having found his love for acting, Naseer joined the National School of Drama (NSD), from there went to the Film and Television Institute of India (FTII), and then to roles in the film industry. In 1987, he was conferred the Padma Shri, and in 2003, the Padma Bhushan.

Many successful people like to say that they were not good in school. So, when one learns that Naseer was a bad student growing up, it is not immediately clear how bad he really was. He failed Class IX thrice (in different schools), and the only reason he was able to stay in school was his father's influence with the local administration. When he did not know the answers to any questions in trigonometry, he penned a short note for the examiner: 'If you know the answers, why ask me? And if you don't, how do you expect me to?' The examiner, clearly not amused by the answer, gave him a failing grade.

The iconic entrepreneur Steve Jobs famously advised

young people to find something they loved to do, and then put their heart into doing it. Some find their passion early on in their life, while others struggle to find it. For Naseer, the moment of finding his passion came sometime in Class 12 at St. Anselm's School in Ajmer. Each class was asked to produce a half-hour play with the best ones to be staged on the school's annual day. No one else in his class came up with any ideas, except for Naseer who suggested they enact scenes from William Shakespeare's *Merchant of Venice*, with himself in the role of Shylock. Naseer's team did not win the competition (they came second), but was appreciated by the audience, and Naseer had found something he enjoyed and wanted to spend more time doing.

Just because Naseer had found he loved acting, it did not mean he was going to be able to make it there. Frustrated with the pressure at home, Naseer ran away to Bombay with dreams of becoming a successful film star. He did manage to get work as an extra in some films *(Aman* (1967) and *Sapnon ka Saudaagar* (1968), for example), but it was not enough to pay for food or boarding.[2] It was clear things were not going his way. Before he could starve, one of his father's friends found him living on the streets, put him on the train back to Meerut (and from where he took a bus-ride to his parents' house in Sardhana, a small town in the Indian state of Uttar Pradesh that dates back to the time of the Mahabharta), where his mother had been crying for days for her son.

Naseer's father wanted him to be a doctor or an engineer. Naseer had neither the interest nor the capability for medical or technical studies. His father's connections helped him get into Aligarh Muslim University to study arts. During his time at the university, Naseer came across some plays staged by the NSD, which he learned was a place where you could study acting and get a monthly stipend. So, after finishing up at Aligarh, he joined the NSD where he did more plays in two years than he had ever done before in his entire life. As his time at the NSD started coming to an end, Naseer became worried about his future. He did not want to go back to his home-town to do theatre, join the Song and Drama division of the Information and Broadcasting Ministry, get a teaching job in a school, find employment in radio or on TV, or work for the repertoire company at the NSD, the paths that most graduates of the nation's prestigious drama school followed.

Around this time, Naseer happened to watch a family drama movie, where all the lead actors had graduated from FTII. It reminded him of the advice he had gotten from others who had recommended the acting course at FTII when he had knocked on their doors for roles. So, he appeared for the entrance test at FTII, got in, and went there for two years. Towards the end, the FTII director and eminent playwright Girish Karnad recommended Naseer to the film-maker Shyam Benegal for a movie he was making. The movie, later named *Nishant,* went onto win the 1977 National Film Award for Best Feature Film in Hindi. Naseer's work in the film was noticed, but only by the critics. No film offers came his way. He auditioned for a newsreader's position on Doordarshan, only to be rejected.

Naseer's FTII colleagues would not have been surprised by his struggle to find work. 'When I was studying at the film institute, I was this student who was given the least chance of succeeding in the film industry', Naseer shared in an interview many years later.[3] Small roles in films followed. It was not until *Sparsh* was released in 1980, that Naseer could claimed to have found a footing in the film industry.

He went on to star in many critically acclaimed Hindi films, such as *Ardh Satya* (1983) and the cult comedy *Jaane Bhi Do Yaaron* (1983). Naseer also starred in many Hindi commercial blockbusters, including *Karma* (1986) and *Tridev* (1989). Yet, Naseer often downplays the parts he has played in commercially successfully movies, preferring instead to talk about the movies that endeared him more to the critics.

When asked to give advice to aspiring actors, Naseer offers that they need to identify their own strengths. 'Try to identify the things which are most essential to you as an actor.'[4] Too many youngsters, he believes, try to copy established actors. Instead of trying to be someone else, they should explore the kind of roles they would be good at as not all actors have the same strengths.

Shiv Kumar Sharma
Santoor Virtuoso

'My story is different from that of other classical musicians', Shiv Kumar Sharma said in an interview. 'While they had to prove their mettle, their talent, their caliber, I had to prove the worth of my instrument. I had to fight for it.'[1] The instrument that made Shiv famous globally was the *santoor*. Before he started playing the *santoor*, the instrument was little known outside Kashmir. Even there it was used only to play a genre of Kashmiri classical music with Persian, Central Asian and Indian roots. Over a long career that spanned seven decades, Shiv propelled the *santoor* onto the world stage, at concerts and recitals in India and around the globe.[2]

Shiv was born on 13 January 1938 in Jammu to Pandit Uma Dutt Sharma and Kesar Devi. His father was a respected vocalist, who came from a family of royal priests. By the time Shiv was born, Uma Dutt had a music school where he taught young children. It was here that Shiv started learning how to sing and play the *tabla* at a very young age. Training with his father also kept Shiv out of trouble and away from the rough boys in the neighbourhood. Even as a child, Shiv would spend hours immersed in music, practicing various instruments in the school. 'There was an obsessive element in my attitude to music even then', Shiv said. 'It was the air I breathed, the reason I lived.'[3]

By age nine, Shiv was an accomplished tabla player, performing on Radio Jammu. In those days, performing on radio was held in very high esteem; only the best musicians were invited for a radio performance. Because of his father's connections and his talent, Shiv also accompanied leading musicians who visited Jammu to do live shows and public performances.

When Shiv was 14, his father gave him a *santoor* and practically charged his teenage son with the mission of elevating the instrument's stature. Shiv was not happy about learning the new instrument his father had brought him. His father was undeterred. 'Mark my words, son', his father told him. 'Shiv Kumar Sharma and the *santoor* will become synonymous in years to come. Have the courage to start something from scratch. You will be recognised as a pioneer.'

Santoor is a trapezoidal wooden instrument whose strings stretch over 25 wooden bridges, played with slim wooden mallets. Playing any instrument well is difficult. The santoor is a particularly challenging instrument to play. It is quite difficult to sustain notes and perform the *meends,* or glides from one note to another, which are essential to the Hindustani musical tradition.

Shiv's first major public performance on the santoor was in 1955, at the Haridas Sangeet Sammelan festival in Bombay (now Mumbai). At 17, he was the youngest participant in the festival. The organisers reluctantly allowed him 30 minutes to play the instrument of his choice, tabla or santoor. He played the santoor for a full hour — to thunderous applause. He was invited back for another recital the next day. While his performance also landed him an offer to make the background score of the famous director V. Shantaram's film, critics were quick to point out the santoor's drawbacks.

The santoor that Shiv's father had gifted him was quite limiting as it was designed for Kashmiri music. Critics and purists alike derided the staccato sound of the santoor, urging him to switch to another instrument. Shiv redesigned the santoor to enable it to play more notes per octave. He modified the seventy-string dulcimer—expanding its range to three full octaves and creating a smoother glissando to allow the player to sustain and slide between notes in emulation of the human voice. Shiv's 100-string santoor was much more suitable for the complex ragas, the melodic framework of Hindustani music, than the one he had got from his father.[4]

Shiv was around twenty-two when he had a bitter argument with his father. Uma Dutt worked at Radio Jammu and as a priest at the royal temple to provide for his family. He wanted his son to do the same. Shiv had also got an offer to work full-time at Radio Jammu, but he wanted to give his full attention to music practice (or *riyaz*). When Shiv refused the job offer, his father told him to leave the house and prove himself. Shiv accepted the challenge and moved to Bombay with INR 500 in his pocket.[5]

Finding work in Bombay proved to be more challenging than Shiv had expected. He did some work for Radio Bombay, but had no regular income. It was not until he started getting work from the film industry that his financial situation improved. During this time, he got offers to act in films, all of which he turned down because he wanted to focus on his music.

Shiv released several albums, beginning with *Call of the Valley* (1967), a collaboration with the acclaimed flautist Pandit Hariprasad Chaurasia and the guitarist Brij Bhushan Kabra. Thereafter, he joined hands with Hariprasad as Shiv-Hari and composed music for their first Hindi film, *Silsila* (1981). Although the movie was not a commercial success at the time, the music became widely popular. 'We had no idea Silsila's music would catch on the way it did'. Shiv reminisced years later, 'I remember when Yash Chopra asked me and

Pandit Hari Prasad Chaurasia to compose music for Silsila, everyone thought he was taking a big risk by signing classical musicians. There is a difference between classical and film music. And it was a tremendous challenge to live up to (film music).' The pair gave music for several other films, including *Chandni* (1989), *Lamhe* (1991) and *Darr* (1993), successfully straddling the worlds of classical and popular music.

Shiv is a recipient of some of India's highest honours, including the Padma Shri in 1991 and the Padma Vibhushan in 2001. He also teaches santoor to the next generation, but does not charge his students any fee. He credits his father with the advice that shaped his work: 'Pay no heed to sweet words of flattery. Listen to your inner voice. Be your own judge. Strive to better your last performance. Always remain humble.'

888

Amitabh Bachchan
The Living Legend of Hindi Cinema

Amitabh Bachchan was born on 11 October 1942 in Allahabad, in present day Uttar Pradesh. His father, Harivansh Rai Bachchan, was a famous Hindi poet and his mother, Teji Bachchan, was a social activist. Though he was born in a family with the surname Srivastava, a Hindu surname common enough in North India, his father used to write poetry under the pen name 'Bachchan' (meaning child-like). Thus, when the time came to be enrolled in a school, Amitabh was given the surname Bachchan.

Amitabh Bachchan completed his secondary schooling from Allahabad and was then enrolled at Sherwood College in Nainital, a hill station in present day Uttarakhand, for higher secondary education. He went on to obtain a Bachelor of Science degree from Kirori Mal College in Delhi in the year 1962. From 1962 to 1969, Bachchan tried his hand at different things but was unsuccessful. He was auditioned for the role of a news reader at All India Radio[1] but was not selected. He worked briefly as a Business Executive at a company called *Bird and Company* in Kolkata and also worked in theatre for some time.

Bachchan's first break in cinema came in the year 1969 when he was offered the role of a narrator in Mrinal Sen's[2] award-winning film *Bhuvan Shome*. Between 1969 and 1972, Bachchan acted in fourteen films out of which twelve were flops and two were hits, namely *Bombay to Goa* in 1972, in which he played the lead role and *Anand* in 1971 in which he played the role of a supporting actor. The years were difficult and by the age of 30, Bachchan was seen as a newcomer who had failed.

However, things changed for Bachchan when the scriptwriter duo Salim Khan and Javed Akhtar, better known as Salim-Javed, spotted Bachchan's talent and wrote the script of the movie *Zanjeer*. The duo was looking for an actor who could play the role of an 'angry young man'. *Zanjeer* was a crime-based movie, whereas most of the films being made at that time in the industry were romantic films.[3] They were unable to find any popular actor of that time who could play the role and eventually they stumbled upon Amitabh Bachchan. The film happened, and the rest is, as they say, history. Bachchan won his first nomination for the Filmfare award[4] for the Best Actor for this movie. The film not only introduced a new hero to the industry, it also brought with it a new acting phenomenon called the 'angry young man'.[5]

Success followed and Bachchan went on to give one superb performance after another in movies such as *Deewar* (1975), *Sholay* (1975), *Trishul* (1978), *Kaala Pathar* (1979) and *Shakti* (1982). He married a Hindi movie star, Jaya Bhaduri, in 1973 and also did films together. *Deewar* has been nominated as one of the 'top 25 Bollywood movies of all time'[6] and *Sholay* was nominated as the 'film of the millennium' in 1999 by BBC. Sholay is the highest inflation-adjusted grosser of all time and the biggest hit in Indian cinema history.[7] These and other movies consolidated Bachchan's reputation as one of the biggest stars of Indian cinema, and also that of the world.

Bachchan took a break from cinema in 1984 and entered politics. He joined the Congress party and contested the Allahabad seat in the 8th Lok Sabha. However, his tenure in politics was short lived. The news linked him to the Bofors scandal[8] that also rocked the Rajiv Gandhi[9] government at that time. Bachchan resigned from his seat and also filed and fought a lawsuit in London. Bachchan won the lawsuit, cleared his name from the Bofors scandal, and received an apology from the journalists accusing him of wrong-doing.[10] However, after this incident, Bachchan moved away from politics for good.

In 1994, Bachchan decided to form the Amitabh Bachchan Corporation Limited (ABCL) that would deal in film production, distribution and event management. While the corporation was successful initially, its forays into film production and event management—it put up the 1996 Miss World contest— went horribly wrong. Bachchan ended up losing money. To fund the growth of the organisation, Bachchan took loans from a bank on personal guarantee. By March 1999, the losses exceed the company's net worth and the creditors came calling to recover their loans. It was the darkest time in Bachchan's life and he was about to lose his house in Mumbai.[11]

'I had a huge financial failure in the corporation that I began. It went bankrupt and it bankrupted me. You sit back and think "What can I do?" and I said, "You are an actor. Go back to acting." So, that's what I did', recollects Bachchan.[12] He then went to Yash Chopra, the director-producer with whom he had worked before and asked for work. He acted in one of the biggest hit movies of his career, *Mohabbatein*, that was released in the year 2002. At around the same time, he also started hosting the quiz show, *Kaun Banega Crorepati*, the Indian adaptation of the British show, *Who Wants to be a Millionaire?* The show became a massive hit and broke many records in terms of viewership. Overtime, Bachchan went back to acting and starred in a number of hits.

Referred to variously as the *Shahenshah* of Bollywood—a

title from his *Shahenshah* (1988)—and also the *Shatabdi ka Mahanayak,* 'Most noteworthy entertainer of the century', a Star of the Millennium, or Big B, Bachchan has acted in more than 200 Indian movies in a career spanning more than five decades, and has won various honours in his profession. In 1999, he was voted the Greatest Star of Stage or Screen by the BBC.[13]

The Government of India honoured him with the Padma Shri in 1984, the Padma Bhushan in 2001 and the Padma Vibhushan in 2015 for his contributions to the arts. The Government of France honoured him with its highest civilian honour, Knight of the Legion of Honour, in 2007 for his exceptional career in the world of cinema and beyond.

☙❦❧

Kattassery Joseph Yesudas
A Voice Gifted by God

A voice so perfect that it could have come down only from the heavens. That is how those familiar with the singing of Kattassery Joseph Yesudas (or, more commonly, Yesudas) describe him. 'Touched by God' in the words of Bappi Lahiri, the popular Indian musician.[1] In the music industry, they call him *Gana Gandharvan* (Celestial Singer or Angel of Music).

Yesudas was born in 1940 in Kochi to a Latin Catholic Christian family. His father Augustine Joseph was a well-known Malayalam classical musician and stage actor. Yesudas started training under his father from a young age, and his talent was strengthened and polished under various gurus (teachers). As Yesudas explained in an interview:

> At the age of five I started to be really interested in music. My first ideal was my father Augustine Joseph Bagavathor. I really respect him as a teacher and as a person. In those days it was very difficult for someone not being Hindu to learn classical Indian Carnatic music. ... It is only through my father's efforts and the strict methods of my gurus that I gained much strength and courage.

Despite his talent and training, success did not come

easy to Yesudas. He was rejected by All India Radio in Thiruvananthapuram, as well as by many other institutions and film studios whose rounds he did in Chennai. Looking for a break, he got in touch with the Kalabhavan at Ernakulam, which encouraged upcoming artistes by organising stage performances. It was here that he met Raman Nambiyath, the producer who introduced Yesudas as a playback singer in the Malyalam film *Kaalpaadukal*. 'The director and composer had apprehensions about giving the newcomer a break, as he had not yet recovered from a bout of fever. However, I made it clear to them that I was ready to bear any loss caused by him singing in my film', Nambiyath recalled years later.[2] The film flopped, but Yesudas was noticed for his singing. From there, Yesudas never looked back.

A few years after his introduction in the Malyalam movie, Yesudas got his break in Hindi films. Once again, there were challenges and obstacles. The first two Hindi films in which Yesudas did playback singing failed to release. The 1976 film *Chhoti Si Baat* (starring Amol Palekar and Vidya Sinha) was the first film where Hindi music lovers heard Yesudas singing. Next year came *Chit Chor* (starring Amol Palekar and Zarina Wahab), which had some of the most popular Hindi songs by Yesudas.

Over a career spanning about six decades, Yesudas is believed to have recorded more than 70,000 songs in various languages: Malayalam, Kannada, Hindi, Tamil, Telugu, Odia, Marathi, and Bengali, as well as Russian, Arabic, and English, among others. His singing has been recognised for a record eight times with the National Film Award for Best Male Playback Singer in three languages (Telugu, Hindi, and Malayalam), the first time in 1972 and most recently in 2017. He has received the Kerala State Film Award for Best Singer a record 25 times, including several times in a row (such as every year from 1979 to 1986 and from 1993 to 1998). At one point,

Yesudas requested the Kerala government to not consider him for the prestigious state award he had won repeatedly, so that young talent could be recognised and appreciated. The Kerala government, however, ignored his request and continued to honour him with the award, which he won most recently in 2014. Interestingly, the 2018 Kerala State Film Award for Best Playback Singer Male went to Vijay Yesudas, the second son of Yesudas.

The list of state awards and private honours (such as the Filmfare award for Best Playback Singer) is too long to mention here. Indeed, there is a whole Wikipedia page dedicated to the awards and nominations received by Yesudas. He received the Padma Shri in 1975, the Padma Bhushan in 2002 and the Padma Vibhushan in 2017. His first major award was in 1969, when he was recognised as the Kerala State Film Best Playback Singer Male Award, and his most recent award was in 2019 when he received the C R Kesavan Vaidyar Award. At the award ceremony in 2019, T P Sreenivasan, the former diplomat turned author, had this to say about the famed singer:

> Giving awards to Yesudas is like making offers to God. We do it for our own satisfaction and sense of duty, as he is beyond the stage of counting his awards and trophies. It makes no difference to him whether it is a handful of flowers or a bag of diamonds we offer to him. His smile and blessings are showered on every one regardless of our wealth and rank. He honours us with his presence and favours us by accepting whatever we offer.[3]

Yesudas married Prabha in 1970. She was eighteen at the time, he was thirty. They have three children together, all boys, of which only one (Vijay) is a professional singer. By all accounts, Yesudas and Prabha have had a happy married life. As Prabha said, 'I thank God for every moment that I spend with him. Though he gets angry pretty easily, it doesn't last long. He gets emotional very easily as he approaches everything with so much honesty.'[4]

Two things stand out about Yesudas, the singer. First, his success, which is a direct result of his talent, hardwork, and dedication to music. Second, the sheer length of time that he has been able to stay at the top of his game. Few people achieve the kind of success he has, and very few can sustain such high levels of success for so long. What is the secret to his spectacular success and its longevity? His passion for music. His wife Prabha shares the secret: 'Music is his first wife. I and the kids come only after that. Like him, we too adore his first wife.'[5] As for Yesudas, the person, it is impressive how he has managed to stay away from controversies. There is no fodder for his critics, no trash-talk or unsavory actions covered in the media to tarnish his clean image.

One of the most popular songs by Yesudas is the devotional *Harivarasanam*, which has been played at the Sabrimala Temple in Kerala for decades at the close of the day. There is a saying that Lord Ayyappan, the presiding deity of the temple, goes to sleep listening to Yesudas singing the Sanskrit hymn (Check it out on youtube, if you want to hear Yesudas's soothing voice).[6]

☙❦❧

Teejan Bai
Retelling Epics

In this day and age, where individuals are failing to remember their conventional practices and see it as something retrogressive and are willing to modernise themselves as well as other people around them, Teejan bai checked out customary workmanship as well as praised her social roots in a manner that brought laurels for her and for the country on different platforms. Teejan bai was born on 8 August 1956 in Ganiyari village, fourteen kilometres to the north of Bhilai in Chattisgarh and belonged to the 'Pardhi' scheduled tribe of the state.

Teejan bai was the eldest among five siblings and took a liking to the Mahabharata when she heard her maternal grandfather, Brijlal Pardhi, singing the epic in the Hindi version composed by Sabal Singh Chauhan, a Chattisgarhi author. She memorised a lot of the Mahabharata and started performing at different places. Though, she had been blessed with a melodious voice, she had to overcome numerous difficulties to practice and pursue what she really loved.

Teejan Bai performs the *Pandavani* in which she recounts stories from the Mahabharata, with melodic intonation. She followed conventional practices but also added innovations to them, making her the first female singing in the *Vedmati Shaili* (style) of Pandavani. In contrast to the traditional approach, Teejan bai performs standing so that anyone can hear her normal throaty voice and inimitable verve, entering what was till then a male stronghold.

Pandavani, in a real sense, implies accounts of Pandavas, the sons of Pandu in the Mahabharata who fought against injustice and emerged victorious. Teejan bai sings stories of the Pandavas with a *tambura*[1] in one hand and at times a *kartal*[2] in the other. As the presentation progresses, the tambura turns into her main prop, at times to embody a mace of Bhima,[3] or Arjuna's[4] bow or chariot, while on another occasion it turns into the hair of Draupadi,[5] permitting her to play different persons effortlessly and with openness. Some of her acclaimed exhibitions are the stories of 'Draupadi's *cheerharan* (disrobing)', 'Dushasana *Vadh* (killing)' and the 'Mahabharata *Yudh* (war)'.

Belonging to a family of bird catchers, who then moved to making mats and brushes and eventually to farm labour, Teejan Bai's life has been difficult. Teejan Bai was married at the age of twelve and was expelled from the 'Pardhi' community for singing the Mahabharata being a woman. She constructed a small hut for herself and started living on borrowed utensils and food from the neighbours. She left her first husband, filed for a divorce and never went back.

Teejan Bai's second marriage was not peaceful either. 'People called me characterless because I sang and danced in public. My second husband used to beat me. What could be more painful for an artist than not being able to perform. I can never forget that difficult path I have left behind', remembers Teejan Bai.[6] She remained determined and strong and this eventually led to success.

At the young age of thirteen, Teejan Bai gave her first exhibition on a stop-gap stage in an adjoining town for a meagre amount of INR 10. Her performance left the audience spellbound and requests for similar performances started coming in from different places. Her big break came when Habib Tanvir, a noted theater character from Madhya Pradesh, saw her ability and invited her to perform before Indira Gandhi, the then Prime Minister of India.

Teejan Bai became famous over time and took part in celebrations of Indian culture and traditions organised in different parts of India and around the world. Beginning in the 1980s, she travelled all around the world as a social and cultural envoy to countries such as Britain, France, Switzerland, Germany, Turkey, Tunisia, Malta, Cyprus, Romania and Mauritius. 'It is heartening for me to take an Indian heritage like the Mahabharata outside my country, to people who have no understanding of the epic. I feel so happy with their response, when I am requested to repeat my performance twice or thrice at one go', she says enthusiastically.[7] Teejan Bai has performed stories from the Mahabharata in Shyam Benegal's[8] acclaimed Doordarshan[9] television series *'Bharat Ek Khoj'* that was based on Jawaharlal Nehru's[10] book, the *Discovery of India*.

Recognising Teejan Bai for her contributions to Indian culture, the Government of India conferred the Padma Shri on her in 1988, the Padma Bhushan in 2003, and the Padma Vibhushan in 2019. She was also awarded the Sangeet Natak Akademi Award in 1995 by the Sangeet Natak Akademi, the country's national academy of dance, music and drama.

Through her unique and indomitable style, Teejan Bai uses her art to portray the difficulties that women like her have to confront in our society. 'My favourite story is *Draupadi cheerharan*. Through this story I want to tell people not to commit atrocities against women. Otherwise, they'll face the fate that befell the *Kauravas*', she says.[11]

It is the sheer energy of her melodious and rustic style of rendition that add to Teejan Bai's charm and charisma. Without thinking twice about the strict worth of the Mahabharata, she has kept on adding fascinating developments. Her accounts are entwined with informal shoptalk where she likewise sings, moves, yells and conveys exchanges through the exhibition. It is her red-hot style that adds to Teejan Bai's mystique. Though she says, 'I don't have the foggiest idea what happens to me when I'm in front of an audience', her fiery exhibition is amazing enough to draw metropolitan elitists into her provincial rhythms.[12] Considerably more than anything else, it is for reminding us the great history *(itihass)* and traditions of our country that Teejan Bai will be best remembered for.

Manoj Bajpayee
A Chameleonic Artist

The idiom 'Try, try and try again until you succeed' is very well known. Unfortunately, it did not seem to have worked for Manoj Bajpayee. Born in the small village of Belwa in Bihar, Manoj wanted to be an actor since childhood. He decided that his chances of becoming an actor would be higher if he got into the National School of Drama (NSD), the premier institution for acting training in the country. He moved to Delhi, got admission to a college, and started doing theatre with a group run by a professor from Satyawati College in Delhi University. After completing his undergraduate studies, he applied to the NSD, but failed to get in. So, he tried again next year. He was rejected again. Not one to give up, he tried again the year after. Rejected again! Manoj was down, but he was not yet done. He applied again, and NSD rejected him, again.[1]

After the first rejection, Manoj was devastated. At one point, he thought of ending his life. As the pain of rejection faded over the next few weeks, as it usually does, he joined a one-year acting program with a theatre group in Delhi. After completing the training program, Manoj appeared again for the NSD entrance exam, which he failed to qualify. By now, several theatre groups were interested in having Manoj act in plays. In addition, Manoj started learning the semi-classical *Chhau* dance popular in the states of Bihar, West Bengal, and Orissa. 'I would train two to three hours every day in an open-air theatre to learn Chhau. This went on for three or four years', Manoj explains.[2]

He devoted himself to learning, working hard to acquire the nuances of acting and the traditional dance-form. Yet, NSD rejected Manoj again the next year. 'By the time, it was the third year, I was used to rejection. Even NSD professors were surprised why I was trying even after getting rejected so many times. My thinking was life would be easier if I was in NSD. I wanted to learn at NSD. But when I didn't get in, I started working hard on the outside. In addition, the amount of time I spent in the NSD library, there is probably no one who used it so much. My life in Delhi revolved around theatre. I never even went to see the Qutub Minar in Delhi. I was focused on learning the skill and craft of acting.'

After getting rejected thrice from the NSD, Manoj turned to Barry John's theatre group.[3] Today, Barry John is famous in India for having trained the likes of Shah Rukh Khan, Freida Pinto, Rana Daggubati, Varun Dhawan, and Jacqueline Fernandez. British by birth, Barry was already well-known among the theatre crowd in Delhi by the time Manoj crossed paths with him. Barry had seen Manoj in a popular play and had been so impressed with his acting that he offered to train Manoj. Once again, Manoj devoted himself fully to acting. After a while, Barry allowed him to act in outside plays. Manoj formed his own acting group, to stage plays.

Around this time, Manoj applied again to the NSD. They rejected him again, but offered him a teaching position. However, Manoj wanted to act on stage and not teach acting to aspiring actors. His dream to act in films seemed to be going nowhere, when suddenly—as if from nowhere—he was offered a role in the movie *Bandit Queen* (1994). The role he got was not the one he had been promised initially, but it did get him on the big screen.[4]

By the time the shooting finished, Manoj had decided to relocate to Mumbai, thinking that producers would be looking for him. Unfortunately, his film role went largely unnoticed. Manoj worked small roles in shows and movies. The next few years were difficult as Manoj had neither money nor opportunities. There were times when Manoj felt lost and helpless, but many of his friends encouraged him to keep going. During this time, the well-known filmmaker Mahesh Bhatt noticed his acting and gave him work, first in a television show and then in a film. The show and the films did not make much of an impact on the audience, but it got Manoj some spending money.

Manoj continued auditioning for work, and it was during one such audition that he met the experimental filmmaker Ram Gopal Varma.[5] When Varma heard that Bajpayee had played the dacoit Man Singh in Bandit Queen, he was shocked. 'I've been trying to locate you for the past five years. No one was even telling me your name. Don't do this small role. I will give you the lead role in my next film.' This was the first time in so many years that someone had mentioned his role in Bandit Queen.

After years of struggle, Manoj had become blasé about all the promises people made to him. Manoj asked for a small role in the movie and also committed to do the role in the next film, an as-yet-unnamed gangster film set in Mumbai. This film, *Satya* (1998), not only changed the course of Manoj's career, it also forever altered the flavor of Mumbai cinema. Manoj's performance in *Satya* inspired several future actors: Irrfan Khan, Nawazuddin Siddiqui, Kay Kay Menon, Pankaj Tripathi, to name a few. *Satya* was also a box-office hit and got Manoj a national award as the 'Best Supporting Actor'.

After *Satya*, Manoj began to get regular work. A couple of movies did well (e.g., *Shool* (1999), *Rajneeti* (2010)), but on the whole, the first decade of the new millennium saw most of Manoj's films crash at the box-office. His films were talked about, but not watched enough.

In 2012, came the film *Gangs of Wasseypur*, where Manoj played the role of a dreaded coal mafia don, which cemented his reputation as one of the finest actors in the industry. For Manoj, successful actors need to constantly hone their craft. 'Acting is a constantly changing art and we must keep upgrading ourselves. I remain open to knowing what others are doing and learning from them. The goal is to constantly grow', he says.[6] He was honoured with the Padma Shri in 2019.

❦❦❦

Public
Affairs

Ujjwal Nikam
Padma Shri 2016

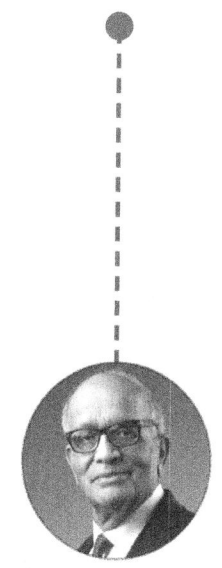

Ravindra Chandra Bhargava
Padma Bhushan 2016

Ujjwal Nikam
Prosecution Powerhouse

Few lawyers in India can claim the kind of success that Ujjwal Nikam has achieved. Perhaps even more surprising, his success did not come from hobnobbing with the rich and famous. So successful is Ujjwal in his chosen profession that there have been times when people have asked for him by name to be appointed public prosecutor. When Mohsin Shaikh — a 28-year-old man in Pune — was murdered, his family requested that Ujjwal be the Public Prosecutor to oppose the bail petition of the main accused.[1] In 2016, he was awarded the Padma Shri.

Ujjwal is the second son of barrister Deorao Nikam and Vimaladevi Nikam, born in 1953. His father was a famous politician in Maharashtra and had also been the chairman of the Khandesh Maratha Mandal, a social organisation of people hailing from the Khandesh region of Maharashtra. His mother had been a foot-soldier in the Indian freedom struggle, though she had refused to accept the Swatantra-Sainik Pension (or freedom fighter pension) in independent India.

Ujjwal's mother wanted him to become a doctor, and he embraced her dream for him. When he did not score enough to pass the rigorous entrance exam for medical studies, he started looking for opportunities elsewhere. At the time, he was not interested in studying law as he did not consider it to have much value in the matrimonial market. However, his father's influence helped him get into S S Maniyar Law College in Jalgaon to train as a lawyer. Frequent visits to the library as a student got him interested in reading, which he believed contributed to his success as a lawyer.

Ujjwal considers his father to be the biggest influence in his life. Yet, defying his father's desire for Ujjwal to start his own law office, he chose to become a District Prosecutor in Jalgaon. Ujjwal's big break came in 1993 when he was appointed Public Prosecutor in the Mumbai serial blasts case, a case concerning a series of twelve bombings over the course of a single day (12 March). At the time, the blasts were the world's worst terrorist attack, with explosions over a three-hour period, starting at the city's stock exchange. The powerful explosives had been packed into scooters and cars, under a manhole cover and in a hotel room.

As Ujjwal delved into the case against the blast accused, he realised that the prosecution had no independent evidence to prove its case.[2] Some of the accused had made confessions, but he knew from his experience that such confessions are often withdrawn in court, which could leave the prosecution empty-handed. Public sentiment was in favor of punishing the accused, and Ujjwal understood that failure to bring them to justice could be the end of his prosecutorial career. With support from the police, Ujjwal turned two of the accused into witnesses for the prosecution, considerably strengthening the prosecution's case.[3]

Ujjwal says that for 13 years, as the Mumbai blast case inched its way through the Indian judicial system, Arthur Road Jail had become a second home for him. This was the jail where prime accused Abu Salem was housed after his extradition from Portugal. During the trial, Ujjwal called Salem a 'merchant of death' and sought life imprisonment for him (because of the terms of the extradition treaty with Portugal, Salem could not be sentenced to death). Yet, even after being found guilty, Salem wrote a letter appreciating the work Ujjwal had done and requested the prosecutor to become his defense attorney. It is rare for an accused to publicly appreciate the prosecuting attorney, and even rarer for him to demand that the prosecutor be invited to join his defense team.[4]

Since then, Ujjwal has been the lawyer for the government on several high-profile cases. As a Public Prosecutor, he handled many well-known cases, such as the murders of Gulshan Kumar (founder of T-Series) and Pramod Mahajan (senior politician and former cabinet minister), Gateway of India blast, and the 2008 Mumbai attacks' trial, among others. His prosecution of Ajmal Kasab, the only attacker captured alive by the police, drew considerable attention, particularly when Kasab claimed to be a minor. Ujjwal requested the court to order a bone ossification test to medically determine the age of the accused. Doctors identified Kasab to be between twenty-two to twenty-four years of age, which allowed the prosecution case to move forward.[5]

By some counts, Ujjwal has helped put over 600 convicts in prison for life and sent more than 35 to the gallows. The cases he has prosecuted range from terrorism to kidnapping and murder.

In his free time, Ujjwal enjoys watching light-hearted movies. He also likes to write poetry, often in Marathi and sometimes in Hindi. His most famous poem is probably the one he shared after Kasab was sentenced to death by the court. Clearly elated at bringing the unrepentant terrorist to justice, Ujjwal wrote, *Badle tumne rang bahut, bahut badle nakab; Fansi takh hamne tumhe la hi diya Kasab* (translation: Your clever tactic of changing colours and masks could not save you from our determination to bring you to the gallows).⁶

Ujjwal believes that an effective lawyer needs to occasionally adopt theatrics and pay attention to non-verbal communication, particularly voice modulation, to get the attention of the judge. His stated philosophy as a public prosecutor is to identify positive aspects in the life of the convicted with an eye towards helping them realise what they could have been or accomplished instead of pursuing the criminal path.

❦❦❦

Ravindra Chandra Bhargava
Scion of Maruti Automobiles

Born on 30 July 1934, Ravindra Chandra Bhargava gained fame as the Chairman of Maruti Suzuki, one of the leading automobile companies in India. Bhargava is an alumnus of Doon School, Uttarakhand and holds a postgraduate degree in mathematics from the Allahabad University. In 1956, he cracked the IAS (Indian Administrative Service) examination and was a batch topper. He then worked in Uttar Pradesh till 1968 and in Jammu and Kashmir till 1973.

Bhargava worked in the Ministry of Energy in New Delhi for fifteen months and was also in the Cabinet Secretariat till 1978. In 1974, Bhargava was a special assistant to Shri K C Pant, the then Union Minister, and had a chance encounter with V Krishnamurthy, the chairman of BHEL[1] at that time. V Krishnamurthy offered Bhargava a job at BHEL asking him, 'Bhargava, why don't you come and join me at BHEL?'[2] Bhargava refused the offer at once.

Four years later in 1978, Bhargava called V Krishnamurthy to check whether the offer made to him was still available. Though Krishnamurthy had stepped down as the director of BHEL, Bhargava was still hired as the Director, Commercial which was specially conceived for him at the public sector giant. However, Bhargava remembers that two years later, 'the new chairman went for a restructuring at the company, abolishing the post I held, as he probably felt I would be a threat to his position in the years to come.'[3]

After a long career in administration and industry, Bhargava's journey with Maruti began in 1981. Recalling the unremarkable start of his remarkable career, Bhargava disclosed that it was Krishnamurthy who had asked him to join Maruti with him. Krishnamurthy was the first Managing Director and Vice Chairman of Maruti, and had been appointed by Indira Gandhi, the then Prime Minister of India.

Their limited experience together at BHEL was enough to convince Krishnamurthy that Bhargava was bright and had the right mix of administrative background and the ability to handle difficult situations. 'I requested the government to let him (Bhargava) work with me in Maruti because he was one of the few IAS officers to have greatly impressed me when he was working with the power ministry in the 1970s', remarked Krishnamurthy.[4] As per Krishnamurthy, Bhargava could articulate his point of view, think out of the box, would not toe the conventional line, but always question assumptions.

According to Bhargava, his transformation from public administration to corporate governance was not as difficult at BHEL as he had worked with the energy ministry. He knew the nature of the work at BHEL as he was the Joint Secretary and Founding Director of the state owned NTPC.[5] Post his stint at BHEL, when he had a chance to work with Krishnamurthy, he decided to put an end to his civil services career. 'I had come to the conclusion that staying on in government was not necessarily a good idea', said Bhargava.[6]

Finally, in 1981, Bhargava joined Maruti Udyog as the Director of Sales and Marketing. The initial years were challenging as Krishnamurthy asked Bhargava to identify potential foreign partners that would help achieve late Sanjay Gandhi's dream of building an indigenous, efficient and affordable car for the Indian market. Bhargava along with D S Gupta, a former BHEL employee, had initially shortlisted French company Renault for its sedan and Renault 18 models, but these did not seem to fit the bill of affordable cars. On the other hand, Germany's Volkswagen, and Japan's Daihatsu and Suzuki were the perfect fit.

In 1982, a top official from Suzuki who was visiting the TVS Motor Company happened to learn about the tie up between Maruti and Daihatsu. The official did not want to lose this opportunity and sent a fax to the Suzuki chairman. 'Three days later, a team from Suzuki was in India to negotiate a deal. The companies signed the deal on 2 October 1982 and fourteen months later on 14 December 1983, Maruti 800 was launched in the Indian market commemorating Sanjay Gandhi's birthday', shared Bhargava.[7]

In 2016, Bhargava was conferred the Padma Bhushan for his contribution and work in public affairs. Bhargava believes that the company is successful because of its employees. Jagdish Khattar, a former Managing Director of Maruti reflected on his experience with Bhargava and mentioned that, 'Bhargava is extremely analytical, has tremendous memory, but things are usually black or white for him. I often used to go by my gut feel. We had debated, but one could persuade him with reason.'[8]

Spending more than forty years in the automaking industry, Bhargava believes that if the Indian government and companies work cohesively, India can surpass China in low-cost manufacturing. He believes that the 'Make-in-India' push by the government will help boost the economy.

He also holds the opinion that the auto industry has flourished over the years because of the people of this country. Their aspiration to own a car pushed the automakers to bring an indigenous, affordable and efficient car. Hence, customers must be the central focus when planning things.

The reason behind the massive success of Maruti 800 was

because it had customers as its focus. 'If the auto industry is to drive the economy and the manufacturing sector, the penetration of cars in India has to move from 25 or 30 per 1,000 to even 200 per 1,000. It requires millions of cars to be made every year. This can happen only when we have a potential customer base which is ready to buy cars despite the economic recessions seen in the past years', believes Bhargava.[9]

Bhargava has had a roller coaster career but he has managed to sail his ship through the waves with his infectious smile and a wink. He was honoured with the Padma Bhushan in 2016.

Others

Chandi Prasad Bhatt
Padma Bhushan 2005

Balkrishna Vithaldas Doshi
Padma Vibhushan 2023
Padma Bhushan 2020
Padma Shri 1976

Chewang Norphel
Padma Shri 2015

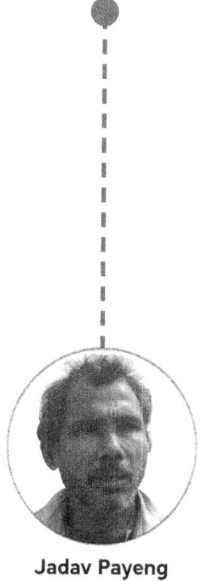

Jadav Payeng
Padma Shri 2015

Simon Oraon
Padma Shri 2016

Chandi Prasad Bhatt
Chipko Movement Pioneer

Many people attribute the birth of modern Indian environmentalism to the public protests that erupted in the 1970s when hundreds of villagers in the Himalayas revolted against deforestation. By hugging trees destined to become timber, these people, many of them women, wanted to protect their soil from erosion, as well as their supplies of water and firewood. The protests launched what many consider India's first ecological movement that became known as 'Chipko,' or embrace.[1] While the Chipko movement has received global attention, the man who inspired and led it—Chandi Prasad Bhatt—remains largely unknown. He was honoured with the Padma Bhushan in 2005.

Bhatt was born on 23 June 1934 in a family of priests that served the temple of Rudranath, part of the 'Panch Kedar', the five Himalayan temples dedicated to Shiva. His father died when Bhatt was still a baby, and he was raised by a single mother. As a boy, Bhatt often walked up to the revered shrine, which alerted him to the local ecological traditions. Walking through the alpine pastures, Bhatt was expected to take off his shoes, so as not to harm the flowers. In a four-kilometer stretch above the Amrit Ganga, a short tributary of the Alakananda river, spitting and coughing was banned as it could pollute the river below. Plucking plants before the festival of Nandashtami (celebration dedicated to Nanda Devi), in September, was taboo. The restrictions were lifted after the festive season, by when the flowers had ripened so that plucking them released their seeds.

Along with his informal learning in folk ecology, Bhatt also pursued formal education in Rudraprayag and Pauri, but could not get a degree. Job opportunities have always been scarce in the Garhwal region. Bhatt joined the Garhwal Motor Owners Union (GMOU) as a Booking Clerk, which allowed him to travel up and down the Alakananda. The job selling bus tickets exposed Bhatt to the cultural diversity of the country, as he met pilgrims from different parts of the country, practicing various trades and professions.

The turning point in Bhatt's life came when he attended a public meeting in Badrinath in 1956 where Jayaprakash Narayan (or JP) was the star speaker. At the meeting, he also met Man Singh Rawat, the local leader of the Sarvodaya movement helmed by Vinoba Bhave. Bhatt was impressed by JP and Rawat. The more he learned about them, the more he wanted to be like them. Rawat's own brother operated three GMOU buses, but he had decided to forego a life of comfort to serve in the Sarvodaya movement. Between 1956 and 1960, Bhatt spent his time-off learning about Sarvodaya from Rawat and his wife. He also went on educative treks with the Rawats including one in 1959, with Vinoba Bhave himself. In 1960, the married Bhatt, who was also now a father, announced that he was committing his life to the Sarvodaya movement.

Bhatt teamed up with a few friends to start a labour cooperative that helped repair houses and build roads, its members sharing the work and wages equally. The 1962 Indo-China war brought drastic change to the area as the Indian government decided to invest heavily in infrastructure development in the mountains bordering China. Road-building brought new jobs, but the local people did not benefit from this as contractors from the plains brought labourers with them. The labour cooperative, with 30 full-time and 700 part-time members, tried to deal with the issue of job discrimination, but the efforts stalled when the cooperative lost money.[2]

In 1964, Bhatt founded the Dashauli Gram Swarajya Sangh (DGSS), for which the foundation stone was laid by Sucheta Kripalani, then Chief Minister of Uttar Pradesh. DGSS focused on local employment generation through the promotion of weaving, apiculture, herb collection, and cottage industries for the sustainable use of forest products. When JP and his wife visited Gopeshwar in 1968, they said the work Bhatt and DGSS was doing reminded them of Mahatma Gandhi's service to the community.

While DGSS had started with the blessings of the state government, its activities sometimes created conflicts with the local bureaucracy. Then, in 1973, the Forest Department refused its request to allot some hornbeam trees to make agricultural tools. To make matters worse, the same trees were then auctioned off to a sports goods company. At Bhatt's prodding, residents of the village adjacent to the forest refused to allow the loggers to cut the trees. The villagers hugged the trees in non-violent protest. No one knew it at the time, but the Chipko movement had been born.

Soon, the protests spread across the Alakananda valley. Another protest in the spring of 1974 made global news when the local villagers, mostly women, hugged the trees. Bhatt was hailed as the 'chief organiser' (*mukhya sanchalak*) of the Chipko movement.[3] The growing popularity of the movement motivated a broadening of its goals. It was no longer just about protesting deforestation, but instead seeking to foster love towards trees in people's hearts.

Under Bhatt's leadership, many tree-plantation and

protection programs were organised. A large focus was on the women, on encouraging them to reforest the barren hillsides around the villages. A study by the Indian Institute of Science showed that the survival rate of saplings in DGSS plantations was in excess of 70 per cent, whereas the figure for Forest Department plantations lay between 20 per cent and 50 per cent.

Bhatt still lives in the Garhwal region of Uttarakhand, where he continues to work on many issues—environment, ecology, economic self-reliance—that first caught his attention more than 30 years back. Bhatt observes: 'Our movement goes beyond the erosion of land to the erosion of human values. The center of all this is humankind. If we are not in a good relationship with the environment, the environment will be destroyed, and we will lose our ground. But if you halt the erosion of human values, humankind will halt the erosion of the soil.'

※※※

Balkrishna Vithaldas Doshi
Building India

Born to a family of furniture makers on 26 August 1927, Balkrishna Vithaldas Doshi initially believed that he would end up following the family profession. Little did he know that he would, one day, embark on his journey to leave an impression of his purposeful art that will be celebrated for ages. With a career of almost seven decades and completing more than 100 projects, Doshi was the first Indian architect to have won the prestigious Pritzker Prize[1] in 2018.

Balkrishna Doshi was a recipient of the Padma Shri in 1976 and the Padma Bhushan in 2020. He was responsible for reforming architecture in India and designing over 100 projects that included buildings of prestigious institutions such as that of the Indian Institute of Management in Bangalore, the National War Memorial at New Delhi and the Centre for Environment and Planning Technology (CEPT) in Ahmedabad.

Doshi's designing skills were an inherited talent, a talent that would eventually channel Doshi's interest towards architecture. Early in his life, his art teacher at the Marathi-medium school in Bombay recognised his skill and motivated him to study architecture. Doshi enrolled at the J J School of Architecture in Bombay in the year 1947 (also the year India got its independence). In 1950, he travelled to London, where he met Le Corbusier and worked in the famous architect's studio in Paris for the next four years. He returned to India and worked on the design of Chandigarh city briefly and then looked after Le Corbusier's projects in Ahmedabad that included buildings such as the Mill Owners' Association Building (1954) and the Villa Sarabhai in Ahmedabad (1955).

Doshi worked with Louis Kahn[2] as an associate to build the Indian Institute of Management at Ahmedabad and continued this association for over a decade. He founded his own studio, *Sangath – Vastu Shilpa* in 1956. *Vastu Shilpa*[3] soon became a place that changed the way architecture was felt, understood and practiced in India. Doshi's philosophy of proactive participation even applies to the office space at *Sangath* – that has an open door, inviting passers-by to drop in.

Some of Doshi's notable projects include The Institute of Indology (1962) built to house rare documents, Tagore Hall and Memorial Theatre (1967) and the Indian Institute of Management, Bangalore (1977-92), amongst many others. *Amdavad ni Gufa* built in 1995 at Ahmedabad to exhibit M F Hussain's[4] artwork was one of Doshi's experimental project that also served as a treat for art lovers. Doshi was inspired by the caves at Ajanta and Ellora and decided to design the interior with ellipses and circles. The cave has no straight walls and is supported by irregular columns depicting a tree trunk. A mystic atmosphere is created by the snouts that allow the sunlight to enter the cave.[5]

Doshi strongly believes that architects should also be looked upon as doctors who are responsible for public health and social welfare. 'Institutions of architecture have an important role in decision-making, planning and development. We need to imagine and create modern, contemporary habitats that respond to the aspirations of society. When we use the term "architecture", we really mean the creation of an environment in response to a lifestyle', he believes.[6]

Citing an observation from his visit to Italy, Doshi noted that the Italian government collaborated with architects to improve historic neighbourhoods. The effort positively influenced the educational system and instilled in students an understanding of the importance of history, heritage and growth with respect to the environment.[7] Recognising the need for higher standards of habitat design that includes a holistic view of the environment and new ways of working and living, he started the Ahmedabad School of Architecture in 1962. Renamed as CEPT, the university is one of the leading universities in India to promote collaborative learning and architecture design.[8]

In his career spanning decades of evolving and creating, Doshi donned a number of hats. He was a thinker, architect and an academician who has been able to 'undo, redo and evolve' with his projects. He was a pioneering architect whose seamless art blends the inside and the outside. His projects are living proof of his talent and vision that speaks of his commitment to the economic, cultural and climatic context of India.[9] 'You have to accept that architecture can be malleable. The whole sense of being an instrument of change has to do with allowing things to take shape as nature does. You may not know it at that time, but when it bears fruit, you will be surprised', he believes.[10]

Can good architecture inspire us to work, live and dream better? Doshi's life and works have, and will surely continue to inspire generations in India and around the world not only to work, live, dream better but also to coexist in harmony with nature.[11] His ability to stay rooted in Indian culture and traditions while at the same time bringing in the best of global knowledge and wisdom is unparalleled. The buildings that he created are not just monuments in bricks and stone, but also pieces of a marvel that will continue to speak about his legacy and impact our society for years to come.

888

Chewang Norphel
Creator of Artificial Glaciers

Ladakh is an Indian region that lies between the Himalayan and Karakoram mountain ranges. The word 'Ladakh' is Tibetan, and means 'land of high passes', which is apt for a place 3000 meters above sea level. Winter temperatures are often lower than 20 degrees Celsius below zero. It is a beautiful place with magnificent scenery around and exquisite beauty. It is also a high-altitude desert, drier than the Sahara because it lies in the rain shadow of the Himalayas. By the time air reaches the Ladakhi side of the mountains, there is no rain left.

Born in 1935, Chewang grew up in a farming family in Leh, Ladakh's biggest town. He had a typical childhood helping parents at home and in fields after school, but with one difference. He found inspiration in his father's cousin who was Ladakh's first engineer and had helped build its airport and its first roads.[1]

Chewang's family had few means. His parents wanted him to join the monastery as they could not afford formal schooling. Instead, Chewang ran away to Srinagar, 400 kilometers away across the rugged mountain passes, for school. There, he cooked and cleaned to pay for his food and a place to stay. After finishing his schooling, Chewang studied Civil Engineering.

After graduating in 1960, Chewang joined the Rural

Development Department of the Jammu and Kashmir government. The job allowed him to contribute infrastructure development in Ladakh, and thus, help with the construction of many schools, bridges and roads in the region. 'Almost all the villages in Ladakh have roads, culverts, bridges, buildings or irrigation systems made by me', he says.[2] Yet, his biggest contribution lies elsewhere.

Scientists who monitor our planet's health generally agree that the earth has been getting warmer. Everywhere on the planet, ice is changing. Arctic sea ice is thinning rapidly, faster than most people realise. The edges of Greenland's ice sheet are shrinking.[3] The famed snows of Kilimanjaro have melted more than 80 per cent over the past century. Glaciers in the Himalayas in India are retreating at such a rapid pace that researchers believe that most central and eastern Himalayan glaciers could virtually disappear in the next 15-20 years.

Rising temperatures and melting ice means more water flows to the oceans from glaciers and icecaps. Ocean water warms and expands in volume. As a result, average global sea level has risen around the world. Estimates range between four to eight inches in the past hundred years. Coastlines are in danger, and if the trend continues, more and more coastal communities will be under water.

Chewang's answer to the climate crisis facing the world: create new glaciers to lock in the flowing waters.[4]

It all started one winter morning when Chewang noticed water dripping from a tap near his house. The tap had been left running throughout winter to stop the pipes from freezing. Chewang noticed that some water froze in the shade of a tree. The rest of the water flowed freely without freezing over. This was Chewang's eureka moment. He wondered if there was a way to slow down mountain streams to create shallow pools where water could be frozen and stored in the winter and then melted in spring.

Chewang began to sketch some designs. Perhaps, streams could be slowed down until the water froze, gradually creating an artificial glacier. Perhaps, wide streams could form frozen waterfalls as they made their way down the mountainside, while narrow streams on steeper slopes could first be diverted to a gentler incline. Perhaps, the shade of the mountain could help freeze the water faster. Maybe, if he could make the glacier come as close as possible to the village, it would help the villagers have water early in spring to irrigate the precious crops. It was all so tentative, so uncertain. There was no guidebook or advice. No one had ever made glaciers before. No one, except nature.

When Chewang shared his idea with villagers and officials to ask for funding, they thought he was crazy. Undeterred, and with only a few people to help him, he built his first experimental glacier in a valley near Phutse village. He constructed canals to divert water from the stream to small catchment areas located some distance from the village. He also made a shaded area to keep the water frozen in winters. When winter ended, there was a sheet of ice under the shade. As the ice melted in the spring, there was water for the villagers to use for irrigation. Happy with the success of the first artificial glacier, the villagers helped him build walls and channels for a bigger glacier, to obtain more water the next year.

For the next two decades, Chewang built many more artificial glaciers in Ladakh.[5] Funding came from the government and not-for-profit organisations. The physical work was mostly done manually using labourers and volunteers. The whole village would work together to construct the artificial glaciers, with people carrying building materials through dangerous terrain on their backs.

Because of Chewang's artificial glaciers, many villages in the area now harvest two crops a year instead of one. The yield is larger, which means some of it can be sold for money.

Plants like potatoes and peas are now grown, fetching more money than the traditional barley crop. Fewer animals have to be sent into the mountains to graze, reducing the risk of losing them to attacks by snow leopards and lynx. Young people, tempted to move away to the cities, can consider living off farming, helping families stay together.

Artificial glaciers are an innovative, locally suitable, and cost-effective means of water storage uniquely suited to the conditions of Ladakh. 'It's a technique to harvest winter waste water in the form of ice. And by creating artificial glaciers at relatively lower altitudes, it was possible to get water when it was needed', Chewang says.[6] In 2015, Chewang was honoured with the Padma Shri.

☙☙☙

Jadav Payeng
Forest Man of India

When a herd of 115 elephants went missing after damaging village property, officials from the forest department in the Indian state of Assam went looking for them. What they saw surprised them. The elephants had taken refuge in a large and dense forest that the officers did not even know existed. As the officers later found out, the forest covered an area of hundreds of hectares. It housed tigers, rhinoceros, deer and rabbits, apes and many varieties of birds, including a large number of vultures.[1] The locals call it *Mulai Kathoni* or Mulai forest; Mulai is Jadav Payeng's nickname.[2]

Jadav began planting trees as a teenager in his native state of Assam on the island of Majuli. He belongs to the Mising tribe, an indigenous community inhabiting parts of the Indian states of Assam and Arunachal Pradesh.[3] The economy of the Misings is based largely on agriculture.

Majuli is a river island formed by the mighty Brahmaputra river. Some estimate it to be the largest river island in the world. Located about 300-400 kms from the state capital Guwahati, Majuli was the cultural capital of the Assamese people for centuries.

When Jadav was 16, Majuli was, as usual, flooded by the Brahmaputra during the monsoons. As the flood waters receded, Jadav saw something that would change his life forever. 'I saw hundreds of snakes that were washed up during the floods, lying dead on the sandbar in the heat once the water dried up.'[4] The sight of dead snakes made him sad. It also got him thinking. He wondered if the same thing could happen to his people as well. The flooding was routine for the villagers and the island was eroding faster than at any time in recorded history.

Jadav wanted to do something. He asked around and was told he could try planting bamboo trees. 'I asked tribal people in a nearby village what I could do and they said that I should plant trees, bamboo in particular, since it could withstand harsh conditions. They gave me 25 saplings and some seeds too', recalled Jadav.[5]

Jadav always knew his life was going to have something to do with nature. It was as if working in nature was his destiny. 'When I was a little boy, a man looked at my palm to read it. He said that my life will take the course of nature.'[6] The palm reader's prophecy came true.

Jadav started planting the saplings and seeds given to him by the tribals. 'It was painful, but I did it. There was nobody to help me', Jadav describes his years in the wilderness. Still a teenager at the time, he started living alone on the sandbar where he had found the dead snakes - spending his days tending the fledgling plants. Planting and taking care of the trees was time-consuming and back-breaking work. 'I stopped going to school', says Jadav about his younger years. He was spending all his time with the plants. School did not seem a priority at that age. Formal education was not prized among the Misings, so Jadav's decision to drop out of school did not raise any eyebrows.

Slowly, the plants began to produce their own seed. He brought red ants from his home village to the sandbar to improve the soil quality. He was stung many times when transporting the ants to the forest, but he was not deterred. As the bamboo took root, he began to introduce other species of trees into the island. The tree plantings are planned according to the arrival of the monsoons. 'I plant in April, May, and June, so that they can benefit from the rains', he states. 'During the rest of the nine months, I collect seeds from within the forest.' Where there were once dead snakes, life began to flourish. Birds and wildlife started visiting the growing forest, and then made it home.[7]

Jadav lives in a small house he built for himself near the forest with his wife and three children. He keeps cows and buffaloes, selling their milk for livelihood. Over the years, he has lost many dairy animals to the wildlife. Wild elephants have damaged his little house many times. Even such personal destruction has failed to dent Jadav's passion for his work. He sees people who encroach on forest land and destroy animal habitats as the reason for animal attacks on human dwellings. Poachers have their eye on his forest and animals too. Every time Jadav travels outside, he asks the forest department officials to take care of the forest in his absence.

A couple of years after the forest department officials came upon the forest, a journalist and wildlife photographer from the nearby city of Jorhat wrote about Jadav in an Assamese newspaper. Other articles in newspapers and media coverage from around the world soon followed. Many documentary films were made on Jadav, at least a couple of which are available for free on youtube. This includes *Forest Man* by William Douglas McMaster and *Foresting Life* by Aarti Srivastava. Jadav is also the subject of an English-language children's book by American writer Sophia Gholz, which has been translated into French and German as well. Sophia sees Jadav as an inspiration and role model for children worldwide.[8]

Jadav's pioneering work has brought him many awards and much recognition. At least two universities have awarded him honorary doctorates. Not bad for a school dropout! In 2015, he received the Padma Shri.

☸ ☸ ☸

Simon Oraon
Protector of Trees

Experts estimate that by 2050, three-quarters of the world's population will be affected by droughts, and an estimated 5 billion (500 crores) people will live in areas that are water scarce for at least a month each year. To put this in perspective, by the time India gets ready to celebrate the 100th anniversary of its independence, much of humanity will be living under drought conditions. It is a sobering scenario that, if it comes to pass, could drastically alter the trajectory of human existence on our planet.

Simon Oraon, who received the Padma Shri in 2016, has spent his life fighting chronic water scarcity in the villages of Jharkhand, a state, known for its lush green forests, that has been reeling from back-to-back droughts for years. Respectfully known as *Baba* in his area, the media refers to him as Jharkhand's waterman. For over 60 years, he has organised pond- and well-digging initiatives to store rainwater, initiating at the same time massive tree plantation drives, changing the lives of thousands of villagers. When the announcement of the Padma Shri was made, Oraon was surprised. 'I had no idea about the award until a friend from the media called up to congratulate me', he said.[1] Soon after he learned about the award, Oraon announced that he would accept the award only if the government became more serious about advancing the interests of farmers.

Growing up in Khaksi Toli village, which comes under the Bero block and is about 30 km from Ranchi (the capital of Jharkhand state), Oraon's family owned eight acres of fallow land. His relatives and neighbors grew a monocrop of paddy, that too with frequent failures. The forest cover had been destroyed by the timber mafia. Every year, after the monsoons, most able-bodied villagers migrated to bigger cities for jobs, leaving the old and infirm behind. When the monsoons failed, which happened quite frequently, drought caused hunger, starvation, and often, death.

Oraon quit school in Class IV to support his parents in the fields. At the time, he was in awe of the massive apparatus that deforested the land around him. 'As a child, I had seen trees in Bero being cut and transported in huge trucks. I was even initially fascinated by these huge machines. But I realised after several years when a severe drought caused total crop failure, how much harm this deforestation was causing. I took the lead, called all the villagers and urged them to stand firm against the mindless cutting of trees.'[2]

Young Oraon began to consider that if a dam is built somewhere near the foothills, water could be blocked and used for irrigation with the use of canals on the plains. Soon, with the help of friends, he constructed the first earthen dam near Gaighat in Bero. The dam, however, was washed away next monsoon. The reconstructed dam too failed to withstand the strong current of water. It was then that the state water resource department intervened to increase the height and width of the dam and strengthen it with concrete. 'This worked, so much so that the dam has not developed any crack till date', said Oraon.[3]

To say that Oraon built a check dam to trap rainwater obscures the resistance he faced when he came up with the unconventional idea to address the problem. 'People scoffed at me when I first presented the idea', he says. 'Officials were apathetic and villagers were not ready to part with an inch of land for submergence in the water of the dam. I won them over by using my own land and by ploughing the barren land of others for those who lost land due to dams."[4]

More small dams followed, often without any help from the local government. Rainwater was captured during the monsoons and channeled through canals to the fields. To prevent soil erosion, Oraon has planted more than 30,000 trees. Once again, he started by planting trees on his family's land. As time passed, neighbours saw his methods helped conserve rainwater and allowed him to plant trees across the area. Farms in the village now yield three crops of vegetables annually, in addition to paddy. There is now a *mandi* in the village from where hundreds of tonnes of vegetables are transported to large cities and towns every month. Water table improved and migration decreased in the area. 'Due to Oraon, we are leading a comfortable life and our children are going to school', says a fellow farmer from the village.[5]

Oraon has been elected Tribal Chieftain (*parha raja*) continuously since 1964. As the head of the *parha* (a confederacy of villages), he presides over its panchayat meetings as well as over the numerous social functions such as community feasts, music and dance events. He has also been appointed brand ambassador of the watershed program of the Rural Development Department of the Government of Jharkhand. Success and fame have, however, not changed much in Oraon's life. He continues to live in a small house. He still gets up before dawn (about 4.30 am in the morning), goes to the farms, diligently checks the plants and trees around the village, takes a round of the forest he has cultivated in the face of tremendous odds, and walks back to his house in time for lunch.

Planting trees has become a central mission of Oraon's

life, and he continues to plant a thousand trees every year. He also protects the trees—no villager dares chop off even a single tree branch without his consent. 'As long as I have the energy to walk and work, I will keep planting trees. These trees give us life and it's our duty to protect them. We should make trees our partners for a green revolution and development', he says.[6]

Conclusion

Life is short; vanities of the world are transient. He alone lives who lives for others; others are more dead than alive.
—Swami Vivekanand

About one hundred years ago, the archaeologist Howard Carter chiseled a hole in the doorway of an as-yet-unexplored vault in Egypt's Valley of the Kings. By candlelight, he peered in to find what has since come to be known as the greatest archaeological discovery of all times. 'Can you see anything?' asked an impatient Lord Carnarvon, his longtime, long-suffering financial backer. 'Wonderful things', Carter responded. Neither Carter nor his patron Lord Carnarvon knew at the time that their brief conversation would one day be considered among the most memorable exchanges in the annals of archaeology. Carter had found the tomb of King Tutankhamun, a little-known boy king who had been laid to rest with a staggering store of treasures, then largely forgotten for 3000 years. The find was one of a handful of the most significant and bountiful discoveries in the unearthing of the ancient world, offering the world a dazzling vision of life on the Nile during the heydays of ancient Egypt and instilling a new sense of national pride and self-determination among modern Egyptians.

Carter, who grew up in England, was an unlikely archaeologist. He had no formal training in archaeology and was scratching out a living selling watercolors to well-heeled tourists in Egypt when he was introduced to George Edward Stanhope Molyneux Herbert, the fifth Earl of Carnarvon. Lord Carnarvon suffered from congenitally poor health, made worse by a near-fatal car accident that left him with badly injured lungs. On the advice of his doctor, he began spending winters on the Nile to breathe Egypt's desert air. Soon, he began relishing Egyptian antiquities as much as Egypt's air, hiring Carter to supervise excavations he was funding in search of artifacts for his growing collection. Carter convinced him to support excavations in the Valley of Kings, which after decades of digging, was generally seen as having already revealed all its hidden treasures.

For the next five years, Carter and his team dug relentlessly in the valley. When the efforts failed to produce any gains, and Lord Carnarvon began to have doubts about the wisdom of digging in the valley, Carter convinced him to continue his support for one last season. A few days later, Carter and his patron were celebrating one of archaeology's greatest triumphs, their names on the front pages of newspapers around the world.

By the time Carter made his historic discovery, he had been labouring in the Valley of Kings for a decade-and-a-half, including through the tumultuous years of the First World War. By the time he found the hidden tomb, Carter had moved 150,000 to 200,000 tons of rubble in the valley. The tomb revealed so much treasure that it took more than a decade of painstaking work to catalogue, pack, preserve, and move the artifacts to a safe location. Yet, many prominent historians are quick to attribute Carter's discovery to 'luck'. He was lucky, they say. Never mind that Carter toiled in the scorching desert heat doing hard, dusty, and sweltering work in a valley that most considered picked over and played out after decades of relentless digging.

One of the easiest ways to dismiss the achievements of others is to attribute their success to luck. In fact, many even attribute their own success to luck. A popular author with multiple books on the *New York Times* best-selling list was asked what role he thought luck played in his career. 'Oh, luck has been everything. I can point to at least ten occasions where pure, dumb luck landed me a huge break in my career', he responded. Many successful people mistakenly credit their success fully to luck. Attributing success to luck makes one more humble and less egoistical, but also erroneously downplays the importance of delayed gratification, smart choices, and hard work. In any situation, there are many people who are similarly advantaged; yet, few succeed, and even fewer succeed spectacularly.

The famed author Jim Collins sees luck as just a spark for success. As he explained it, 'luck, good and bad, happens to everyone, whether we like it or not'. Successful people seek opportunities in their circumstances, as they proactively 'grab luck events and make much more of them'. Thomas Jefferson, the third President of the United States, reportedly said, 'I am a great believer in luck. I find that the harder I work, the more luck I seem to have.'

Once we move beyond attributions of luck, we hear two major stories about success and the human capacity for extraordinary achievement. The first story is that successful people are born. According to this view, we are either born with innate qualities (talent, you may call it) or are born in the right time and place. For an example of the talent logic, consider the innumerable accounts of successful people that start with talking about their precocious qualities as young children. Jeff Bezos, the founder of Amazon and one of the richest men in the world, we are told, was barely three years old when he took a screwdriver to his crib with the goal of dismantling it (he was unsuccessful at it). For an example of the time-place logic, consider the runaway success of the *Outliers: The Story of Success*, which argues that success is a result of when one was born. The real reason, Bill Gates succeeded, the book *Outliers* tells us, is that he was born in 1955 —just the right time to be born to take advantage of the personal computer age —(never mind the more than four million other children born in the US the same year). The famous investor Warren Buffett has repeatedly declared that if someone wanting to be successful could pick the best time and place to be born, it would undoubtedly be 'today and in America'.

The second story tells us that extraordinary success comes from acquiring the right pedigree by going to the right school or college, preferably, both. This explanation has an unbelievable hold on people's minds around the world, influencing their decisions and actions in stunningly predictable ways. The lengths to which people go to get into the right kindergarten in Los Angeles, the right private school in New Delhi, and the right college in South Korea, are all testament to the strength of this story. Get into the right educational institution, and you are on the path to success, goes the thinking.

There is another story about achievement that is not often recognised, and scarcely understood. It is the story that we find in our exploration of the lives of 75 achievers discussed in this book. It is a story that is more powerful and more common among those who become successful. This story may not have the popular appeal of the birth logic or the pedigree logic, but presents before us a few common attributes that were exhibited by people who made it big in their lives. As we documented the stories of 75 Indian mavericks who not just excelled in their respective fields, but also set a shining example before others that success comes—sooner or later—to people who believe they can! Below, we briefly describe some common personal attributes that we found in these 75 individuals.

Learning Mindset, Self-belief and Grit
It is said that 'great works are performed, not by strength but by perseverance'. One of the qualities that we found emerge consistently in the life stories of individuals documented in this book is the 'learning mindset'. The individuals—in their pursuit of excellence—remained unfazed by the failures that they met. In the face of failures, these individuals exhibited a tremendous appetite for learning and improving their skills. One of the exemplary quotes to exhibit this point came from G V Krishna Reddy who said about his life, 'with very little knowledge of the trade, I was unsure of myself but gradually learned the ropes by facing the challenges, working hard, remaining self-disciplined and committed — the four virtues that remained constant in the path of my life'.

We found that by facing the challenges with courage and with the self-belief and a zeal to learn, these individuals surmounted life's challenges and emerged successful. They stood determined in the face of hardships and kept surging forward with the belief that life would open some doors for them even if it shut a few.

Humility
Mahatma Gandhi once remarked, 'It is unwise to be too sure of one's own wisdom. It is healthy to be reminded that the strongest might weaken and the wisest might err.' A common characteristic we observed among the people we write about in this book is that these individuals exhibited extreme humility. Jim Collins in his book *Good to Great* writes that the highest form of leadership (level 5 leadership) is a combination of

humility and indomitable spirit. Successful people don't just exhibit learning mindset, grit and determination, they also combine it with humility and a sense of modesty.

Attesting to the importance of humility in successful individuals, a Managing Director of Godrej reflected about Adi Godrej, 'My fondest memory of Mr Godrej and his brother Nadir is them having lunch in the same canteen as the factory staff every day.' Ratan Tata lived for years in the same simple apartment in the Bakhtawar area of Colaba in Mumbai that is more suitable for a bachelor who loves reading and dogs than for one of the richest Indians.

Hard work and Leading by Example

After humility, determination and learning mindset comes the importance of hard work and leading by example. The leaders and individuals documented in this book never shied away from leading from the front and putting in the effort needed to go all the distance. Mr Naik very aptly observed the importance of hard work and leading by example when he mentioned that 'Everyone should aspire to become a role model in that sense, and discipline is one of the key factors. Initially, in the 1990s, when we had to submit bids to ONGC, we had people who would work through the night and then straightaway in the morning go to submit the tenders. I used to sit up with them till 2 am. I would then go home and return before they finally left the office in the morning to submit the tenders. I didn't have to do it. But my being there would give them strength. If the boss is doing so much, they would think, then so can we.'

Every single individual whom we studied for this book put in tremendous hard work. It is very rightly said 'hard work beats talent when talent doesn't work hard'. One of the messages we hope readers can take away from this book is that hard work and talent make a deadly combination, and if talent is in scarce quantity, hard work can even make up for the lack of talent. One of the cases in point is that of Deepika Kumari, India's famous archer. As a colleague from Deepika's training academy tells us, 'She would always do two times of what she was told during the drills. With her frail structure, her body would easily give up, but she would keep running, doing other drills, double than others.' What Deepika lacked was physical prowess, and she more than made up for it with hard-work and persistence.

Positive Human Values (Compassion and Empathy)

One of the qualities we observed in the heroes (and heroines) we write about in this book is their sense of compassion and empathy for others (people around them and the environment). People were often motivated to take up the causes that they worked for observing the pain and suffering around them. Also, they worked in order to leave a better world for the next generation. They showed a tremendous amount of responsibility and ownership for society and children. Almost all the musicians we write about in this book have observed that music must be included in the school curriculum and could be used as an intervention to educate our children about positive values like compassion, non-violence and non-addiction.

People like Dr Shetty took up their calling after seeing children suffering from heart problems at birth. Dr Kler decided to become a neonatologist seeing the death of a baby boy who died due to asphyxia, that is the inability to breathe due to long, difficult labour. And Jadav Payeng took upon himself the onerous task of planting a forest on an island seeing the sight of snakes that had been washed up during the floods and had died due to the heat once the water dried up. Such stories show us that the value of compassion and empathy is important not just to become good individuals but also plays a significant role in our lives as they can give us a higher purpose to live and work for. As Mark Twain famously said, 'We are born twice—first, the day we were born, and second, the day we figure out why.' Compassion and empathy towards our people and the environment is a useful way to figure out the purpose of our lives.

Patriotism

The last quality that we would like to talk about through this book is that of patriotism – a sense of belonging to our motherland and working towards making it stronger and better. The seventy-five individuals that we describe in this book, and many more Padma awardees, have made India proud through their work and contributions in different fields. As Azim Premji mentioned while pledging USD 7.6 billion worth of Wipro stocks to charity raising his total lifetime donations to USD 21 billion in 2019, 'I was deeply influenced by Gandhi's notion of holding one's wealth in trusteeship, to be used for the betterment of society and not as if one owned it.' Many industry stalwarts have started foundations and charitable arms that are working towards improving the quality of healthcare, education and other facilities in the country.

Scientists have improved the stature of India in technology and science through their contributions. As Dr Bhatkar mentioned, 'Great nations are not built on borrowed technology', and Dr Ramasami observes 'It (science policy) should enable faster and sustainable inclusive growth of the nation, and I think open our space for strategic partnerships with the developed world for global good and for sustainable global growth by also serving the needs of the unserved, underserved markets of the world… Economics that hurt the moral being of an individual or of a nation are immoral and sinful. Therefore, I would like to talk about pro-poor technologies for the world.' India has truly been shaped by the generous and patriotic dispositions of such individuals.

Concluding Thoughts

While success may be achieved through luck or through right education, we hope this book highlights to the readers, the importance of some fundamental qualities that prepare us better to achieve success in our lives. Each of the individuals discussed in the book did not wait for luck to happen to them. Rather, many of them overcame unthinkable hardships in their lives, tremendous personal losses, suffering and tragedies and lack of right opportunities and resources. What they banked on was their hardwork, determination, self-belief and willingness to learn without bothering about where the learning came from. They used compassion and empathy towards others to stay humble and grounded in the face of success and kept working to make the most of their lives.

Finally, when they got an opportunity, they gave back to their country in greater proportion what they had received from it in the hope that what was denied to them (or to their generation) should not be denied to the next generation. This book is a celebration of such wonderful lives that have not just changed and shaped the destiny of millions, and also of their country (India) and society through their work!

End Notes

INTRODUCTION

1. Patel, D. 2020. *Naoroji: Pioneer of Indian Nationalism.* Harvard University Press, Boston (MA, USA).
2. Milani, A. 2008. Eminent Persians: *The Men and Women Who Made Modern Iran.* Syracuse University Press, Syracuse (NY, USA).
3. Sampath, V. 2022. *Bravehearts of Bharat: Vignettes from Indian History.* Penguin Viking, Haryana (India)
4. https://www.asercentre.org/survey/p/418.html
5. https://economictimes.indiatimes.com/news/politics-and-nation/corrupt-are-becoming-role-models-for-youth-in-india-narayana-murthy/articleshow/11679687.cms?from=mdr
6. https://archive.nytimes.com/india.blogs.nytimes.com/2012/03/20/in-india-history-literally-rots-away/

SCIENCE AND ENGINEERING

Kiran Mazumdar Shaw
The Self-made Female Billionaire

1. https://www.bbc.com/news/business-45547352
2. https://businessconnectindia.in/biocon-kiran-mazumdar-shaw-success-story/
3. https://www.forbes.com/profile/kiran-mazumdar-shaw/?sh=527ecacb59ad
4. https://www.reliancemoney.co.in/from-entrepreneur-to-mit-board-member-the-inspiring-story-of-kiran-mazumdar-shaw
5. https://www.ft.com/content/756b2922-9a0a-11dd-960e-000077b07658

6. https://www.asianage.com/age-on-sunday/290919/meet-the-ultimate-myth-breaker.html

Brahma Singh
The Horticultural Scientist
1. Interview with Brahma Singh, September 22, 2022
2. https://www.britannica.com/topic/ghost-pepper

Thirumalachari Ramasami
Pioneering Advances in Leather Science
1. Thirumalachari Ramasami. Retrieved from: https://clri.org/Admin/Leaders/DrTRProfile.html
2. Ibid.
3. Dr Thirumalachari Ramasami. Retrieved from: https://web.archive.org/web/20130115234608/http://dst.gov.in/about_us/secretary-resume.htm
4. Thirumalachari Ramasami. Retrieved from: https://en.wikipedia.org/wiki/Thirumalachari_Ramasami
5. CSIR-Central Leather Research Institute. Retrieved from: https://clri.org/AboutUs.aspx?A=12
6. Dr Thirumalachari Ramasami. Retrieved from : https://web.archive.org/web/20130115234608/http://dst.gov.in/about_us/secretary-resume.htm
7. Thirumalachari Ramasami. Retrieved from: https://clri.org/Admin/Leaders/DrTRProfile.html
8. Nayudamma Award for leather scientist. Retrieved from: https://archive.ph/20130125111126/http://www.hindu.com/2008/12/06/stories/2008120656000600.htm#selection-281.1-281.38
9. Thirumalachari Ramasami: The role of science and technology policy in developing countries. Retrieved from: https://fordschool.umich.edu/video/2017/thirumalachari-ramasami-role-science-and-technology-policy-developing-countries
10. Dr Thirumalachari Ramasami. Retrieved from: https://web.archive.org/web/20130115234608/http://dst.gov.in/about_us/secretary-resume.htm
11. Ibid.
12. Thirumalachari Ramasami. Retrieved from: https://clri.org/Admin/Leaders/DrTRProfile.html
13. Thirumalachari Ramasami: The role of science and technology policy in developing countries. Retrieved from: https://fordschool.umich.edu/video/2017/thirumalachari-ramasami-role-science-and-technology-policy-developing-countries

Koppillil Radhakrishnan
Leading India's Space Odyssey

1. My Odyssey: Memoirs of the Man behind the Mangalyaan Mission. Penguin UK. ISBN 9789385990380
2. K Radhakrishnan: How ISRO chief, man behind Mars mission, is retooling the organization. Retrieved from: https://economictimes.indiatimes.com/k-radhakrishnan-how-isro-chief-man-behind-mars-mission-is-retooling-the-organization/articleshow/25719213.cms
3. India's space odyssey: ISRO creates history in 2014. Retrieved from: https://indianexpress.com/article/technology/science/indias-space-odyssey-isro-creates-history-in-2014/
4. Walk The Talk with ISRO Chairman Dr K Radhakrishnan An interview. Retrieved from https://www.youtube.com/watch?v=Om_wAEDUG7k
5. India's space odyssey: ISRO creates history in 2014. Retrieved from: https://indianexpress.com/article/technology/science/indias-space-odyssey-isro-creates-history-in-2014/
6. K Radhakrishnan interview: Success due to tireless efforts of ISRO. Retrieved from: https://www.hindustantimes.com/india/k-radhakrishnan-interview-success-due-to-tireless-efforts-of-isro/story-Uz4BU6xpPeU8kHmTUamBlO.html
7. https://www.wsj.com/articles/BL-IRTB-26643?mod=trending_now_video_5
8. ISRO working on manned space mission: Dr K Radhakrishnan. Retrieved from: https://economictimes.indiatimes.com/news/science/isro-working-on-manned-space-mission-dr-k-radhakrishnan/articleshow/45742817.cms
9. 365 days: Nature's 10. Retrieved from: https://doi.org/10.1038/516311a
10. Padma Bhushan Dr Koppillil Radhakrishnan calls upon Ahmedabad University's class of 2022 to leave a legacy behind and make a difference to society. Retrieved from: https://timesofindia.indiatimes.com/padma-bhushan-dr-koppillil-radhakrishnan-calls-upon-ahmedabad-universitys-class-of-2022-to-leave-a-legacy-behind-and-make-a-difference-to-society/articleshow/96030655.cms
11. New ISRO chief a noted Kathakali dancer. Retrieved from: https://www.indiatoday.in/web-exclusive/story/new-isro-chief-a-noted-kathakali-dancer-59234-2009-10-25

Padmanabhan Balaram
Mastermind of Molecular Symphony

1. Face to face with Professor P Balaram. Retrieved from: https://www.ias.ac.in/article/fulltext/reso/024/06/0697-0710
2. Ibid.
3. Ibid

Nambi Narayanan
Integral to India's Satellite Launch Vehicle Development

1. Nambi Narayanan: The fake spy scandal that blew up a rocket scientist's career. Retrieved from: https://www.bbc.com/news/world-asia-india-49836270
2. Ibid.
3. Ibid.
4. Enemies of India tried their best to decimate Indian space progress destroyed a brilliant scientist : All need to be punished to hell. Retrieved from: https://www.indianpolitics.co.in/enemies-of-india-tried-their-best-to-decimate-indian-space-progress-destroyed-a-brilliant-scientist-all-need-to-be-punished-to-hell/
5. Who is Nambi Narayanan? Retrieved from: https://www.indiatoday.in/movies/celebrities/story/who-is-nambi-narayanan-1786357-2021-04-02
6. Ibid.
7. The 1994 espionage case that led to Isro scientist Nambi Narayanan's arrest. Retrieved from: https://www.hindustantimes.com/india-news/the-1994-espionage-case-that-led-to-isro-scientist-nambi-narayanan-s-arrest-101618555565896.html
8. Told CBI the truth: Ex-ISRO scientist Nambi Narayanan. Retrieved from:https://www.ndtv.com/india-news/told-cbi-the-truth-ex-isro-scientist-nambi-narayanan-2477311
9. Once falsely accused of being a spy, ISRO scientist Nambi Narayanan honoured With Padma Bhushan. Retrieved from: https://www.indiatimes.com/trending/human-interest/once-falsely-accused-of-being-a-spy-isro-scientist-nambi-narayanan-honoured-with-padma-bhushan-363846.html

Madabusi Santanam Raghunathan
Maths Genius

1. More about MS Raghunathan. Retrieved from: https://web.archive.

org/web/20140610013607/http://mathstat.uohyd.ernet.in/people/msr/more-about-msr
2. Raghunathan Madabusi Santanam. Retrieved from: https://twas.org/directory/raghunathan-madabusi-santanam
3. Professor M S Raghunathan. Retrieved fromt: http://www.math.tifr.res.in/~dani/msrfr.pdf
4. Indian Fellow. Retrieved from: https://www.insaindia.res.in/detail.php?id=N75-0584
5. Professor M S Raghunathan. Retrieved from: http://www.math.tifr.res.in/~dani/msrfr.pdf
6. Ibid.
7. M S Raghunathan. Retrieved from: https://en.wikipedia.org/wiki/M._S._Raghunathan
8. Professor M S Raghunathan. Retrieved fromt: http://www.math.tifr.res.in/~dani/msrfr.pdf
9. M S Raghunathan. Retrieved from: https://en.wikipedia.org/wiki/M._S._Raghunathan
10. Professor M S Raghunathan. Retrieved from: http://www.math.tifr.res.in/~dani/msrfr.pdf
11. India a world mathematics power, says Professor Raghunathan. Retrieved from: https://www.thehindu.com/sci-tech/science/India-a-world-mathematics-power-says-Professor-Raghunathan/article16327362.ece

Vijay Bhatkar
Architect of India's Param Supercomputers

1. The Little Known Story of How India's First Indigenous Supercomputer Amazed the World in 1991. Retrieved from: https://www.thebetterindia.com/82076/india-first-supercomputer-param-cdac-vijay-bhatkar/
2. Vijay P Bhatkar. Retrieved from: https://en.wikipedia.org/wiki/Vijay_P._Bhatkar
3. Dr Vijay P Bhatkar - A rare interview to MoneyLIFE. Retrieved from: http://www.suchetadalal.com/?id=d7ab4ff7-d795-9425-492e8be60719&base=sections&f&t=Dr.Vijay+P+Bhatkar+-+A+rare+interview+to+MoneyLIFE
4. Ibid.
5. Ibid.

6. The Little Known Story of How India's First Indigenous Supercomputer Amazed the World in 1991. Retrieved from: https://www.thebetterindia.com/82076/india-first-supercomputer-param-cdac-vijay-bhatkar/
7. How India's First Indigenous Supercomputer Amazed the World. Retrieved from: https://defenceupdate.in/how-indias-first-indigenous-supercomputer-amazed-the-world/
8. The Little Known Story of How India's First Indigenous Supercomputer Amazed the World in 1991. Retrieved from: https://www.thebetterindia.com/82076/india-first-supercomputer-param-cdac-vijay-bhatkar/
9. Ibid.
10. Yesterday's supercomputers are today's laptops: Bhatkar. Retrieved from: https://www.livemint.com/Industry/jmNVLeBoYXUbJzFJBTdNLK/Yesterdays-supercomputers-are-todays-laptops-Bhatkar.html
11. Father of India's first supercomputer becomes Nalanda University's Chancellor. Retrieved from: https://www.newindianexpress.com/nation/2017/jan/28/father-of-indias-first-supercomputer-becomes-nalanda-universitys-chancellor-1564421.html
12. Vijay Bhatkar, Head of RSS-affiliated science body, named Nalanda University Chancellor. Retrieved from: https://thewire.in/education/vijay-bhatkar-nalanda-university
13. Dr Vijay Bhatkar. Retreived from: https://web.archive.org/web/20200811160013/https://actionforindia.org/afi-forum-2016/pic/Dr.Bhatkar.html
14. Multiversity. Retrieved from: https://www.multiversity.co.in/about-us/

CIVIL SERVICES

Parveen Talha
Trailblazer in Narcotics Control and UPSC Leadership

1. https://www.youtube.com/watch?v=K7mPd-ADBHk
2. https://www.youtube.com/watch?v=V99Sak2BErs
3. https://www.business-standard.com/article/pti-stories/first-muslim-woman-to-enter-civil-services-awarded-padma-shri-114042700109_1.html

Vinod Rai
A Stalwart in Public Financial Accountability

1. Vinod Rai: Auditor or Crusader. Retrieved from: https://www.

livemint.com/Politics/XwBXRyhEwFuLWhDGj9vEvN/Vinod-Rai-Auditor-or-crusader.html
2. Vinod Rai: DPOC Member. Retrieved from: https://www.ifrs.org/groups/due-process-oversight-committee/profiles/vinod-rai/.
3. Vinod Rai demits office: A CAG that India will miss. Retrieved from: https://www.moneylife.in/article/vinod-rai-demits-office-a-cag-that-india-will-miss/32807.html.
4. Vinod Rai: Auditor or crusader. Retrieved from: https://www.livemint.com/Politics/XwBXRyhEwFuLWhDGj9vEvN/Vinod-Rai-Auditor-or-crusader.html.
5. Ibid.
6. CAG Vinod Rai: An accountant who's calling government to account. Retrieved from: https://economictimes.indiatimes.com/news/politics-and-nation/cag-vinod-rai-an-accountant-whos-calling-government-to-account/articleshow/15540142.cms?utm_source=contentofinterest&utm_medium=text&utm_campaign=cppst
7. Not just an accountant's angst. Retrieved from: https://www.business-standard.com/article/opinion/not-just-an-accountant-s-angst-114092401401_1.html
8. Vinod Rai demits office: A CAG that India will miss. Retrieved from: https://www.moneylife.in/article/vinod-rai-demits-office-a-cag-that-india-will-miss/32807.html
9. Vinod Rai: Auditor or crusader. Retrieved from: https://www.livemint.com/Politics/XwBXRyhEwFuLWhDGj9vEvN/Vinod-Rai-Auditor-or-crusader.html

Venkatarman Krishnamurthy
Father of Public Sector Undertakings in India

1. Krishnamurthy, V. (2014). At the Helm: A Memoir. HarperCollins Publishers India.

Moosa Raza
A Storied Journey of Diplomacy

1. AFSPA is a great issue for the Kashmiri, not Art. 370; 10-12 States enjoy similar protection: Moosa Raza, former J&K Chief Secretary. Retrieved from: https://www.thehinducentre.com/the-arena/current-issues/article27010864.ece
2. Less obvious presence of forces, a welcome change:Moosa Raza. Retrieved from: https://www.tribuneindia.com/2003/20031130/edit.htm#1

TRADE AND INDUSTRY

Shiv Nadar
The PC Man

1. https://www.knma.in/
2. https://www.forbes.com/global/2011/0718/heroes-philanthropy-11-shiv-nadar-vidyagyan-getting-them-young.html?sh=7ce44fc825e9
3. https://www.indiatimes.com/trending/human-interest/shiv-nadar-founder-of-hcl-technologies-success-story-548745.html
4. https://timesofindia.indiatimes.com/city/trichy/nadar-says-hindi-shaped-his-career-asks-students-to-learn-it/articleshow/67842025.cms

Azim Hashim Premji
Shaping India's IT Landscape

1. Full Story | George Fernandes and the Infamous IBM Exit. Retrieved from: https://thewire.in/government/full-story-george-fernandes-and-the-infamous-ibm-exit
2. Wipro joins Billion dollar club. Retrieved from: https://www.financialexpress.com/archive/wipro-joins-billion-dollar-club/104100/
3. Azim Premji. Retrieved from: https://web.archive.org web/20131227000058/http://www.worldofceos.com/dossiers/azim-premji
4. Azim Premji. Retrieved from: https://www.britannica.com/biography/Azim-Premji
5. Azim Premji. Retrieved from: https://web.archive.org/web/20110424130953/http://www.time.com/time/specials/packages/article/0,28804,2066367_2066369_2066101,00.html
6. Azim Premji. Retrieved from: https://timesofindia.indiatimes.com/topic/azim-premji
7. Azim Premji. Retrieved from: https://themuslim500.com/profiles/azim-premji/
8. Azim Premji. Retrieved from: https://www.bloomberg.com/billionaires/profiles/azim-h-premji/
9. Azim Premji. Retrieved from: https://www.britannica.com/biography/Azim-Premji
10. Azim Premji. Retrieved from: https://timesofindia.indiatimes.com/topic/azim-premji

11. Azim Premji. Retrieved from: https://www.wipro.com/leadership/azim-h-premji/
12. Premji to donate more to philanthropic causes. Retrieved from: https://epaper.indianexpress.com/c/11343877
13. Asia's 2019 heroes of philanthropy: Catalysts for change. Retrieved from: https://www.forbes.com/sites/gracechung/2019/12/02/asias-2019-heroes-of-philanthropy-catalysts-for-change/?sh=552310176d98
14. Azim Premji donates half of his wealth. Retrieved from: https://web.archive.org/web/20130310062218/http://www.in.com/news/business/azim-premji-donates-half-of-his-wealth-50187456-in-1.html
15. Ibid.
16. Azim Premji retains 'India's most generous' tag, donated ₹27 crore per day | Full List. Retrieved from: https://www.indiatvnews.com/business/news-edelgive-hurun-india-philanthropy-2021-list-azim-premji-mukesh-ambani-shiv-nadar-india-s-top-10-most-generous-person-list-742739
17. Azim Premji. Retrieved from: https://www.wipro.com/leadership/azim-h-premji/

Venu Srinivasan
Driving Innovation and Excellence in India's Industrial Sector

1. Venu Srinivasan is Autocar Professional's Man of the Year 2021. Retrieved from: https://www.autocarpro.in/feature/venu-srinivasan-is-autocar-professional-man-of-the-year-2021-80765
2. Ibid.
3. Padma Bhushan Venu Srinivasan down memory lane. Retrieved from: https://www.themachinemaker.com/machinemaker/venu-srinivasan-padma-bhushan-awardee-1911#:~:text=from%20May%201979.,TVS%20Motor%20Company%20soon%20after.
4. Venu Srinivasan is Autocar Professional's Man of the Year 2021. Retrieved from: https://www.autocarpro.in/feature/venu-srinivasan-is-autocar-professional-man-of-the-year-2021-80765
5. Ibid.
6. Venu Srinivasan: The man who took TVS from mopeds to BMW. Retrieved from:https://www.moneycontrol.com/news/technology/auto/venu-srinivasan-the-man-who-took-tvs-from-mopeds-to-bmw-6704811.html

7. Venu Srinivasan, Chairman TVS Motor Company, awarded Padma Bhushan for his contribution to the field of trade and industry. Retrieved from: https://theprint.in/ani-press-releases/venu-srinivasan-chairman-tvs-motor-company-awarded-padma-bhushan-for-his-contribution-to-the-field-of-trade-and-industry/763313/

Anand Gopal Mahindra
Transformative Leadership

1. Jagadish Chandra Mahindra. Retrieved from: https://en.wikipedia.org/wiki/Jagdish_Chandra_Mahindra
2. Anand G Mahindra, MBA 1981. Retrieved from: https://www.alumni.hbs.edu/stories/Pages/story-bulletin.aspx?num=1994
3. Ibid.
4. MUSCO, now known as Mahindra Sanyo Special Steel Private Limited is a manufacturer of speciality rings, stampings and steel, and is headquartered in Mumbai.
5. Anand Mahindra. Retrieved from: https://en.wikipedia.org/wiki/Anand_Mahindra
6. Ibid.
7. Anand Mahindra Success Story: An Inspirational Journey. Retrieved from: https://insider.finology.in/success-stories/anand-mahindra-success-story
8. Ibid.
9. Anand G Mahindra, MBA 1981. Retrieved from: https://www.alumni.hbs.edu/stories/Pages/story-bulletin.aspx?num=1994
10. Anand Mahindra Success Story: An Inspirational Journey. Retrieved from: https://insider.finology.in/success-stories/anand-mahindra-success-story
11. Ibid
12. Anand G Mahindra, MBA 1981. Retrieved from: https://www.alumni.hbs.edu/stories/Pages/story-bulletin.aspx?num=1994
13. 25 most powerful businesspeople in Asia. Retrieved from: https://money.cnn.com/galleries/2011/news/international/1104/gallery.asia_most_powerful.fortune/25.html
14. Anand Mahindra Success Story: An Inspirational Journey. Retrieved from: https://insider.finology.in/success-stories/anand-mahindra-success-story
15. Anand Mahindra Success Story: An Inspirational Journey. Retrieved from: https://insider.finology.in/success-stories/anand-mahindra-success-story

16. Mahindra gives $10M for Humanities Center. Retrieved from: https://news.harvard.edu/gazette/story/2010/10/anand-mahindra-gives-10m-for-humanities-center/
17. ET Awards: Mahindra & Mahindra wins Corporate Citizen award for empowering the girl child. Retrieved from: https://economictimes.indiatimes.com/news/company/corporate-trends/et-awards-mahindra-mahindra-wins-corporate-citizen-award-for-empowering-the-girl-child/articleshow/60369125.cms?utm_source=contentofinterest&utm_medium=text&utm_campaign=cppst
18. Anand Mahindra, Lakshmi Mittal among world's greatest leaders: Fortune magazine. Retrieved from: https://www.thehindu.com/news/national/anand-mahindra-lakshmi-mittal-among-worlds-greatest-leaders-fortune-magazine/article5811270.ece
19. 25 most powerful businesspeople in Asia. Retrieved from: https://money.cnn.com/galleries/2011/news/international/1104/gallery.asia_most_powerful.fortune/25.html

G V Krishna Reddy
Shaping Infrastructure Landscapes

1. Chhatrapati Shivaji International Airport Terminal 2, Mumbai, India. Retrieved from: https://www.airport-technology.com/projects/terminal-2-chhatrapati-shivaji-international-airport-mumbai/
2. Who is GV Krishna Reddy? A story of an illustrious business career and active social action. Retrieved from: https://www.thecitizen.in/index.php/en/NewsDetail/index/12/19995/Who-is-GV-Krishna-Reddy-A-story-of-an-illustrious-business-career-and-active-social-action---
3. Ibid.
4. Ibid.
5. GVK EMRI. Retrieved from: https://en.wikipedia.org/wiki/GVK_EMRI
6. Who is GV Krishna Reddy? A story of an illustrious business career and active social action. Retrieved from: https://www.thecitizen.in/index.php/en/NewsDetail/index/12/19995/Who-is-GV-Krishna-Reddy-A-story-of-an-illustrious-business-career-and-active-social-action---
7. Munneru river is a tributary of the Krishna rives and flows in the Khammam district of Telangana and Krishna district of Andhra Pradesh.

8. Face Challenges, Work Hard. Retrieved from: https://www.businesstoday.in/magazine/from-the-mag/story/face-challenges-work-hard-says-gvk-reddy-founder-and-chairman-gvk-87308-2017-
9. Ibid.

Adi Burjorji Godrej
Architect of the Godrej Group

1. https://www.fortuneindia.com/long-reads/adi-godrej-humility-redefined/109622
2. https://failurebeforesuccess.com/ardeshir-godrej/
3. https://www.youtube.com/watch?v=I22AwvH-vBw
4. https://www.youtube.com/watch?v=CHSB4Cu1mhc
5. https://www.businessworld.in/article/Sales-Is-Vanity-Profit-Is-Sanity-Cash-Is-Reality/08-11-2014-71548/

Nagavara Ramarao Narayan Murthy
Founding Father of Infosys

1. https://www.nytimes.com/1999/12/16/world/india-s-high-tech-and-sheepish-capitalism.html
2. https://www.livemint.com/news/india/why-narayana-murthy-rejected-air-india-and-two-other-jobs-to-join-less-paying-iim-ahmedabad-11680616532596.html
3. https://toistudent.timesofindia.indiatimes.com/news/leadership/narayana-murthy-shares-life-lessons/76805.html
4. https://economictimes.indiatimes.com/tech/ites/government-helped-infosys-at-its-critical-hour-nr-narayana-murthy/articleshow/50845768.cms?from=mdr
5. https://economictimes.indiatimes.com/markets/stocks/news/narayana-murthy-shares-9-lessons-learnt-as-an-entrepreneur-from-his-infosys-days/articleshow/92782337.cms?from=mdr

Rajendra Singh Pawar
Pioneering IT Education

1. Rajendra Singh Pawar - Alumni Affairs, IITD. Retrieved from: https://alumni.iitd.ac.in/home/index.php/1995/11/23/mr-rajendra-singh-pawar/
2. NIIT Limited. Retrieved from: https://www.google.com/finance/quote/D:NSE?sa=X&ved=2ahUKEwjno4eywZT9AhVZ_3MBHVkaCcgQ3ecFegQIJxAh
3. Rajendra Singh Pawar - The Scindia School. Retrieved from: https://www.scindia.edu/scindia_management/rajender-singh-pawar/

4. First-mover advantage ensured our leadership in IT training space: Rajendra S. Pawar, NIIT. Retrieved from: https://www.dqindia.com/first-mover-advantage-ensured-leadership-training-space-rajendra-s-pawar-niit/
5. Ibid.
6. Ibid.
7. Rajendra Singh Pawar Padma Bhushan awarded In 2011. Retrieved from: http://www.edubilla.com/award/padma-bhushan/rajendra-singh-pawar/
8. Technology will be a subservient tool in education: Rajendra Singh Pawar, Chairman and Co-Founder, NIIT Group and Founder, NIIT University. Retrieved from: http://bweducation.businessworld.in/article/Technology-Will-Be-A-Subservient-Tool-In-Education-Rajendra-Singh-Pawar-Chairman-And-Co-Founder-NIIT-Group-And-Founder-NIIT-University-/31-08-2020-314857/
9. Ibid.

Anil Kumar Manibhai Naik
Industrial Titan

1. https://www.forbes.com/sites/anuraghunathan/2015/03/30/indias-mr-infrastructure-a-m-naik-of-larsen-toubro-completes-50-years-at-the-conglomerate/?sh=e0ba7483485a
2. https://www.suchetadalal.com/?id=4f28061f-8177-7bb2-492e8bb5b8ad&base=sections&f&t=AM+Naik+-+A+rare+interview+to+MoneyLIFE
3. Merchant, M. 2017. The Nationalist: How A.M. Naik Overcame Great Odds to Transform Larsen & Toubro into a Global Powerhouse. Harper Business, India.
4. https://www.maneeshmedia.com/anilkumar-manibhai-naik/
5. https://www.businesstoday.in/magazine/cover-story/story/best-ceos-india-larsen-toubro-am-naik-interview-28991-2012-01-12

Ratan Tata
Luminary of Industrial Innovation

1. Piramal, G & Herdeck, M. 1985. India's Industrialists: Volume 1.
2. https://www.businesstoday.in/trending/story/jamsetji-tata-has-provided-us-with-inspiration-ethics-says-ratan-tata-324576-2022-03-03
3. Gaurav, K. 2020. Ratan Tata Says His Grandmother Taught Him To Retain His Dignity At All Costs. Republic World, February 12.

4. https://www.virsanghvi.com/People-Detail.aspx?Key=3
5. https://parsikhabar.net/individuals/came-close-to-getting-married-four-times-ratan-tata/3062/
6. Piramal, G. Business Maharajas. Penguin, India.
7. Sanghvi, V. 2007. Men of Steel: India's Business Leaders in Candid Conversation. Lotus Roli Books.

SPORTS

Mithali Raj
Batting Through Boundaries

1. https://organiser.org/2017/11/20/70395/general/r47acc7c9/
2. Das, S. 2018. Free hit: The story of women's cricket in India. Harper Sports India.
3. Raj, M. 2018. Unguarded. Penguin Books.
4. https://www.thecricketmonthly.com/story/1041251/the-sleepy-girl-who-woke-up-a-generation
5. https://www.newindianexpress.com/sport/2015/jan/27/Surprised-by-Padma-Mithali-Remembers-Late-Coach-Sampath-710055.html
6. https://www.thecricketmonthly.com/story/1041251/the-sleepy-girl-who-woke-up-a-generation
7. Das, S. 2018. Free hit: The story of women's cricket in India. Harper Sports India
8. https://www.thestatesman.com/sports/indian-womens-cricket-mithali-raj-calls-it-a-day-1503079198.html

Mahendra Singh Dhoni
Cricket Icon and Revered Captain

1. International Cricket Council, cricket's apex governing body.
2. Tournament played between the cricketing teams from the sub-continent.
3. Indian Premier League is a men's 20-over cricketing tournament held in India
4. Dhoni's leadership. Retrieved from: http://epaper.lokmat.com/articlepage.php?articleid=LOK_JLLK_20220325_5_3
5. MECON (Metallurgical and Engineering Consultants (India) Limited) is a central-government public sector undertaking that provides engineering consulting to companies.
6. Ranchi rocker. Retrieved from: https://www.tribuneindia.com/2006/20060429/saturday/main1.htm

End Notes | 343

7. Vinoo Mankad Trophy is a national-level under-19 ODI tournament organized by the Board of Control for Cricket in India (BCCI).
8. Dhoni: The Kharagpur story. Retrieved from: https://www.telegraphindia.com/west-bengal/dhoni-the-kharagpur-story/cid/1497897
9. TRDO — a system that unearthed Dhoni, Ishant and Raina — gets a thumbs up. Retrieved from: https://www.thehindu.com/sport/cricket/trdo-a-system-that-unearthed-dhoni-ishant-and-raina-gets-a-thumbs-up/article7298917.ece
10. Highest scores by wicket keepers. Retrieved from: https://in.rediff.com/cricket/2005/apr/06dhoni.htm
11. India versus Sri Lanka. Retrieved from: https://www.espncricinfo.com/series/sri-lanka-tour-of-india-2005-06-218259/india-vs-sri-lanka-3rd-odi-223634/full-scorecard
12. Kapil Dev is a former Indian cricketer who led his team to win the 1983 world cup.
13. On this Day: MS Dhoni's India clinched T20 World Cup with memorable triumph over Pakistan. Retreived from: https://www.firstpost.com/firstcricket/sports-news/on-this-day-ms-dhonis-india-clinched-t20-world-cup-with-memorable-triumph-over-pakistan-8847001.html
14. MS Dhoni celebrates anniversary of ICC World Cup 2011 win with CSK teammates. Retrieved from: https://www.wionews.com/sports/ms-dhoni-celebrates-anniversary-of-icc-world-cup-2011-win-with-csk-teammates-467785
15. MS Dhoni. Retrieved from: https://en.wikipedia.org/wiki/MS_Dhoni
16. MS Dhoni's Padma Bhushan award remind stars of 2011 Cricket World Cup win. Retrieved from: https://www.hindustantimes.com/cricket/ms-dhoni-s-padma-bhushan-award-reminds-stars-of-2011-cricket-world-cup-win/story-0EHBp2bZFa5GTFczZyZa3K.html

Rahul Sharad Dravid
Upholding the Spirit of Cricket

1. Meet Rahul Sharad Dravid. Retrieved from: https://timesofindia.indiatimes.com/home/sunday-times/deep-focus/Meet-Rahul-Sharad-Dravid/articleshow/1675924.cms
2. The great wall of India. Retrieved from: https://web.archive.org/web/20110716094607/http://www.verveonline.com/29/people/rahul/full.shtml

3. Ranji trophy is a domestic first-class cricketing tournament organised in India. It is one of the most reputed domestic cricketing tournament in the country.
4. A three-sided one-day international (ODI) tournament hosted by India and played between India, New Zealand and West Indies.
5. Javagal Srinath is an Indian cricketer who played in the Indian national team as a fast baller. He also belongs to Karnataka.
6. Dravid returns to where it all began. Retrieved from: https://web.archive.org/web/20150924195402/http://www.espncricinfo.com/england-v-india-2011/content/story/523876.html
7. Rahul Dravid in Tests. Retrieved from:https://web.archive.org/web/20150920132508/http://stats.espncricinfo.com/ci/engine/player/28114.html?class=1;filter=advanced;orderby=start;season=1996;-season=1996%2F97;season=1997;season=1997%2F98;template=results;type=batting;view=innings
8. Rahul Dravid. Retrieved from: https://web.archive.org/web/20140326192118/http://stats.espncricinfo.com/ci/engine/player/28114.html?class=2%3Bspanmax1%3D31%2B-dec%2B1998%3Bspanval1%3Dspan%3Btemplate%3Dresults%3Btype%3Dbatting
9. India in New Zealand ODI series. Retrieved from: https://web.archive.org/web/20160105112712/http://stats.espncricinfo.com/ci/engine/records/batting/most_runs_career.html?id=778%3Btype%3Dseries
10. Most runs in 1999 world cup. Retrieved from: https://web.archive.org/web/20151017171232/http://www.khelnama.com/130620/cricket/features/golden-debuts-day-sourav-ganguly-rahul-dravid-lords/10043
11. Batting records. Retrieved from: https://web.archive.org/web/20190525232013/http://stats.espncricinfo.com/ci/engine/stats/index.html?class=11;filter=advanced;orderby=runs;season=2002;-season=2002%2F03;season=2003;season=2003%2F04;-season=2004;season=2004%2F05;season=2005;season=2005%2F06;season=2006;template=results;type=batting
12. Full text of Rahul Dravid's retirement speech. Retrieved from: https://www.indiatoday.in/sports/cricket/story/rahul-dravid-retirement-speech-95431-2012-03-08
13. Is Rahul Dravid the greatest middle-order batsman of all time? Retrieved from: https://www.bbc.com/sport/cricket/17310407
14. Ibid.
15. International Cricket Council is Cricket's apex body.

Pankaj Advani
Cue Sports Pro

1. We need to focus a bit more on sports that do not feature in the Olympics: Pankaj Advani. Retrieved from: https://thebridge.in/cue-sports/need-focus-sports-do-not-feature-olympics-pankaj-advani-26831
2. Pankaj Advani finishes on a high, claims top position. Retrieved from: https://economictimes.indiatimes.com/news/sports/pankaj-advani-finishes-on-a-high-claims-top-position/articleshow/87258107.cms?utm_source=contentofinterest&utm_medium=text&utm_campaign=cppst
3. Pankaj Advani gets his due, says no hard feelings against government. Retrieved from: https://www.dtnext.in/sports/2018/01/26/pankaj-advani-gets-his-due-says-no-hard-feelings-against-government
4. Feels great when people say things like 'he is the Messi of our sport': Pankaj Advani. Retrieved from: https://timesofindia.indiatimes.com/sports/more-sports/others/feels-great-when-people-say-things-like-he-is-the-messi-of-our-sport-pankaj-advani/articleshow/87186842.cms

Mary Kom
The Boxing Phenomenon

1. This chapter, including all direct quotes, are from Mary Kom's autobiography Unbreakable (co-authored with Dina Serto).

Pullela Gopichand
A Beacon of Excellence in India's Sporting Legacy

1. Prakash Padukone is a former Indian badminton player who won the 'All England Open Badminton Championship' in 1980. He was also the world number 1 in 1980.
2. The 'All England Open Badminton Championship' is the world's oldest and one of the most prestigious badminton championships. It was upgraded to the Super Series Premier Status in 2011. A super series premier status offers higher ranking points and higher prize money to the players.
3. P Gopichand. Retrieved from: https://www.webindia123.com/personal/sports/gopi.htm

4. Star Maker. Retrieved from: https://www.telegraphindia.com/culture/star-maker/cid/492520
5. Dhyana app brings Pullela Gopichand as mental fitness trainer: Here's what you need to know. Retrieved from: https://www.indiatvnews.com/technology/news-dhyana-app-brings-pullela-gopichand-as-mental-fitness-trainer-670607

P V Sindhu
The Shuttle Queen

1. India's second highest sporting honour given for outstanding performance and contributions in sports.
2. The Rise of the Badminton Star PV Sindhu. Retrieved from: https://www.entrepreneur.com/en-in/lifestyle/the-rise-of-the-badminton-star-pv-sindhu/288710
3. A badminton academy run by Pullela Gopichand in Hyderabad.
4. Ibid.
5. Aiming for the stars. Retrieved from: https://web.archive.org/web/20121108060446/http://www.hindu.com/mp/2008/04/10/stories/2008041050140300.htm
6. Ibid.
7. Badminton Gold for Sindhu. Retrieved from: https://www.thehindu.com/news/cities/Hyderabad/badminton-gold-for-sindhu/article2446408.ece/amp/
8. Ibid.
9. Charting PV Sindhu's course through world badminton rankings. Retrieved from: https://olympics.com/en/news/pv-sindhu-ranking-bwf-badminton-history
10. When PV Sindhu became Indian badminton's golden girl. Retrieved from: https://olympics.com/en/featured-news/indian-badminton-pv-sindhu-how-bwf-world-championships-gold-2019
11. Heralding a new era: PV Sindhu's silver lining in an emphatic Olympic debut. Retrieved from: https://olympics.com/en/news/indian-badminton-pv-sindhu-olympics-rio-2016-silver-medal-carolina-marin
12. The rise and rise of Brand Sindhu. Retrieved from: https://www.business-standard.com/article/current-affairs/the-rise-and-rise-of-brand-sindhu-117090300847_1.html
13. The highest paid female athletes. Retrieved from: https://www.forbes.com/sites/kurtbadenhausen/2018/08/21/the-highest-paid-female-athletes-2018/

Bachendri Pal
Summit Conqueror

1. National Adventure Foundation (NAF) is one of the oldest and most reputed organisations dedicated to the promotion of adventure activities and sports as a 'growth and development oriented, positive, activity' among the youth of the country.
2. The day Bachendri conquered the Everest and a lot more. Retrieved from: https://economictimes.indiatimes.com/news/sports/the-day-bachendri-conquered-the-everest-and-a-lot-more/articleshow/75914249.cms?utm_source=contentofinterest&utm_medium=text&utm_campaign=cppst
3. How Bachendri Pal became the first Indian woman to climb Mount Everest!. Retrieved from: https://www.thebetterindia.com/113258/bachendri-pal-first-indian-woman-mount-everest/#:~:text=Share%20it%20now!&text=%E2%80%9CMy%20heart%20stood%20still,My%20Journey%20to%20the%20Top
4. Bachendri Pal: The first Indian woman to climb the Mount Everest. Retrieved from : https://feminisminindia.com/2022/05/25/bachendri-pal-the-first-indian-woman-to-climb-the-mount/
5. Tata Steel Adventure Foundation. Available at: https://www.tata.com/newsroom/tata-people-bachendri-pal-tata-steel-adventure-foundation ment-speech-95431-2012-03-08
6. Is Rahul Dravid the greatest middle-order batsman of all time? Retrieved from: https://www.bbc.com/sport/cricket/17310407
7. Ibid.

Vishwanathan Anand
India's Grandmaster

1. Murray, H J R (1913). A history of chess. Clarendon Press.
2. https://www.nytimes.com/2010/08/09/world/asia/09india.html
3. https://www.indiatoday.in/magazine/sport/story/19870831-vishwanathan-anand-wins-world-junior-chess-title-in-the-philippines-799241-1987-08-30
4. Anand, V. Mind Master: Winning Lessons from a Champion's Life. Hachette Books
5. https://www.espn.com/chess/story/_/id/29967952/how-sp-balasubrahmanyam-helped-teenage-viswanathan-anand-break
6. https://archive.nytimes.com/india.blogs.nytimes.com/2013/04/03/a-conversation-with-chess-champion-viswanathan-anand/

Abhinav Bindra
Hitting Bull's Eye

1. This profile, including the direct quotes, are based on Bindra's book: Bindra, A. (2013). A shot at history: My obsessive journey to Olympic Gold. Harper Collins.

Harry Boniface Prabhu
A Pioneer of the Sport in India

1. https://newzhook.com/story/12553/
2. https://timesofindia.indiatimes.com/what-a-racquet/articleshow/49780.cms
3. https://timesofindia.indiatimes.com/what-a-racquet/articleshow/49780.cms
4. https://www.hindustantimes.com/pune-news/there-are-no-barriers-for-disabled-people-says-boniface-prabhu-a-quadriplegic-wheelchair-tennis-champion/story-OvsjQ63ePVk5MOe7OASUrO.html
5. https://www.hindustantimes.com/pune-news/there-are-no-barriers-for-disabled-people-says-boniface-prabhu-a-quadriplegic-wheelchair-tennis-champion/story-OvsjQ63ePVk5MOe7OASUrO.html

Love Raj Singh Dharmshaktu
Summiteer Extraordinary

1. https://www.nytimes.com/2019/05/30/sports/everest-bodies-global-warming.html
2. https://www.thestatesman.com/exclusive-interviews/saturday-interview-standing-atop-everest-magical-1502944186.html
3. https://www.thehindu.com/features/magazine/no-work-on-any-expedition-was-below-my-dignity/article4746016.ece
4. https://www.ft.com/content/2dbe8716-2dec-11e2-9988-00144feabdc0
5. https://www.thehansindia.com/life-style/discouragements-make-life-more-interesting-says-loveraj-singh-683403#:~:text=%22There%20is%20no%20short%20cut,preparation%20to%20conquer%20the%20Everest.

Arunima Sinha
Conquering the Mountain

1. This profile, and the direct quotes here, are based on Sinha's autobiography: Sinha, A. 2014. Born Again on the Mountain: A Story of Losing Everything and Finding it Back. Penguin Books India.

Deepika Kumari
Bowstring of Ambition

1. https://sportscafe.in/archery/articles/2016/jul/27/deepika-kumari-4-years-after-that-windy-day-in-london-rio-offers-redemption
2. https://www.deccanherald.com/sports/other-sports/world-number-1-archer-deepikas-journey-from-an-emaciated-12-year-old-to-indias-olympic-medal-prospect-1011044.html
3. https://www.thenationalnews.com/arts-culture/film/deepika-kumari-from-poverty-in-rural-india-to-olympic-archery-1.710332
4. https://www.hindustantimes.com/lifestyle/art-culture/a-common-aim-meet-champion-archers-deepika-kumari-and-atanu-das-101619787966328.html
5. Dubey, A., & Mukherjea, S. (2019). She Dared: Women in Indian Sports. Rupa Publications India.

Devendra Jhajharia
Paralympic Legend

1. Devendra Jhajharia: Inspirational story of India's para javelin thrower. Retrieved from: https://www.kreedon.com/devendra-jhajharia-indias-paralympic-javelin-thrower-athlete-story/?amp
2. Devendra Jhajharia: The one-armed javelin genius. Retrieved from: https://www.livemint.com/news/business-of-life/devendra-jhajharia-the-one-armed-javelin-genius-1541214608239.html
3. Ibid.
4. Tokyo Paralympics 2020: Driven by 'junoon', Devendra Jhajharia takes aim at making history again. Retrieved from: https://www.firstpost.com/sports/tokyo-paralympics-2020-driven-by-junoon-devendra-jhajharia-takes-aim-at-making-history-again-9921391.html
5. The Dronacharya award is given to outstanding coaches in sports in India. The award is named after Drona, the master teacher of princes in the Indian epic, Mahabharata.

6. The Paralympic games (also known as the Paralympics or the Games of the Paralympiad) is a periodic series of international multisport events that involves athletes with a range of physical disabilities. Started in 1948, the Paralympics has become one of the largest international sporting events. It is governed by the International Paralympic Committee (IPC) and are organised in parallel and in a similar manner to the Olympic games.
7. The FESPIC Games, short for the Far East and South Pacific Games for the Disabled, is a major multi-sport event for disabled athletes in Asia and South Pacific. The games were first organised in 1975.
8. Indian Javelin thrower Devendra Jhajharia wins silver medal at IPC Para-athletics meet. Retrieved from: https://www.sportskeeda.com/sports/indian-javelin-thrower-devendra-jhajharia-wins-silver-world-para-athletics-meet
9. Ibid.
10. Devendra Jhajharia: The one-armed javelin genius. Retrieved from: https://www.livemint.com/news/business-of-life/devendra-jhajharia-the-one-armed-javelin-genius-1541214608239.html
11. Jhajharia competes in the F46 category where 'F' stands for field event and 45-47 is for 'upper limb(s) deficiency, impaired muscle power or impaired range of movement'.
12. Tokyo Paralympics 2020: Driven by 'junoon', Devendra Jhajharia takes aim at making history again. Retrieved from: https://www.firstpost.com/sports/tokyo-paralympics-2020-driven-by-junoon-devendra-jhajharia-takes-aim-at-making-history-again-9921391.html
13. Jhajharia's wife Manju was a national-level kabaddi player.
14. Dad I topped, now it's your turn: Daughter told Jhajharia. Retrieved from: http://timesofindia.indiatimes.com/articleshow/54328463.cms?utm_source=contentofinterest&utm_medium=text&utm_campaign=cppst
15. Devendra Jhajharia: Inspirational story of India's Para Javelin Thrower. Retrieved from: https://www.kreedon.com/devendra-jhajharia-indias-paralympic-javelin-thrower-athlete-story/?amp

SOCIAL WORK

Saalumarada Thimmakka
Compassionate Environmentalist

1. http://www.goodnewsindia.com/Pages/content/inspirational/thimmakka.html

2. https://blogs.worldbank.org/endpovertyinsouthasia/80-thimmakka-has-planted-more-8000-saplings
3. https://www.aljazeera.com/features/2013/10/13/childless-woman-who-mothered-trees
4. https://www.femina.in/trending/achievers/meet-the-105-year-old-environmentalist-from-karnataka-135934.html
5. https://bookofachievers.com/articles/saalumarada-thimmakka-the-mother-to-more-than-8000-trees

Anil Prakash Joshi
Making Rural India Economically Independent

1. Science for Equity, Empowerment & Development Division whose emphasis is placed on equity in development, so that the benefits of technological growth reach the majority of the population, particularly the disadvantaged sections, leading to an improved quality of life for every citizen of the country.
2. Institute Lecture: In Conversation with Dr. Anil Joshi. Retrieved from: http://watchout.iitr.ac.in/2020/03/lecture-dr-anil
3. Ibid.
4. Dr. Anil Prakash Joshi. Retrieved from: https://www.jamnalalbajajfoundation.org/awards/archives/2006/science-and-technology/anil-prakash-joshi
5. Green activist Anil Prakash Joshi bats for Gross Environment Product. Retrieved from: https://www.thestatesman.com/india/green-activist-anil-prakash-joshi-bats-for-gross-environment-product-1502713405.html

Hari Pal Singh Ahluwalia
The Summit Of The Mind

1. http://www.the-south-asian.com/April-June2010/Major-HPS_Ahluwalia.htm
2. Ahluwalia, H P S 2016. Higher than Everest: Memoirs of a Mountaineer. Niyogi Books.
3. Ahluwalia, H P S 2001. The Everest Within. Hemkunt Publishers Pvt. Ltd.
4. https://www.isiconline.org/
5. https://theprint.in/india/remembering-major-h-p-s-ahluwalia-mountaineer-army-man-social-worker-a-fighter-forever/804177/

Arunachalam Muruganantham
The Pad Man

1. https://www.bbc.com/news/magazine-26260978
2. https://www.gqindia.com/content/pad-man-akshay-kumar-inspiration-arunachalam-muruganantham
3. https://www.thehindubusinessline.com/blchangemakers/period-story-how-padman-muruganantham-arunachalam-scripted-a-hygiene-revolution/article62222233.ece
4. https://economictimes.indiatimes.com/news/politics-and-nation/meet-arunachalam-muruganantham-the-man-who-wore-a-sanitary-pad-to-break-a-taboo/game-changer/slideshow/58340287.cms
5. https://www.bbc.com/news/magazine-26260978
6. https://interactive.aljazeera.com/aje/shorts/india-menstruation-man/
7. https://www.thehindubusinessline.com/blchangemakers/period-story-how-padman-muruganantham-arunachalam-scripted-a-hygiene-revolution/article62222233.ece

Tulsi Gowda
Cultivating Trees

1. https://economictimes.indiatimes.com/magazines/travel/visit-the-400-year-old-tribes-of-halakki-vokkaligas-and-sidhis-in-uttara-kannada/articleshow/46771930.cms?from=mdr
2. https://www.goheritagerun.com/halakki-vokkaliga-discover-powerful-community-uttara-kannada/
3. https://www.thebeacon.in/2021/06/10/tulsi-gowda-barefoot-ecologist-brings-forests-to-life/
4. https://www.newindianexpress.com/good-news/2021/nov/09/30000-trees-and-counting-encyclopedia-of-forest-tulasi-gowda-elated-at-receiving-padma-shri-2381475.html
5. https://indusscrolls.com/indias-barefoot-activist-tulsi-gowda-brings-forests-to-life
6. https://www.newsbharati.com/Encyc/2021/11/13/Tulsi-Gowda.html

Bindeshwar Pathak
The Man behind Sulabh Shauchalaya

1. https://yourstory.com/2015/08/dr-bindeshwar-pathak
2. https://www.indiatoday.in/india/east/story/sulabh-founder-bindeshwar-pathak-beats-poverty-caste-barrier-emerges-unusual-entrepreneur-of-bihar-india-today-156862-2013-03-22

3. http://www.goodnewsindia.com/index.php/Magazine/story/sulabh/P1/
4. https://www.news18.com/news/mission-paani/bindeshwar-pathak-activist-who-once-saw-no-loo-in-his-big-house-helped-indians-build-millions-of-toilets-4453640.html
5. https://www.sulabhinternational.org/founders-profile-dr-bindeshwar-pathak/

Baburao Hazare
Campaigning for Mankind

1. https://www.theatlantic.com/international/archive/2011/12/the-amazing-rise-of-anna-hazare-indias-gandhi-like-protest-leader/249542/
2. https://economictimes.indiatimes.com/anna-hazare-reborn-in-battlefield-of-khem-karan/articleshow/8005166.cms?from=mdr
3. https://timesofindia.indiatimes.com/anna-hazare-the-guest-editor/top-headlines/i-was-re-born-in-the-battlefield-of-khem-karan/articleshow/8002771.cms
4. https://www.readersdigest.in/features/story-why-god-saved-anna-hazare-127487
5. Sharma, M. (2006). The making of moral authority: Anna Hazare and watershed management programme in Ralegan Siddhi. Economic and Political Weekly, 41(20), 1981-1988.
6. https://pulitzercenter.org/stories/occupy-delhi-gandhian-take-corruption

LITERATURE AND EDUCATION

Sitakant Mahapatra
Weaving Words into Timeless Tapestries

1. Sitakant Mahapatra, 1937. Available at: https://www.loc.gov/acq/ovop/delhi/salrp/sitakantmahapatra.html
2. Primitive poetry represents the textual practices (structures, grammar) that allow a closer understanding of the verbal practices carried out in cultures that do not have access to writing. It is also called 'wild', 'tribal' or 'archaic'poetry.
3. Primitive poetry and a poet. Retrieved from: https://www.proquest.com/docview/499586128/fulltextPDF/C65619599D3846B7PQ/1?accountid=27540
4. Poetry comes from the soul and it can be written in your mother tongue: Sitakant Mahapatra on his love for Odia and literature.

Retrieved from: https://www.edexlive.com/people/2019/jan/04/padma-vibhushan-sitakant-mahapatra-tells-us-about-his-love-for-books-poetry-and-literature-4925.html
5. India's National Academy of Letters bestows the Sahitya Akademi Award to authors of outstanding books of literary merit published in Indian languages (22 languages recognised by the Indian constitution along with English and Rajasthani language).
6. Jnanpith Award is the oldest and the highest Indian literary award presented annually by the Bharatiya Jnanpith – a literary and research organisation found in 1944 and located in Delhi to undertake systematic research and publication of Indian languages such as Sanskrit, Prakrit, Pali, etc. – to an author for his/her 'outstanding contribution towards literature'.
7. Sitakant Mahapatra. Retrieved from: https://en.wikipedia.org/wiki/Sitakant_Mahapatra
8. Sitakant Mahapatra Jnanpith award awarded in 1993. Retrieved from: http://www.edubilla.com/award/jnanpith-award/sitakant-mahapatra/
9. Tagore Peace award for Odia poet Sitakant Mahapatra. Retrieved from: https://www.newindianexpress.com/states/odisha/2017/apr/29/tagore-peace-award-for-odia-poet-sitakant-mahapatra-1599062.html
10. Padma Vibhushan for Sitakant Mahapatra. Retrieved from: https://timesofindia.indiatimes.com/city/bhubaneswar/padma-vibhushan-for-sitakant-mahapatraashok/articleshow/7363220.cms
11. Padma Vibhushan for Sitakant Mahapatra Ashok. Retrieved from: https://timesofindia.indiatimes.com/city/bhubaneswar/padma-vibhushan-for-sitakant-mahapatraashok/articleshow/7363220.cms

Ruskin Bond
Crafting Tales of Charm and Nostalgia
1. British air force
2. The name is Bond, Ruskin Bond - All India News. http://www.allindianewssite.com/7396/the-name-is-bond-ruskin-bond/#ixzz1a4Nlgw20
3. John Llewellyn Rhys Prize was a prize given annually for the best work of literature by an author aged 35 or less from the Commonwealth countries written in English and published from the UK.
4. Booked by Bond. Retrieved from: https://www.thehindu.com/features/kids/booked-by-bond/article5465474.ece

5. Escape to life. Retrieved from: https://www.nytimes.com/1957/03/17/archives/escape-to-life.html
6. Booked by Bond. Retrieved from: https://www.thehindu.com/features/kids/booked-by-bond/article5465474.ece
7. The name is Bond, Ruskin Bond - All India News http://www.allindianewssite.com/7396/the-name-is-bond-ruskin-bond/#ixzz1a4Nlgw20
8. Ibid.
9. My writings reflect my lonely childhood: Ruskin Bond. Retrieved from: https://indianexpress.com/article/lifestyle/life-style/my-writings-reflect-my-lonely-childhood-ruskin-bond/
10. Ruskin Bond: His life as a story. Retrieved from: https://www.livemint.com/Leisure/p2iFf1n3LuKRvXJV2e1YqJ/Ruskin-Bond-His-life-as-a-story.html
11. Khorana, Meena G. (2003). The life and works of Ruskin Bond. Praegar, Greenwood. p. 1–10. ISBN 9780313311857.
12. The award is given by India's National Academy of Letters to writers of outstanding books published in any of the 22 languages recognised by the Indian constitution alongwith English and Rajasthani.
13. At 81, Ruskin Bond's tryst with his tireless pen continues. Retrieved from: https://www.hindustantimes.com/books/at-81-ruskin-bond-s-tryst-with-his-tireless-pen-continues/story-6st8jXIEz5E-WadwoBGfWNP.html
14. A Landour day with Ruskin Bond. Retrieved from: https://web.archive.org/web/20160108202224/http://www.thehindubusinessline.com/todays-paper/tp-life/article1027118.ece

MT Vasudevan Nair
Doyen of Malayalam Literature

1. https://www.tribuneindia.com/2005/20050417/spectrum/book8.htm
2. https://english.mathrubhumi.com/special-pages/mathrubhumi-100-years/mt-vasudevan-nair-opens-up-about-his-early-days-at-mathrubhumi-1.7346212
3. https://timesofindia.indiatimes.com/life-style/books/features/celebrated-malayalam-author-mt-vasudevan-nair-to-be-given-2019-puthoor-award/articleshow/68450561.cms
4. https://www.indiatoday.in/magazine/indiascope/story/19960215-madathu-thekkeppattu-vasudevan-nair-a-masters-of-post-independence-indian-literature-834831-1996-02-14

5. https://www.indiatoday.in/magazine/indiascope/story/19960215-madathu-thekkeppattu-vasudevan-nair-a-masters-of-post-independence-indian-literature-834831-1996-02-14

Shekhar Gupta
Shaping Discourse in Indian Media Landscape

1. Gupta, S. 2017. Walk the talk. Rupa Publications.
2. Gupta, S. 2015. Anticipating India: The Best of National Interest. Harper Collins.
3. https://www.outlookindia.com/magazine/story/confessions-of-a-shakhahari/295285
4. https://theprint.in/opinion/remembering-haryana-girl-becoming-heroic-astronaut/33159/
5. Gupta, S. 2017. Walk the talk. Rupa Publications.

Neelam Kler
Nurturing Health and Hope for infants

1. Branch of paediatrics that deals with the health of new born babies.
2. Babies that are born before the normal gestation period of 36-40 weeks.
3. Neonatologist Neelam Kler awarded Padma Bhushan. Retrieved from: https://www.dailypioneer.com/2014/sunday-edition/neonatologist-neelam-kler-awarded-padma-bhushan.html
4. Neelam Kler. Retrieved from: https://en.wikipedia.org/wiki/Neelam_Kler#cite_note-preterm_babies-2
5. Neonatologist Neelam Kler awarded Padma Bhushan. Retrieved from: https://www.dailypioneer.com/2014/sunday-edition/neonatologist-neelam-kler-awarded-padma-bhushan.html
6. Meet the Padma-Bhushan awardee doctor giving premature babies a new hope! Retrieved from: https://www.thebetterindia.com/140504/dr-neelam-kler-neonatologist-premature-babies/
7. Neonatologist Neelam Kler awarded Padma Bhushan. Retrieved from: https://www.dailypioneer.com/2014/sunday-edition/neonatologist-neelam-kler-awarded-padma-bhushan.html
8. Neelam Kler only physician to be conferred Padma Bhushan. Retrieved from: https://www.business-standard.com/article/news-ians/neelam-kler-only-physician-to-be-conferred-padma-bhushan-114012600504_1.html
9. Ibid.

10. Neonatologist Neelam Kler awarded Padma Bhushan. Retrieved from: https://www.dailypioneer.com/2014/sunday-edition/neonatologist-neelam-kler-awarded-padma-bhushan.html
11. Dr T S Kler and wife Dr Neelam Kler conferred with honorary fellowship of Punjab Academy of Sciences. Retrieved from: https://www.financialexpress.com/happening-now/dr-ts-kler-and-wife-dr-neelam-kler-conferred-with-honorary-fellowship-of-punjab-academy-of-sciences/42134/
12. Meet the Padma-Bhushan awardee doctor giving premature babies a new hope! Retrieved from: https://www.thebetterindia.com/140504/dr-neelam-kler-neonatologist-premature-babies/
13. Giving life to premature babies, Dr. Neelam Kler is the hope of countless mothers. Retrieved from: https://www.indianwomenblog.org/giving-life-to-premature-babies-dr-neelam-kler-is-the-hope-of-countless-mothers/?amp_markup=1

Devi Prasad Shetty
Revolutionising Medical Care

1. The Henry Ford of heart surgery. Retrieved from: https://www.wsj.com/articles/SB125875892887958111#articleTabs%3Darticle
2. Dr Devi Prasad Shetty. Retrieved from: https://www.narayanahealth.org/leadership/board-of-directors/dr-devi-shetty
3. Dr. Devi Prasad Shetty – Brief Profile. Retrieved from: https://www.narayanahealth.org/bangalore/cardiac-surgery-adult-cardiac-surgery-paediatric/dr-devi-prasad-shetty
4. Dr. Devi Prasad Shetty. Retrieved from: https://www.narayanahealth.org/leadership/board-of-directors/dr-devi-shetty
5. When I did a 100 heart operations in 1989, I knew it was possible to start a revolution in cardiac surgery: Dr Devi Shetty. Retrieved from https://www.indiatoday.in//magazine/anniversary/story/20210104-when-i-did-a-100-heart-operations-without-a-single-fatality-1753003-2020-12-26?onetap=true
6. Mary Teresa Bojaxhiu, also known as Mother Teresa, was an Albanian-Catholic nun who founded the Missionaries of Charity in 1950. She was awarded the Nobel Peace Prize in 1979 for her social and charitable work.
7. Ibid
8. Ibid
9. Heart surgery in India for $1,583 costs $106,385 in U.S. Retrieved from: https://www.bloomberg.com/news/articles/2013-07-28/heart-surgery-in-india-for-1-583-costs-106-385-in-u-s-#xj4y7vzkg

10. The Henry Ford of heart surgery. Retrieved from: https://www.wsj.com/articles/SB125875892887958111#articleTabs%3Darticle
11. Business Process Award Winner 2011. Available at: https://web.archive.org/web/20120602131115/http://www.economistconferences.co.uk/innovation/businessprocessawardwinner2011
12. Ibid.
13. Yeshasvini Health Insurance Scheme by Karnataka Government. Retrieved from https://www.policybazaar.com/health-insurance/govt-scheme/yeshasvini/
14. Who is Devi Shetty, head of Karnataka's Covid task force? Retrieved from: https://www.deccanherald.com/state/top-karnataka-stories/who-is-devi-shetty-head-of-karnataka-s-covid-task-force-985836.html
15. Henry Ford was an American industrialist who developed the idea of assembly lines and mass production for cars. He was the founder of the Ford Motor company.
16. India's philanthropist-surgeon delivers cardiac care Henry Ford-style. Retrieved from: https://www.npr.org/sections/goatsandsoda/2015/01/05/375142025/india-s-philanthropist-delivers-cardiac-surgery-henry-ford-style
17. Ibid.

Tsering Landol
An Advocate for Women's Health

1. How Ladakh's 1st gynaecologist changed the face of women's health in India's cold desert. Retrieved from: https://www.thebetterindia.com/183379/ladakh-first-gynaecologist-tsering-landol-inspirational-padma-shri/
2. Tejasvini: An interview with Tsering Landol, first woman Doctor from Ladakh. Retrieved from: https://www.youtube.com/watch?v=LOIr306ci2M
3. Hamam is a Turkish-origin heating system that uses wood to heat water in tanks.
4. Extraordinary Indians: How Padma Shri and Padma Bhushan recipient Tsering Landol became a pioneer of women's health in Ladakh. Retrieved from: https://www.readersdigest.in/features/story-extraordinary-indians-how-padma-shri-and-padma-bhushan-recipient-tsering-landol-became-a-pioneer-of-womens-health-in-ladakh-127104

Suresh Hariram Advani
Defeating Illness to Become Hope for Millions

1. Meet Dr Suresh Advani: India's first and best-known oncologist. Retrieved from: https://economictimes.indiatimes.com/meet-dr-suresh-advani-indias-first-and-best-known-oncologist/articleshow/21245370.cms
2. House job is a one-year internship where the new medical graduates are expected to work under the supervision of an experienced doctor to gain clinical experience.
3. Meet Dr Suresh Advani who pioneered bone-marrow transplant for leukaemia in India. Retrieved from: https://economictimes.indiatimes.com/news/company/corporate-trends/meet-dr-suresh-advani-who-pioneered-bone-marrow-transplant-for-leukaemia-in-india/articleshow/21194570.cms?from=mdr
4. In 1990, Dr Thomas won the Nobel Prize for his work on the development of cell and organ transplantation.
5. Myeloid leukaemia is a cancer that forms in the bone marrow of patients.
6. Ibid.
7. Meet Dr Suresh Advani: India's first and best-known oncologist. Retrieved from:https://economictimes.indiatimes.com/meet-dr-suresh-advani-indias-first-and-best-known-oncologist/articleshow/21245370.cms?utm_source=contentofinterest&utm_medium=text&utm_campaign=cppst
8. Dr Suresh Advani: An unshackled soul. Retrieved from:https://www.expresshealthcare.in/life-healthcare/dr-suresh-advani-an-unshackled-soul/176506/
9. Acute shortage of cancer specialists is the most critical issue: Suresh Advani. Retrieved from:https://www.livemint.com/Politics/vc1zSELfssdUI46r2W0AqM/Our-most-critical-issue-is-the-acute-shortage-of-cancer-spec.html

Saroja Vaidyanathan
Keeping Bharatanatyam Alive

1. https://thedanceindia.com/the-triumph-of-an-artistic-soul/
2. https://tamilnation.org/hundredtamils/saroja.htm

Ilaiyaraaja
Creating Timeless Melodies that Transcend Generations

1. Dalit is a word used to refer to backward classes (scheduled caste, scheduled tribe) in India.
2. Vaigai dam is built across the Vaigai river in the Theni district of Tamil Nadu.
3. Performance is an important component of a musical composition: Ilaiyaraaja. Retrieved from: https://www.thehindu.com/entertainment/music/performance-is-an-important-component-of-a-musical-composition-ilaiyaraaja/article61450194.ece
4. A kutcheri is a place where musicians used to present their performances and musical achievements (inventions) before the kings.
5. M S Viswanathan (24 June 1928 – 14 July 2015) was a famous Indian music director, actor and singer of the Tamil film industry. He had composed more than 800 songs for Tamil, Malayalam and Telegu films.
6. Salil Chowdhury (19 November 1925 – 5 September 1995) was a famous Indian poet, writer, song writer and music director. He wrote and composed songs mainly for Bengali, Hindi and Malayalam films.
7. Gurusala Krishnadas Venkatesh (21 September 1927 – 17 November 1993) was a famous Indian song composer who mainly worked for Kannada movies during 1960-80.
8. To appreciate Ilaiyaraaja's anti-caste politics, you have to listen to his music. Retrieved from: https://www.huffpost.com/archive/in/entry/to-appreciate-ilaiyaraaja-s-anti-caste-politics-you-have-to-listen-to-his-music_in_5eda5614c5b6817661649db5
9. Ibid.
10. Performance is an important component of a musical composition: Ilaiyaraaja. Retrieved from: https://www.thehindu.com/entertainment/music/performance-is-an-important-component-of-a-musical-composition-ilaiyaraaja/article61450194.ece
11. To appreciate Ilaiyaraaja's anti-caste politics, you have to listen to his music. Retrieved from: https://www.huffpost.com/archive/in/entry/to-appreciate-ilaiyaraaja-s-anti-caste-politics-you-have-to-listen-to-his-music_in_5eda5614c5b6817661649db5
12. Ibid.

Channulal Mishra
Maestro of Hindustani Classical Music

1. A gharana in Indian classical music is a system of social organization which links its musicians and dancers to a particular style of music or dance (through training, apprenticeship or by adherence). Kirana is a small town in Haryana.
2. Swarmandal (or surmandal) is a trapezoidal or rectangular shaped plucked string instrument that originated from India and is often used as an accompanying instrument by musicians.
3. A doyen's lessons. Retrieved from: https://www.dailypioneer.com/2017/vivacity/a-doyens-lessons.html
4. The magic of Pt. Chhannulal Mishra. Retrieved from: https://www.thehindu.com/entertainment/music/the-magic-of-pt-chhannulal-mishra/article29584250.ece
5. Padma Bhushan is too little, too late: Pt. Channulal Mishra. Retrieved from: https://www.thehindu.com/features/friday-review/music//article59915448.ece
6. A doyen's lessons. Retrieved from: https://www.dailypioneer.com/2017/vivacity/a-doyens-lessons.html

Ajoy Chakrabarty
Weaving Harmonic Tapestries with Emotion

1. Ustad Munawar Ali Khan is the son of Ustad Bade Ghulam Ali Khan, who was an Indian Hindustani classical vocalist, from the Patiala gharana.
2. Pt. Ajoy Chakrabarty – A class apart. Retrieved from: https://www.indiaforums.com/forum/topic/485320
3. How Padma awardee Ajoy Chakrabarty pursued music against odds. Retrieved from: https://www.thehindu.com/entertainment/music/ajoy-chakrabarty-the-seeker/article30931067.ece
4. Interview | Indian classical music needs boost. Retrieved from: https://www.deccanchronicle.com/nation/in-other-news/141221/classical-music-as-compulsory-subject-is-improbable-vocalist.html
5. Pandit Ajoy Chakrabarty; Shrutinandan. Retrieved from: https://ajoychakrabarty.com/#
6. Book Review: Pandit Ajoy Chakrabarty. Retrieved from: https://www.freepressjournal.in/book-reviews/book-review-pandit-ajoy-chakrabarty

7. Padma honours for Ajoy Chakrabarty, Manilal Nag. Retrieved from: https://timesofindia.indiatimes.com/city/kolkata/padma-honours-for-ajoy-chakraborty-manilal-nag/articleshow/73621920.cms
8. Prof. Rohini M. Godbole, Senapathy 'Kris' Gopalakrishnan and Pt. Ajoy Chakrabarty to receive honorary doctorate degrees from IIT Kanpur. Retrieved from: https://indiaeducationdiary.in/prof-rohini-m-godbole-senapathy-kris-gopalakrishnan-and-pt-ajoy-chakrabarty-to-receive-honorary-doctorate-degrees-from-iit-kanpur/
9. Ibid.
10. Mujib Borsho: Padma Bhushan Ajoy Chakrabarty unveils Raag Maitri to celebrate India-Bangladesh friendship. Retrieved from: https://www.indiablooms.com/life-details/AC/5829/mujib-borsho-padma-bhushan-ajoy-chakrabarty-unveils-raag-maitri-to-celebrate-india-bangladesh-friendship.html
11. Ajoy Chakraborty: 'There are few compositions that can actually carry the weight and demands of a raga.' Retrieved from: https://web.archive.org/web/20050506120503/http://www.hinduonnet.com/thehindu/mp/2005/03/19/stories/2005031901280300.htm

Hari Prasad Chaurasia
Reawakening the Bansuri

1. Akhara is a place for practice of Indian martial arts. The place includes provisions for boarding and lodging of players too.
2. Teaching the wind to sing: Pandit Hariprasad Chaurasia on blowing life into a reed. Retrieved from: https://indianexpress.com/article/lifestyle/art-and-culture/teaching-the-wind-to-sing-pandit-hariprasad-chaurasia-on-blowing-life-into-a-reed-4868654/
3. Ibid.
4. Mumbai's film industry.
5. Santoor is a trapezoid-shaped hammered dulcimer, and a variation of the Iranian Santur.
6. Surbahar is a plucked string instrument of the Hindustani classical music. Sometimes, it is also known as bass sitar.
7. Ibid.
8. Learning from the master: Corporate lessons from flute maestro Pandit Hariprasad Chaurasia. Retrieved from: https://www.firstpost.com/business/learning-from-the-master-corporate-lessons-from-flute-maestro-pandit-hariprasad-chaurasia-2188663.html

9. Flamboyant flautist. Retrieved from: https://web.archive.org/web/20160116154405/http://www.india-today.com/itoday/06071998/arts2.html

Zakir Hussain
Taking the Tabla to the World

1. https://www.nytimes.com/2009/05/01/arts/music/01huss.html
2. https://www.nytimes.com/2000/02/06/nyregion/ustad-alla-rakha-80-master-of-hindustani-classical-music.html
3. https://fountainink.in/essay/finding-his-own-way-in-a-world-of-tradition
4. Kabir, N. M. 2018. Zakir Hussain: A Life in Music. Harper Collins India.
5. https://www.npr.org/transcripts/375637915

A R Rahman
Musical Genius and Oscar-Winning Composer

1. https://www.indiatoday.in/magazine/society-and-the-arts/films/story/19940115-ar-rahman-makes-history-with-record-breaking-audio-cassette-sales-of-his-debut-film-roja-808663-1994-01-14
2. https://www.rediff.com/movies/slide-show/slide-show-1-extract-of-the-book-a-r-rahman-the-spirit-of-music/20110418.htm
3. https://www.thenewsminute.com/article/30-years-roja-movie-gave-us-musical-marvel-ar-rahman-166867
4. https://content.time.com/time/magazine/article/0,9171,629407,00.html
5. https://www.nytimes.com/2009/02/21/arts/music/21rahm.html
6. https://www.khabar.com/magazine/entertainment/the_secret_behind_the_allure_of_a._r._rahman.aspx

Sudarsan Pattnaik
Building Castles on Sand

1. https://www.globaltimes.cn/content/1179214.shtml
2. https://www.wsj.com/articles/BL-IRTB-19203
3. https://www.globalindian.com/story/indian-artists/sudarsan-pattnaik-how-a-school-dropout-became-a-world-renowned-sand-artist/
4. https://www.wsj.com/articles/BL-IRTB-19203

5. https://www.globalindian.com/story/indian-artists/sudarsan-pattnaik-how-a-school-dropout-became-a-world-renowned-sand-artist/
6. https://www.parentcircle.com/sand-artist-sudarsan-pattnaiks-message-to-children/article

Naresh Chander Lal
Theater Wunderkind

1. http://www.andamansheekha.com/16813/
2. https://www.youtube.com/watch?v=M1rQvtqc_T0&t=2410s
3. https://www.youtube.com/watch?v=M1rQvtqc_T0&t=2410s
4. http://www.andamansheekha.com/19939/
5. https://dt.andaman.gov.in/DetailNews.aspx?newsid=JEw5zQ3Ybe-BaxsG9iZloTTTMCfZQ+Cf77iT30Krl/7g=

Ram Narayan
Shaping the Soulful Resonance of Classical Indian Music

1. https://www.clevelandart.org/sites/default/files/documents/program-notes-for-performances/2013-01-18_KronosQuartet_Program-web-vF-REV.pdf
2. Qureshi, R B 2007. Master musicians of India: Hereditary sarangi players speak. Routledge.
3. https://www.theglobeandmail.com/news/toronto/first-female-sarangi-musician-shares-love-of-folk-tradition/article13413524/
4. https://www.nytimes.com/2011/12/06/arts/music/sultan-khan-indian-classical-musician-and-sarangi-player-dies-at-71.html
5. Qureshi, R B 2007. Master musicians of India: Hereditary sarangi players speak. Routledge.

Naseerudin Shah
Masterful Actor of Film and Theater

1. From Shah, N. 2014. And Then One Day: A Memoir. Hamish Hamilton.
2. https://www.youtube.com/watch?v=3-4VjMgnnRQ
3. https://www.outlookindia.com/website/story/entertainment-news-naseeruddin-shah-have-done-everything-i-wanted-dont-have-any-desires-left/406570
4. https://indianexpress.com/article/entertainment/bollywood/naseeruddin-shah-interview-crying-mistaken-for-good-acting-watch-video-4965582/

Shiv Kumar Sharma
Santoor Virtuoso

1. https://www.nytimes.com/2022/05/15/world/asia/pandit-shiv-kumar-sharma-dead.html
2. https://www.theguardian.com/music/2022/may/15/shivkumar-sharma-obituary
3. Sharma, S K, & Puri, I. (2018). Journey with a hundred strings: My life in music. Penguin India.
4. https://www.theguardian.com/music/2022/may/15/shivkumar-sharma-obituary
5. Sharma, S K, & Puri, I. (2018). Journey with a hundred strings: My life in music. Penguin India.

Amitabh Bachchan
The Living Legend of Hindi Cinema

1. India's official broadcaster
2. An Indian writer, director and screenwriter known for his works in Hindi, Bengali and Telegu
3. The Hindi film industry is often called Bollywood.
4. Annual awards that honour artistic and technical talent in the Hindi film industry.
5. Revisiting Prakash Mehra's Zanjeer: The film that made Amitabh Bachchan. Retrieved from: https://indianexpress.com/article/entertainment/bollywood/revisiting-prakash-mehra-zanjeer-the-film-that-made-amitabh-bachchan-4714064/
6. Deewaar was the perfect script: Amitabh Bachchan on 42 years of the cult film. Retrieved from: https://www.hindustantimes.com/bollywood/deewaar-was-the-perfect-script-amitabh-bachchan-on-42-years-of-the-cult-film/story-x2hy87zQ0ebVlsVMV59U2I.html
7. Sholay. Retrieved from: https://archive.ph/20120630155123/http://www.ibosnetwork.com/asp/filmbodetails.asp?id=Sholay#selection-651.6-651.95
8. The Bofors scandal was a major weapons-contract political scandal that occurred during the 1980s and 1990s, in which Indian National Congress politicians, including the then Indian prime minister, Rajiv Gandhi was reported to be involved.
9. The then Prime Minister of India.
10. Muqaddar Ka Sikandar. Retrieved from: https://www.tribuneindia.com/2001/20010304/spectrum/main1.htm

11. Backstory: When the Amitabh Bachchan magic faded briefly. Retieved from: https://www.cnbctv18.com/business/companies/backstory-when-the-amitabh-bachchan-magic-faded-briefly-11380222.htm
12. Abhishek Bachchan reveals he dropped out of college to support dad Amitabh when he was broke. Retrieved from: https://www.indiatoday.in/movies/celebrities/story/abhishek-bachchan-reveals-he-dropped-out-of-college-to-support-dad-amitabh-when-he-was-broke-1885460-2021-12-08
13. Bollywood star tops the poll. Retrieved from: http://news.bbc.co.uk/2/hi/entertainment/381017.stm

Kattassery Joseph Yesudas
A Voice Gifted by God

1. https://www.filmfare.com/interviews/king-of-ooh-la-la-land-262.html
2. http://archive.indianexpress.com/news/book-traces-yesudas-s-growth-as-playback-singer/843529/
3. https://www.onmanorama.com/news/global-indian/2019/12/13/column---why-bestowing-awards-on-yesudas-is-like-devotional-offe.html
4. https://www.onmanorama.com/entertainment/music/2020/01/10/yesudas-birthday-special-note-wife-prabha.html
5. https://www.onmanorama.com/entertainment/music/2020/01/10/yesudas-birthday-special-note-wife-prabha.html
6. https://www.thenewsminute.com/article/ayyappas-door-sabarimala-yesudas-sings-harivaraasanam-song-he-immortalised-50277

Ujjwal Nikam
Prosecution Powerhouse

1. https://indianexpress.com/article/india/mohsin-shaikh-murder-case-family-writes-to-cm-seeks-appointment-of-ujjwal-nikam-as-public-prosecutor-4488386/
2. https://www.youtube.com/watch?v=FwtlOfOSV3k
3. https://www.dailymotion.com/video/x8ax7u8
4. https://www.youtube.com/watch?v=YHpCDQXD-Ds
5. https://www.youtube.com/watch?v=UZGmBeYMAqk
6. https://www.youtube.com/watch?v=Wj0brY3ZqJ0

Ravindra Chandra Bhargava
Scion of Maruti Automobiles

1. Established in 1956, the Bharat Heavy Electrical Limited (BHEL) is an Indian government owned power generation equipment manufacturer.
2. A year into Maruti, I made a crucial decision: R C Bhargava. Retrieved from: https://www.indiatoday.in/magazine/anniversary/story/20210104-a-year-into-maruti-i-made-a-crucial-decision-1753023-2020-12-27
3. Ibid.
4. A witness to history. Retrieved from: https://www.financialexpress.com/archive/a-witness-to-history/640994/
5. National Thermal Power Corporation (NTPC) Limited is an Indian public sector organisation that is engaged in the generation of electricity and allied activities.
6. Ibid.
7. A year into Maruti, I made a crucial decision: R C Bhargava. Retrieved from: https://www.indiatoday.in/magazine/anniversary/story/20210104-a-year-into-maruti-i-made-a-crucial-decision-1753023-2020-12-27
8. R C Bhargava: Meet the man who helped drive Maruti in India. Retrieved from: https://economictimes.indiatimes.com/news/company/corporate-trends/rc-bhargava-meet-the-man-who-helped-drive-maruti-in-india/articleshow/50858313.cms?utm_source=contentofinterest&utm_medium=text&utm_campaign=cppst
9. Words don't help sales, need 'concrete action' from govt: Maruti Chairman R C Bhargava. Retrieved from: https://economictimes.indiatimes.com/industry/auto/auto-news/words-dont-help-sales-need-concrete-action-from-govt-maruti-chairman-rc-bhargava/articleshow/85620628.cms?utm_source=contentofinterest&utm_medium=text&utm_campaign=cppst

Chandi Prasad Bhatt
Chipko Movement Pioneer

1. https://web.archive.org/web/20100211130523/http://www.hinduonnet.com/mag/2002/06/02/stories/2002060200010100.htm
2. Shepard, M. 1987. Gandhi today: A report on Mahatma Gandhi's successors. Simple Productions.

3. https://scroll.in/magazine/905320/the-forgotten-story-of-how-the-chipko-andolan-pioneer-chandi-prasad-bhatt-saved-badrinath-temple

Balkrishna Vithaldas Doshi
Building India

1. Known as the Nobel Prize for Architecture
2. Louis Isadore Kahn (20 February, 1901 – 17 March, 1974) was an Estonian-born American architect who worked in Philadelphia, USA. He served as a professor of architecture at the Yale School of Architecture from 1947 to 1957, and as a professor of architecture at the School of Design, University of Pennsylvania from 1957 till his death. At the time of his death, he was considered one of the foremost architects of his time.
3. Now known as Vastushilpa Consultants: see https://www.sangath.org/home/
4. Maqbool Fida Husain (17 September, 1915 – 9 June, 2011) was one of most celebrated and internationally recognised Indian artists of the 20th century who was known for executing bold, vibrantly coloured paintings in a modified Cubist form—a form where subjects are analysed, broken up, and reassembled in an abstract form rather than depicting them in a single form or perspective.
5. Amdavad ni Gufa by architect B V Doshi. Retrieved from: https://www.thetilesofindia.com/global-architects/amdavad-ni-gufa-by-architect-b-v-doshi/
6. The man of the hour: Dr B V Doshi. Retrieved from: https://www.thehindu.com/life-and-style/dr-bv-doshi-has-received-the-padma-bhushan/article30701594.ece
7. Ibid.
8. Doshi was not only the founder and campus architect but has also served as a dean for the University
9. Architect B V Doshi wins the Padma Bhushan. Retrieved from: https://www.thetimesofindia.com/tiles-news/architect-b-v-doshi-wins-the-padma-bhushan/
10. Architects should be doers, not creators: Balkrishna Doshi on winning UK Honour. Retrieved from: https://indianexpress.com/article/india/architect-balkrishna-doshi-winning-uk-honour-7666541/
11. The spaces created by Doshi could inspire generations. Retrieved from: https://www.livemint.com/opinion/columns/the-spaces-created-by-doshi-could-inspire-generations-11674580424354.html

Chewang Norphel
Creator of Artificial Glaciers

1. https://homegrown.co.in/homegrown-creators/how-one-man-single-handedly-solved-ladakh-s-water-crisis
2. https://www.thebetterindia.com/14672/man-creates-artificial-glaciers-chewang-norphel-ladakh/
3. https://www.pbs.org/newshour/show/ice-sheets-in-greenland-antarctica-melting-faster-than-previously-thought-research-shows#.
4. Carey, M. (2007). The history of ice: how glaciers became an endangered species. Environmental History, 12(3), 497-527.
5. https://theamericanscholar.org/the-crisis-up-close/
6. https://economictimes.indiatimes.com/defaultinterstitial.cms

Simon Oraon
Protector of Trees

1. https://www.hindustantimes.com/india/jharkhand-s-waterman-gets-padma-shri-for-waging-war-against-drought/story-7PgYljQmbDBeahSVg4gjrJ.html
2. https://www.jeasa.org/jharkhands-waterman-84-years-old-padmashree-simon-oraon
3. http://archive.indianexpress.com/news/a-73yearold--who-saves-rainwater-and-jungles/719667/
4. https://indianexpress.com/article/news-archive/web/a-73yearold-who-saves-rainwater-and-jungles/
5. https://indianexpress.com/article/news-archive/web/a-73yearold-who-saves-rainwater-and-jungles/
6. https://www.thebetterindia.com/49868/jharkhand-waterman-simon-oraon-afforestation-baba-khaksi-toli-ranchi/

Made in the USA
Monee, IL
03 May 2026

49438691R00236